Ariane understands that the reader is curious and draws us into the artist's world! She leads us through thoughtful skill-building exercises to improve their visual acuity and ability to see like an artist. An exceptional artist and educator, Ariane directs us through the steps of really seeing our world and the beauty it demonstrates every day. Don't delay learning these simple methods to improve your vision and enjoy both our natural and human-made world!

CLAIRE ELISABETH CLUM
Director of Education
Boca Raton Museum of Art
Editor of FAEA *Fresh Paint*

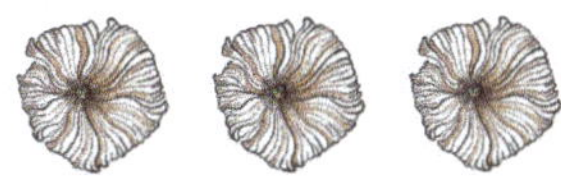

Ariane recently came to teach at our art studio in Florence, Italy with her book, "How to See Like an Artist." Our study abroad students and others loved the experience with her and left feeling inspired. Her unique guidebook teaches everyone exactly how to sharpen visual skills to see like an artist. Ariane encourages everyone to actively pursue a more fulfilling life by tapping into the innate creative nature we all share. All it takes is a little practice with her inspirational book. We also believe that being creative is good for the heart, mind, and soul of everyone! Ariane's book proves this point!

HAILEY AND VICTORIA HODGE
Vino & Vinci Art Studio
Florence, Italy

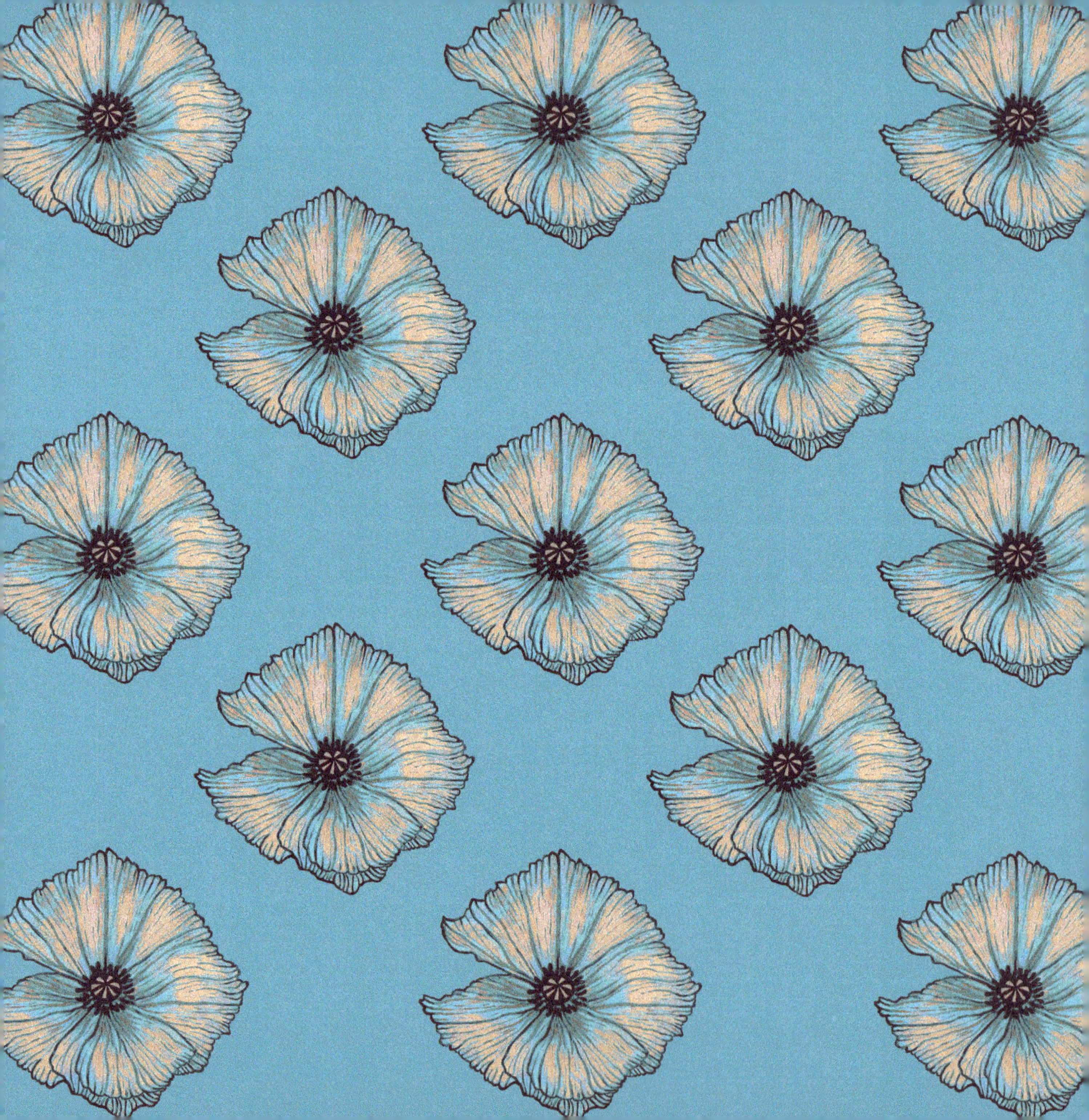

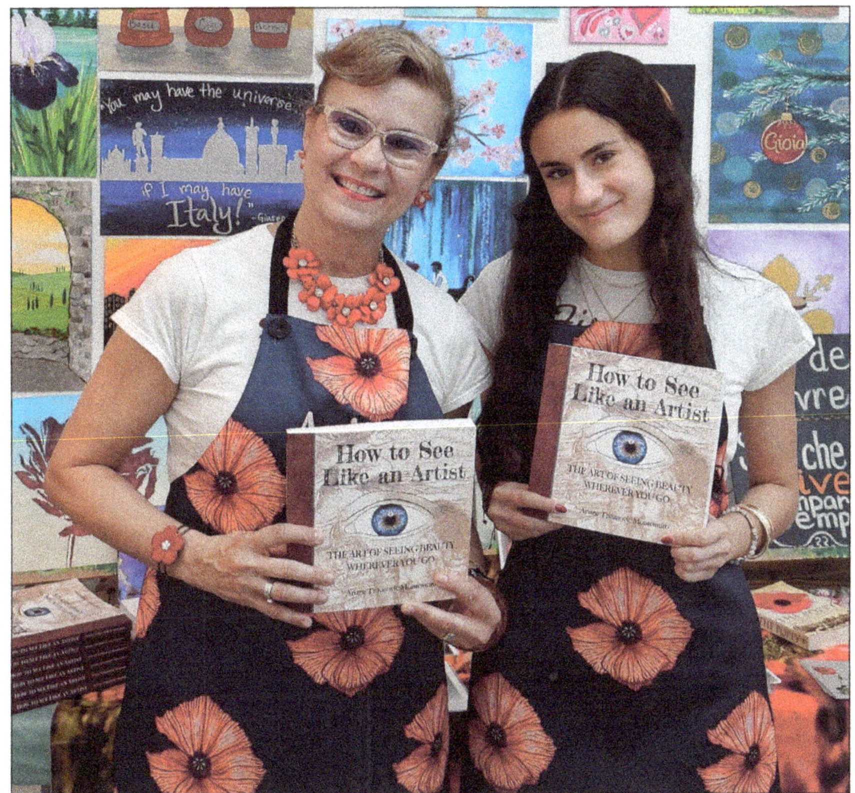

The author pictured here with her daughter teaching in Florence, Italy with her book, "How to See Like an Artist."

After a challenging period in Ariane Trifunovic Montemuro's life, she decided to change gears and look for new inspiration and joy. She discovered that poppy flowers delight her to no end!

She then started a poppy design business. Subsequently, she wrote this book to share her newfound joy in addition to helping people find theirs.

Her classes inspire everyone to begin a lifelong pursuit of beauty by simply learning how to sharpen one's observation skills.

The author is passionate about teaching people to see like an artist because she believes this perspective benefits one's mental health. To inquire about her classes, email arianeart@gmail.com.

The author maintains that once you practice the skill of seeing like an artist, you absolutely will begin to see new beauty and possibilities in your life!

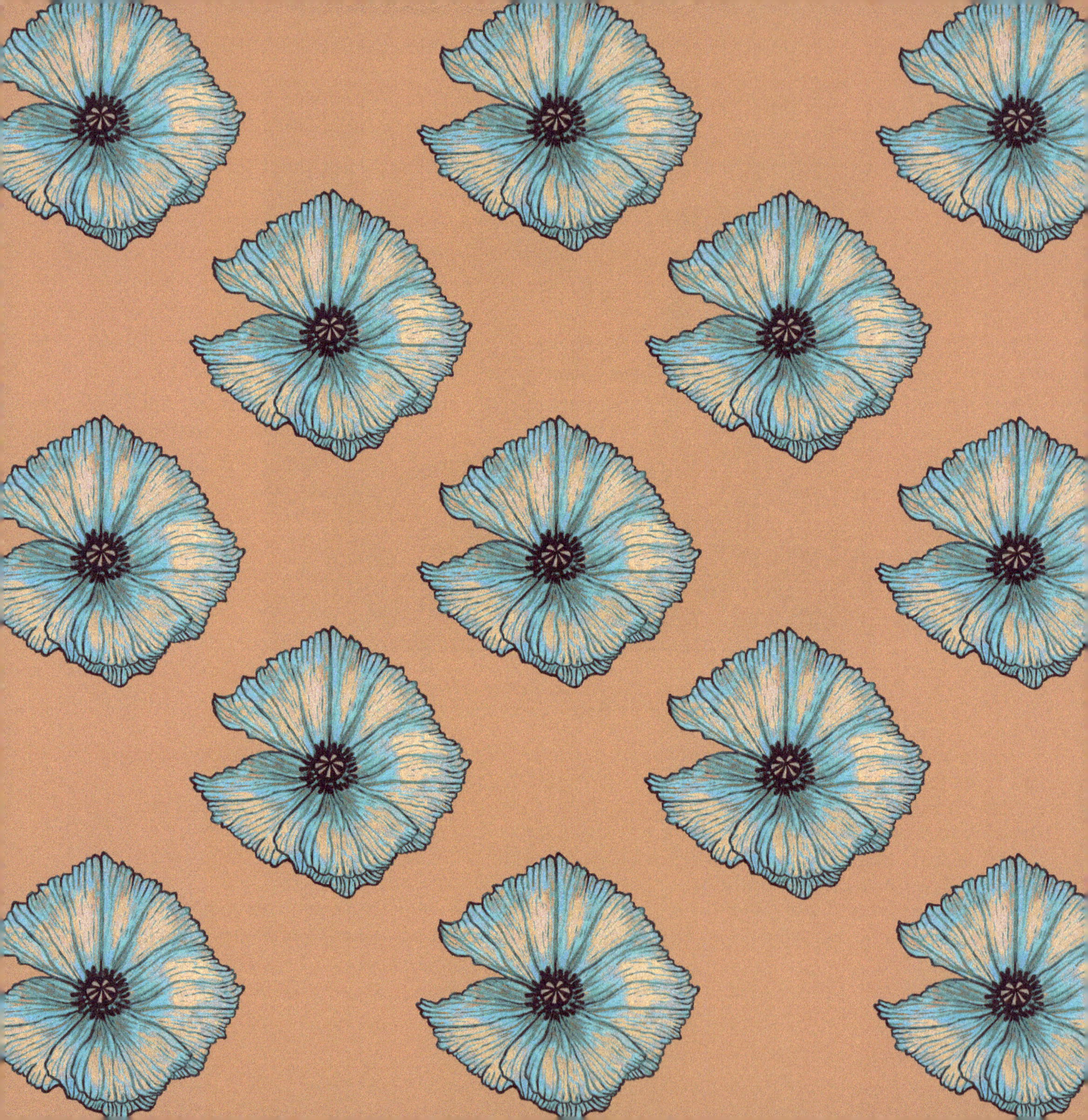

How to See Like an Artist!

The Art of Seeing Beauty Wherever You Go

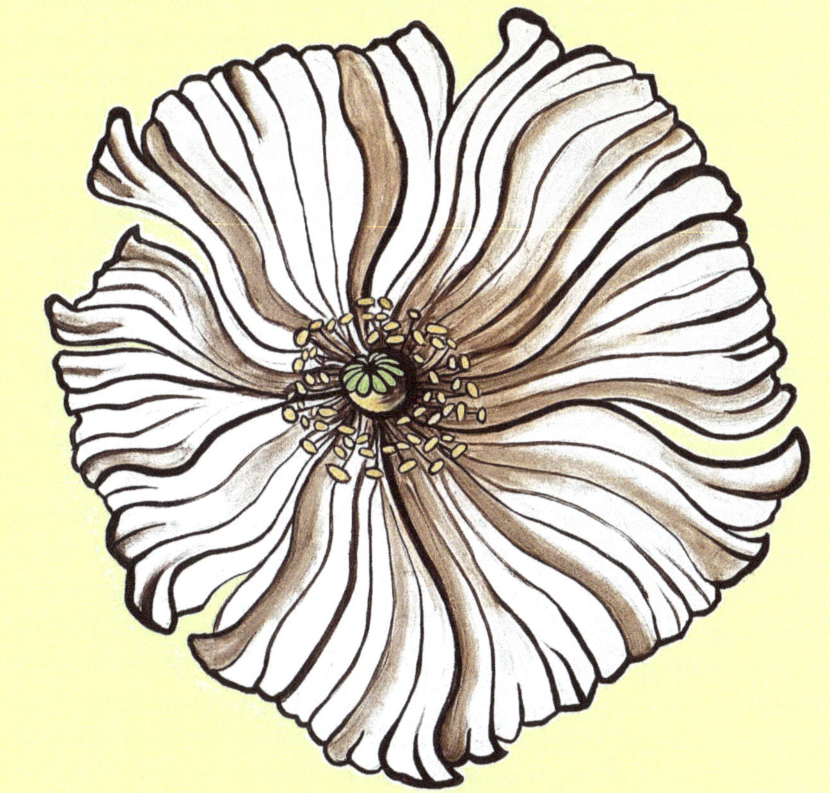

Ariane Trifunovic Montemuro

Ideas into Books: Westview

Kingston Springs, Tennessee

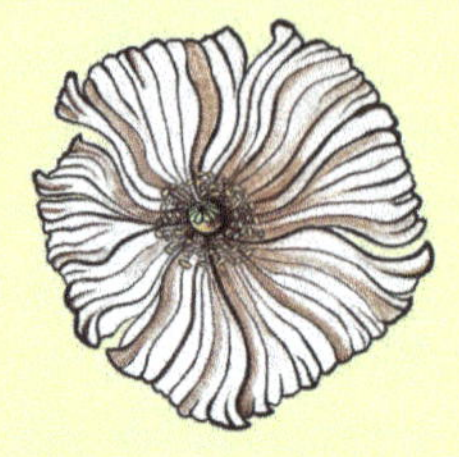

***Ideas into Books*®**
W E S T V I E W
P.O. Box 605
Kingston Springs, TN 37082
www.publishedbywestview.com

ISBN 978-1-62880-290-0

First edition, 2024

Cover and Title Page Graphic Design
Jeri Wofford

Book Graphic Design
Elaine P. Millen, TeknoLink Marketing Services, www.teknolinkmarketingservices.com

Editing Guidance
Anthony Montemuro, M.D.

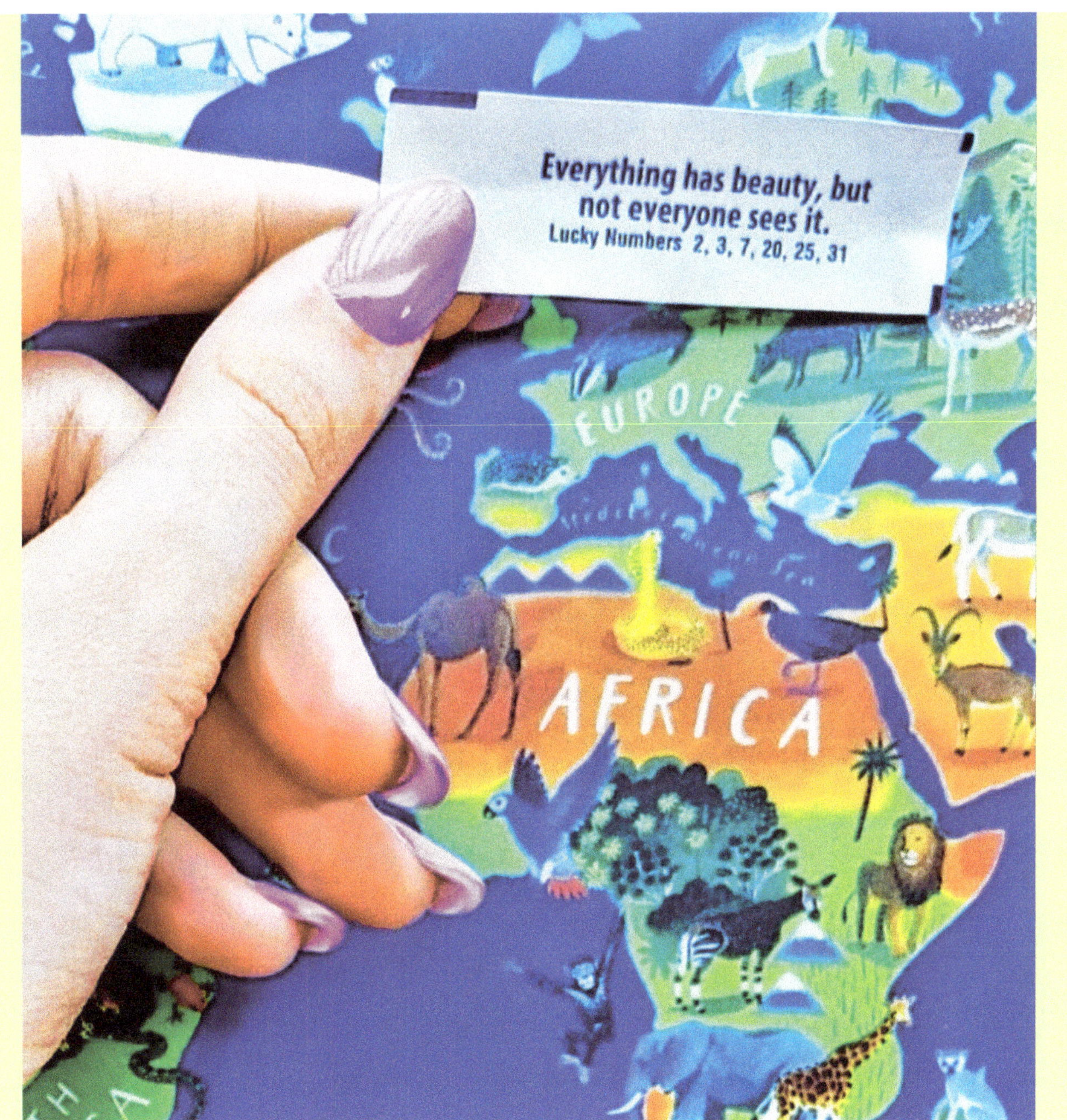
Everything has beauty, but
not everyone sees it.
Lucky Numbers 2, 3, 7, 20, 25, 31
EUROPE
AFRICA

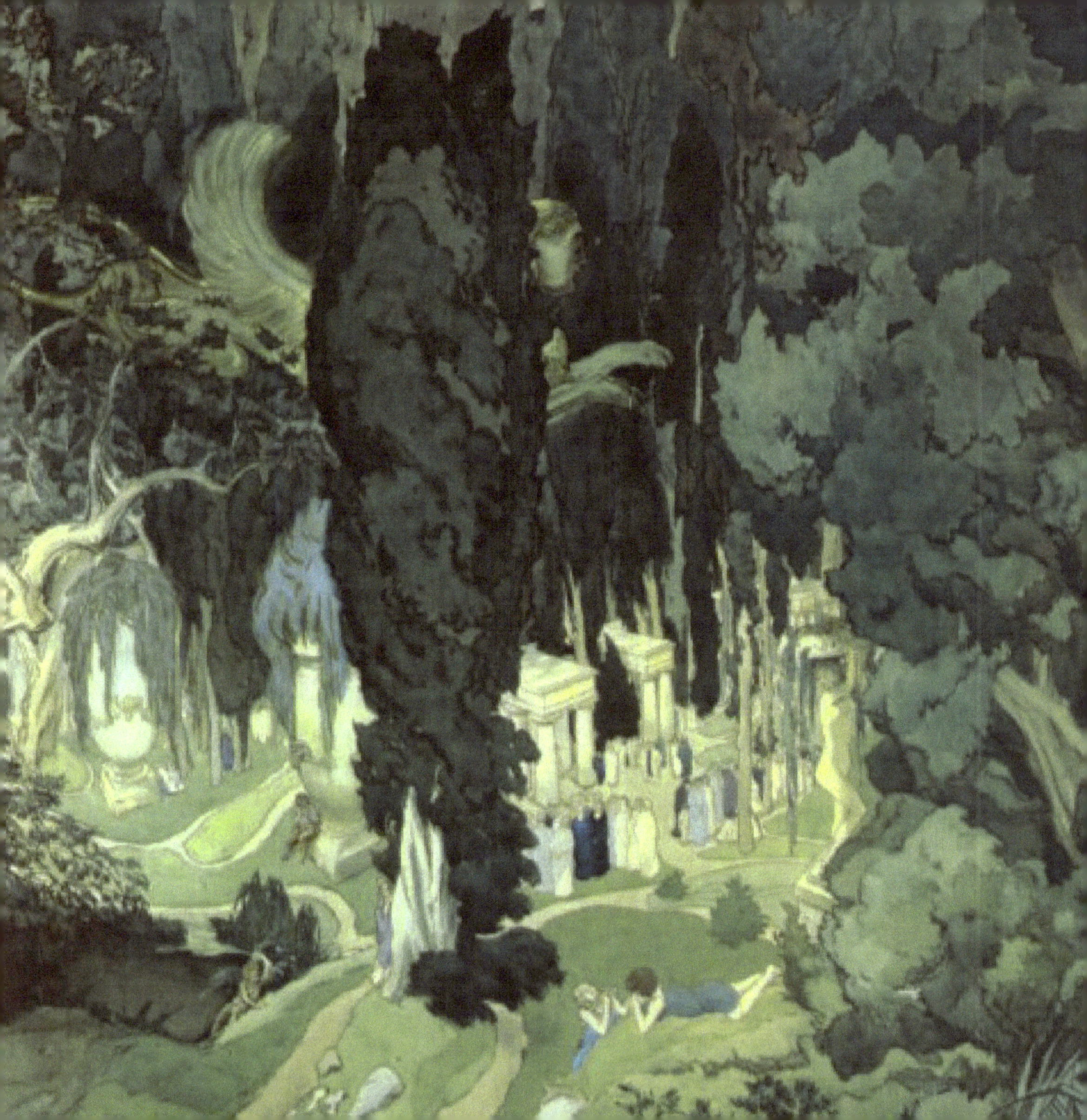

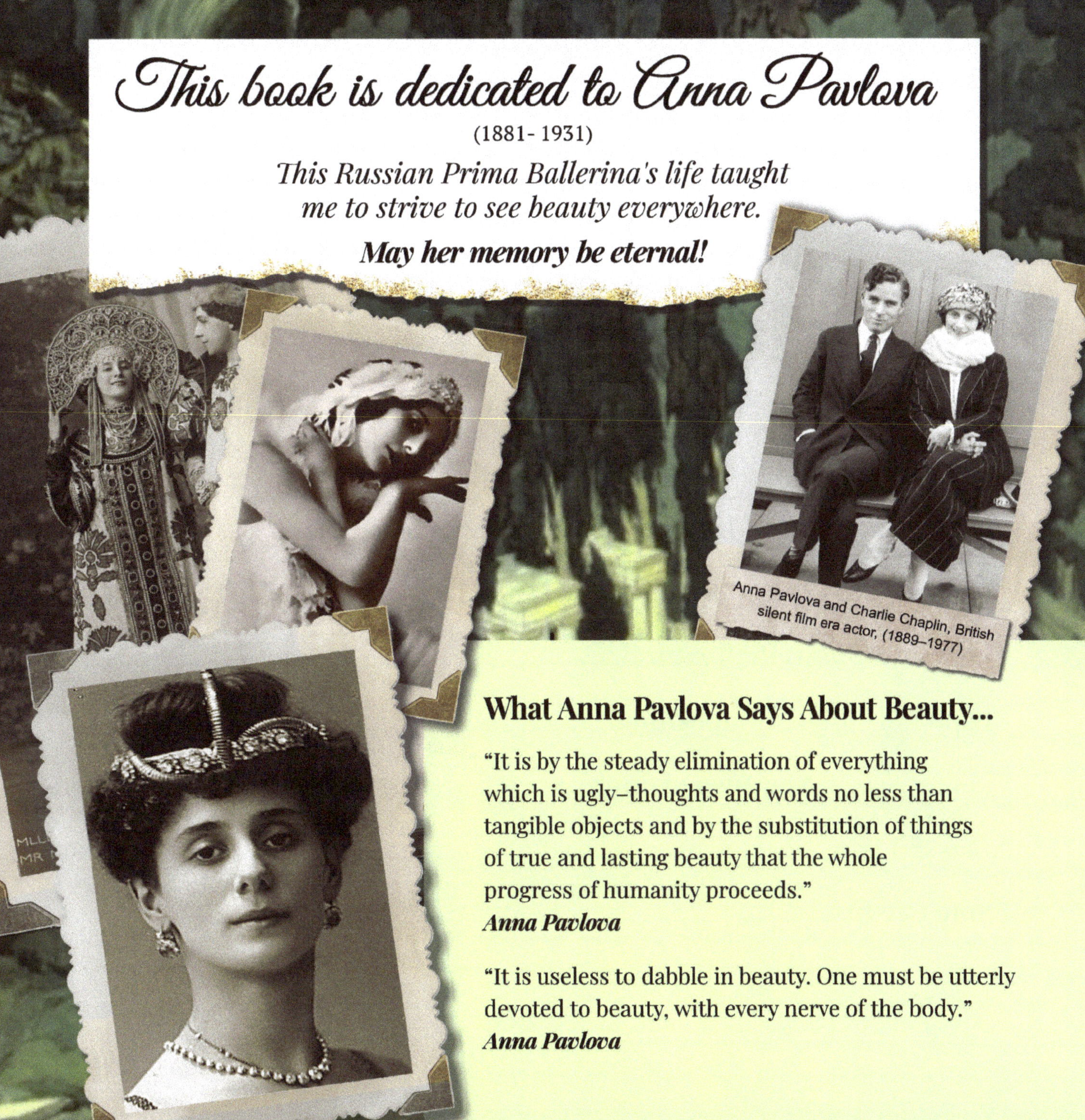

This book is dedicated to Anna Pavlova

(1881- 1931)

This Russian Prima Ballerina's life taught me to strive to see beauty everywhere.

May her memory be eternal!

Anna Pavlova and Charlie Chaplin, British silent film era actor, (1889–1977)

What Anna Pavlova Says About Beauty...

"It is by the steady elimination of everything which is ugly–thoughts and words no less than tangible objects and by the substitution of things of true and lasting beauty that the whole progress of humanity proceeds."
Anna Pavlova

"It is useless to dabble in beauty. One must be utterly devoted to beauty, with every nerve of the body."
Anna Pavlova

Table of Contents

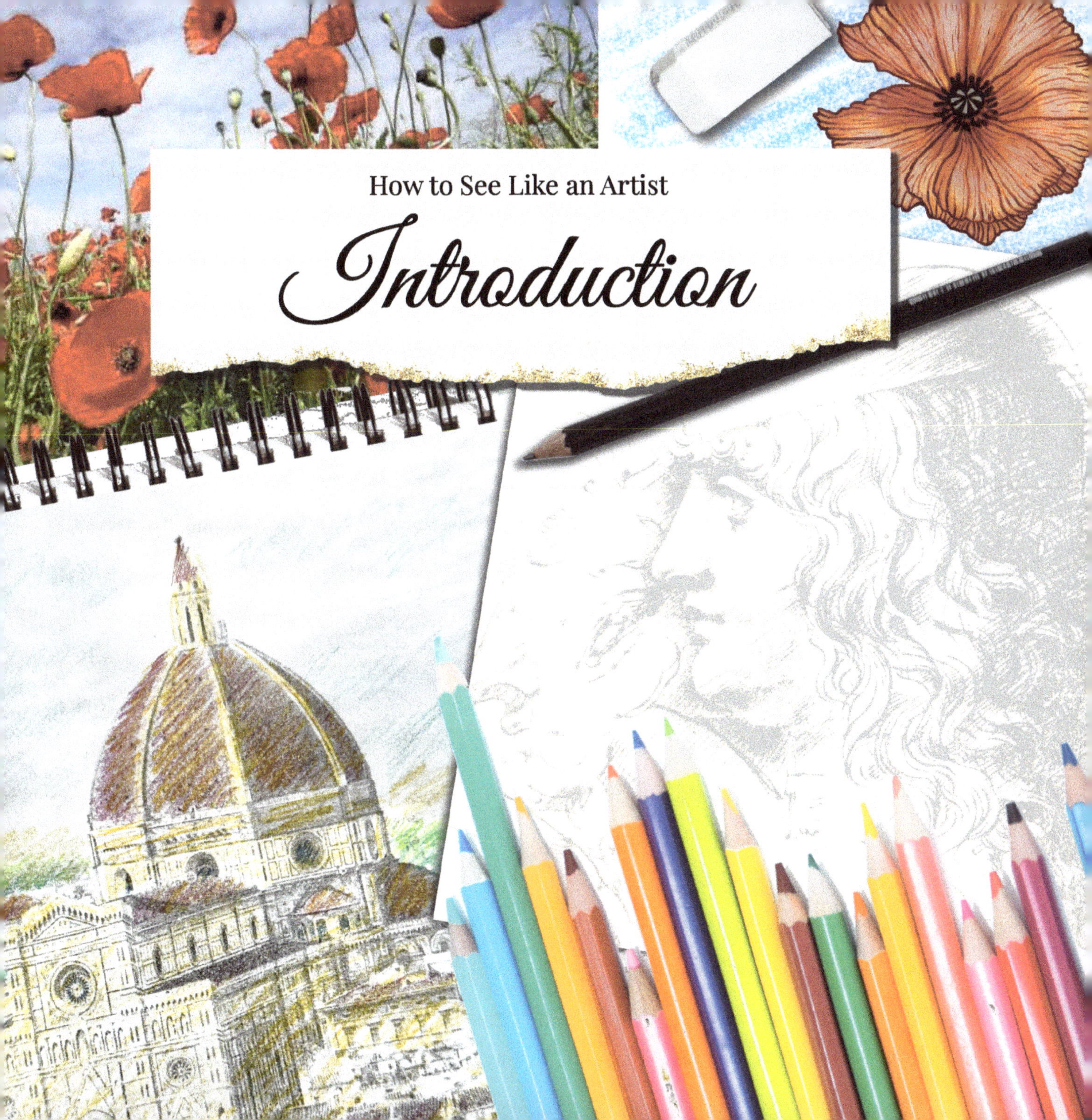
How to See Like an Artist
Introduction

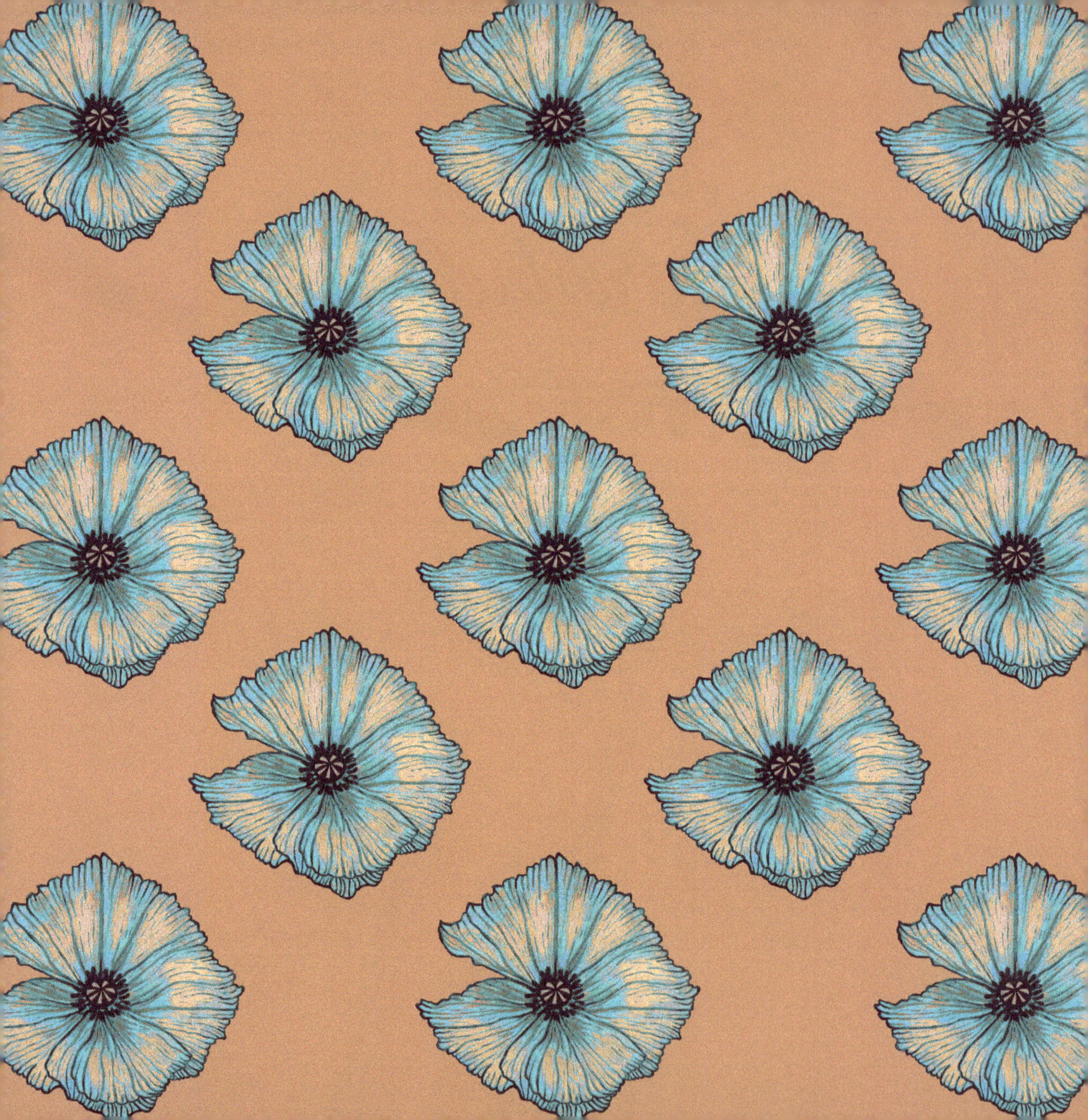

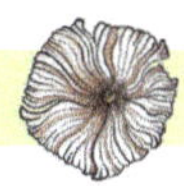

Introduction

Our world is filled with so much beauty.

It fills our souls with awe, wonder, and happiness. The beauty we encounter in our lives inspires us in many different ways.

What's unfortunate is that we are often distracted by virtual realities and become blind to the real physical world surrounding us. We miss out on the beauty that could potentially transform each of us. If we allow it, beauty can inspire our hearts and provide opportunities for growth and positive change in our lives.

That's why it's so important to pause and practice looking at the world around us with the ***eyes of an artist***. Whether we think of ourselves as artists or not, it benefits us to refocus and practice observing our world in this way. **Doing so can prove to be life-changing.**

This book is about training our eyes to see like an artist. We may live in the same world, but the truth is artists notice many things others overlook.

We need to see the beauty in our lives. I remember my watercolor teacher in college once telling our class if Armageddon arrived and only two people remained on earth, *one would decorate the other's coconut bowl*. This unforgettable comment struck me to the core, and it still does. The truth is that our souls long for beauty. **Beauty serves a holy purpose in our lives. It nourishes our souls.**

If we are attentive and work at understanding the basic design elements presented in this book, we will find beauty in our lives. It will hit us when we least expect it. The good news is that learning the basic design elements will serve us in many positive and transformational ways. We will discover that beauty inspires joy and new ideas in our everyday lives.

The inspiration received from a chance encounter with what we find beautiful ignites a flame in our hearts. This, in turn, leads us to create even more beauty. A new journey unfolds. Some people might be inspired to start a new business or try a new fashion style. Others might write a book, compose a song, design jewelry, create a painting, or a new recipe.

The bottom line is that a meaningful encounter with beauty often precipitates a change in our hearts. Inspiration hits us like a Mack truck, and we act on it. The door to new beginnings opens.

Ultimately, perceiving beauty can result in a special purpose for *each of us*.

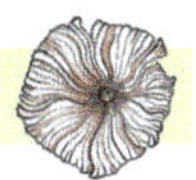

However, coming face to face with beauty and recognizing it takes effort. We must look for it. Our eyes and hearts need a bit of training to find it. **This little book will help you practice seeing by learning the basics of art education**.

One day, I absolutely knew I would write this book. I felt I had to share my impressions of everyday beauty that we often miss. A heartfelt passion overtook me. I had to find a way to encourage and guide others how to see the way I see, ***like an artist***.

This all happened after being filled with an overwhelming emotion of delight and wonder with what surrounded me on a recent trip to Italy. I did not want to forget the everyday beauty that caught my eye, from door knockers to outdoor drinking fountains. I bought a sketchbook and began to collect snippets of beautiful images and draw them. I was so overwhelmed by the everyday beauty I experienced on my travels that I could not contain my enthusiasm. My joy resulted in this little book.

All this beauty made me reflect upon what I had learned in art school years ago. It was the thing that surprised me the most. My college fine arts teacher once said that anyone can learn to draw. He explained that it's not necessarily an inherited skill; each of us can learn to draw with patience and practice. In time, I began to understand how correct his statement was.

Just like learning to draw, the way we see is a skill we can develop and refine. **The truth is that any of us can develop the skill of seeing like an artist.** Step by step, learning how will lead us to recognize beauty in unexpected and wonderful new ways.

Mastering this skill is easier than you might imagine. All you have to do is become familiar with the basic design elements of art. This book outlines the elements that artists use: **line**, **shape**, **form** — including how form exists in space — **color**, **texture**, and **composition**. All it takes is a little time, attention, and practice, and you can begin to find your own unique way of seeing beauty in the world.

Part of the fun of seeing beauty is deciding what you like or don't like. Once you discover what floats your boat, a whole world of creative possibilities opens up. After this, you may discover wonderful new ways of expressing what you see and feel. Then you can incorporate this in your life.

The best part is when we see the world with the eyes of an artist, beauty surprises us at every turn!

I hope in time, you, too, will be inspired to share your unique impressions of beauty with others!

It's time to behold the beauty!

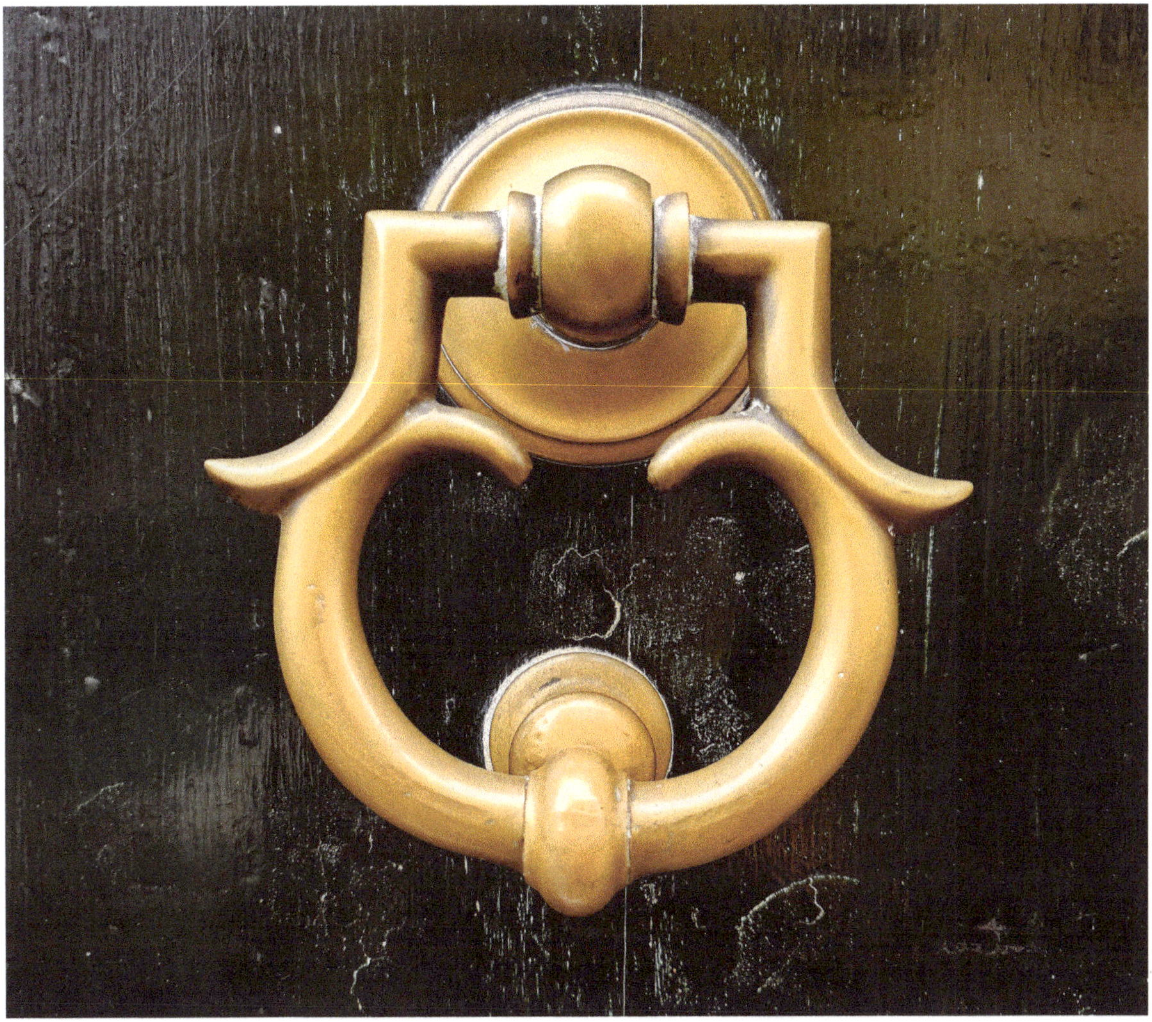

The elegant beauty of a door knocker.

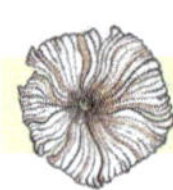

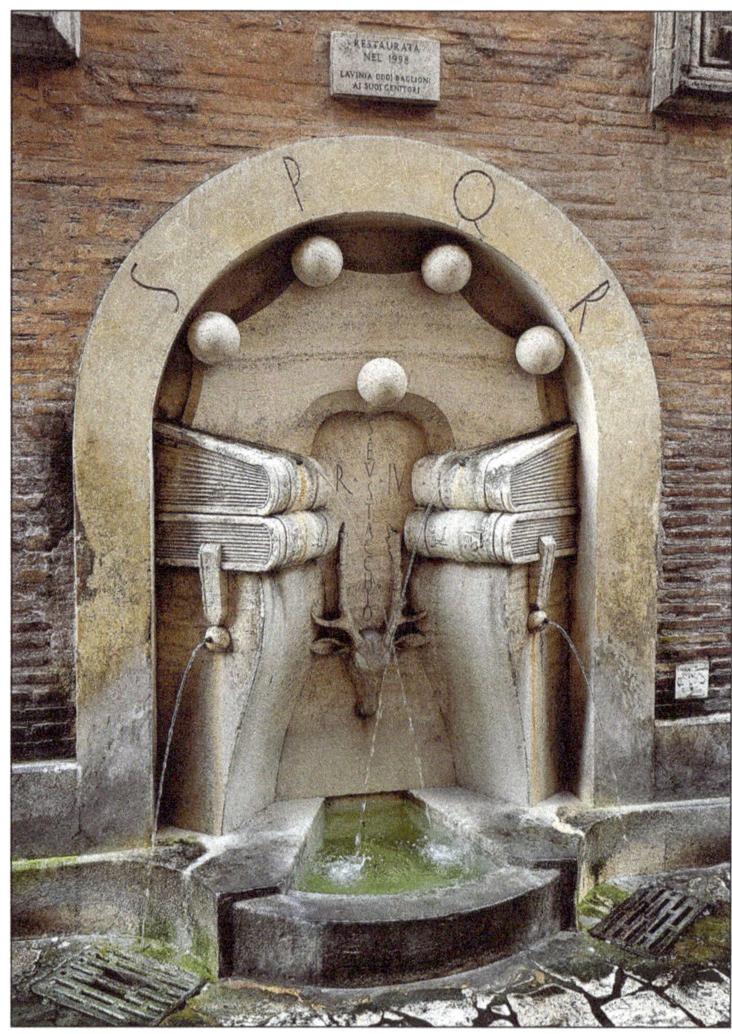

The timeless beauty of a Roman drinking fountain.

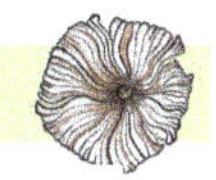

What you need to get started:

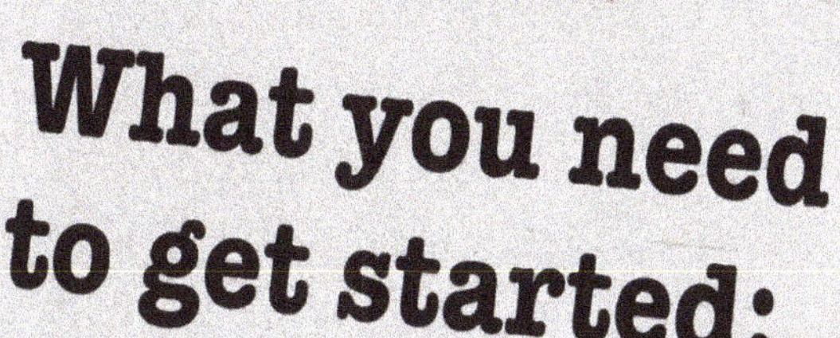

- A pencil for drawing

- A set of colored pencils

- An eraser

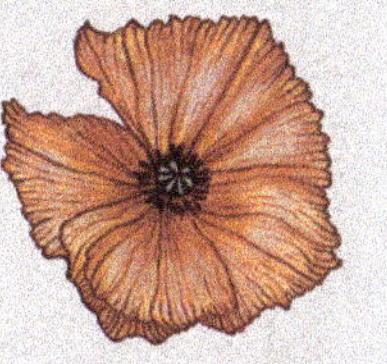

Introductory Learning Tips:

As you read this book, **study each photo carefully**. Contemplate the caption under the photo, if there is one. What is the caption telling you to look for? With time, your eyes will begin to adjust to a new way of looking at the world. They will become sensitive to perceiving each design element presented in this book. **Little by little, you will notice details you never saw before.** If you have a sketchbook, make sure to keep it in a convenient spot. This way you can draw and document what inspires you at any given moment. I keep mine in my car. Be sure to take it with you when you travel.

It's important to remember that perceiving beauty is a *lifelong pursuit*.

Once you begin to see like an artist, the creative spark inside will ignite, and your original ideas will begin to blossom, giving way to new possibilities at any stage in life!

Get ready. Beauty awaits you!

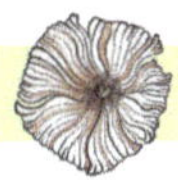

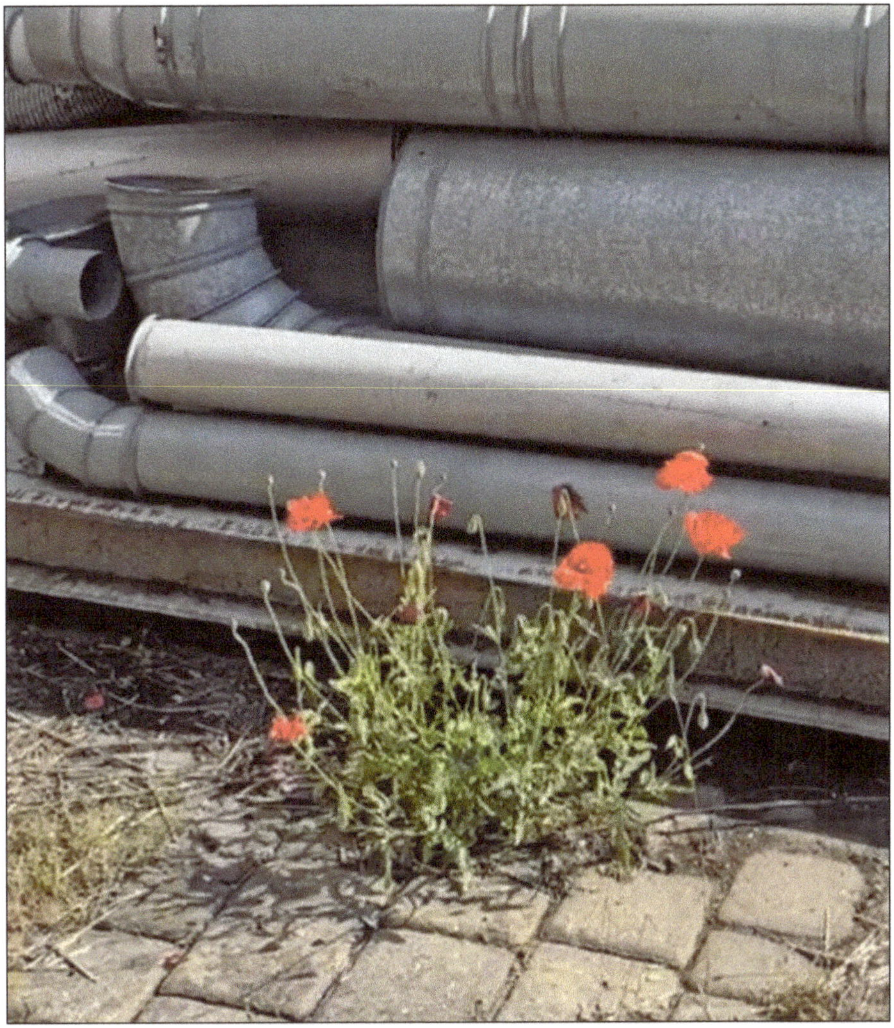

See the lines, shapes, form, color, texture, and composition. Don't just see the junkyard!

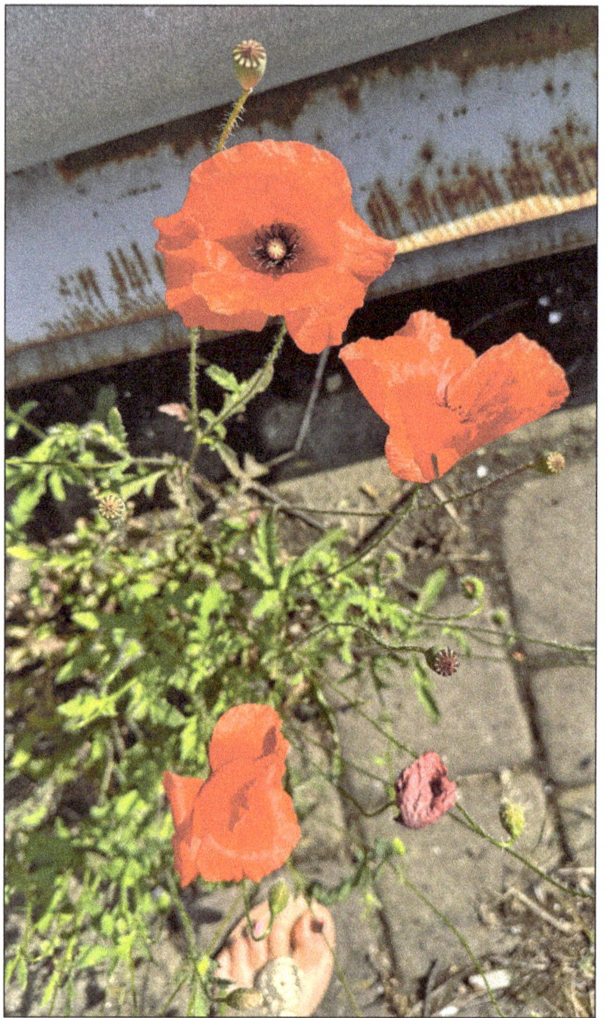

See the beautiful poppies!

Did you know the poppy flower is part of the weed family?

The poppy flowers on these two pages are blooming in a junkyard in Florence, Italy, courtesy of Hailey and Victoria Hodge.

Hailey and Victoria were surprised and delighted when they stumbled upon these beautiful Tuscan poppies blossoming in a junkyard. They are owners of Vino & Vinci art studio, in Florence — **www.vinoevinci.com**.

Amidst piles of junk, they noticed the bright, red flowers with the eyes of an artist and sent the author these photos of her favorite flower in an unexpected place.

Seeing beauty is a choice we can all make!

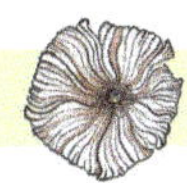

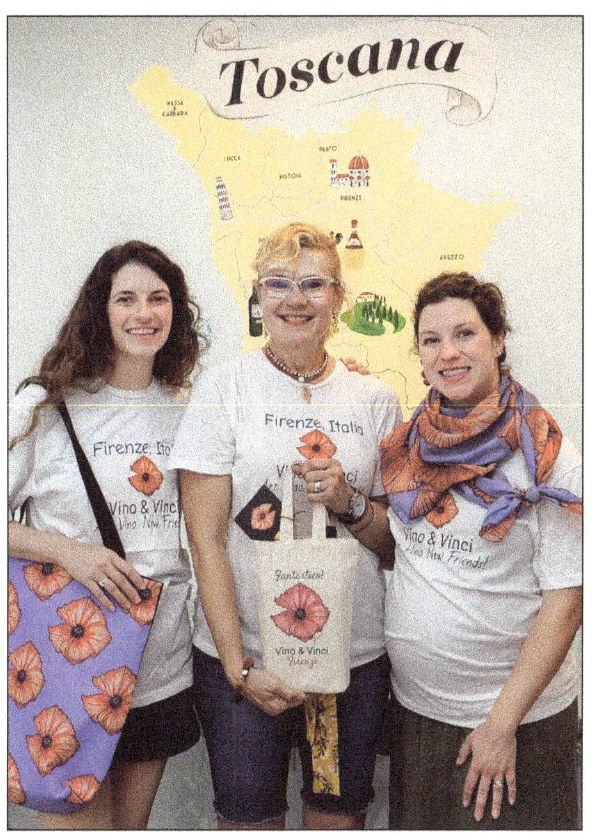

Poppy flowers come in every color under the sun! Inspired by the beauty of one little poppy flower, the author was prompted to start her business: ***www.poppieswithapurpose.com***. She is pictured here standing between Hailey and Victoria, owners of Vino & Vinci, an amazing art studio in Florence, Italy. All are wearing the author's original poppy designs.

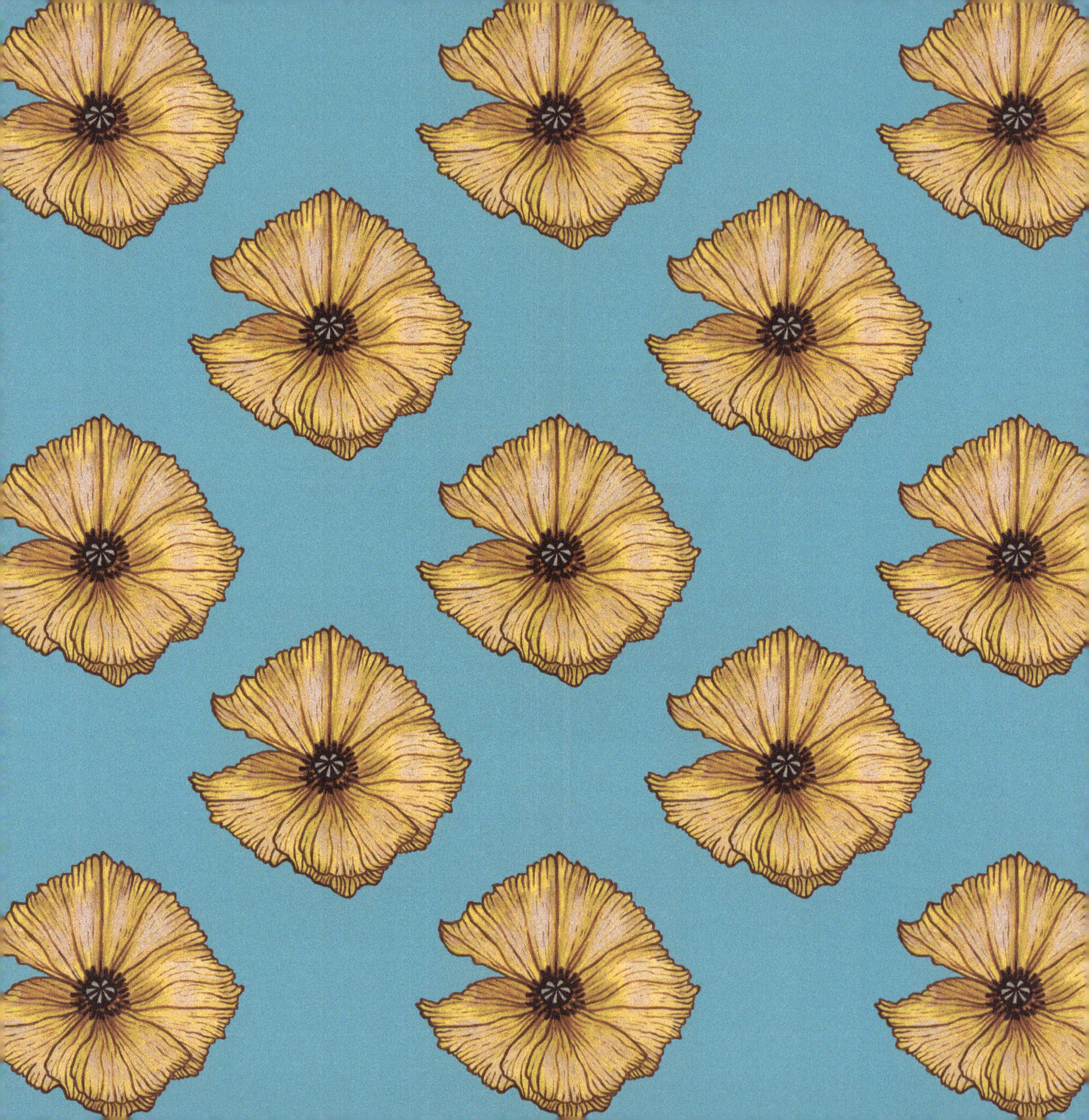

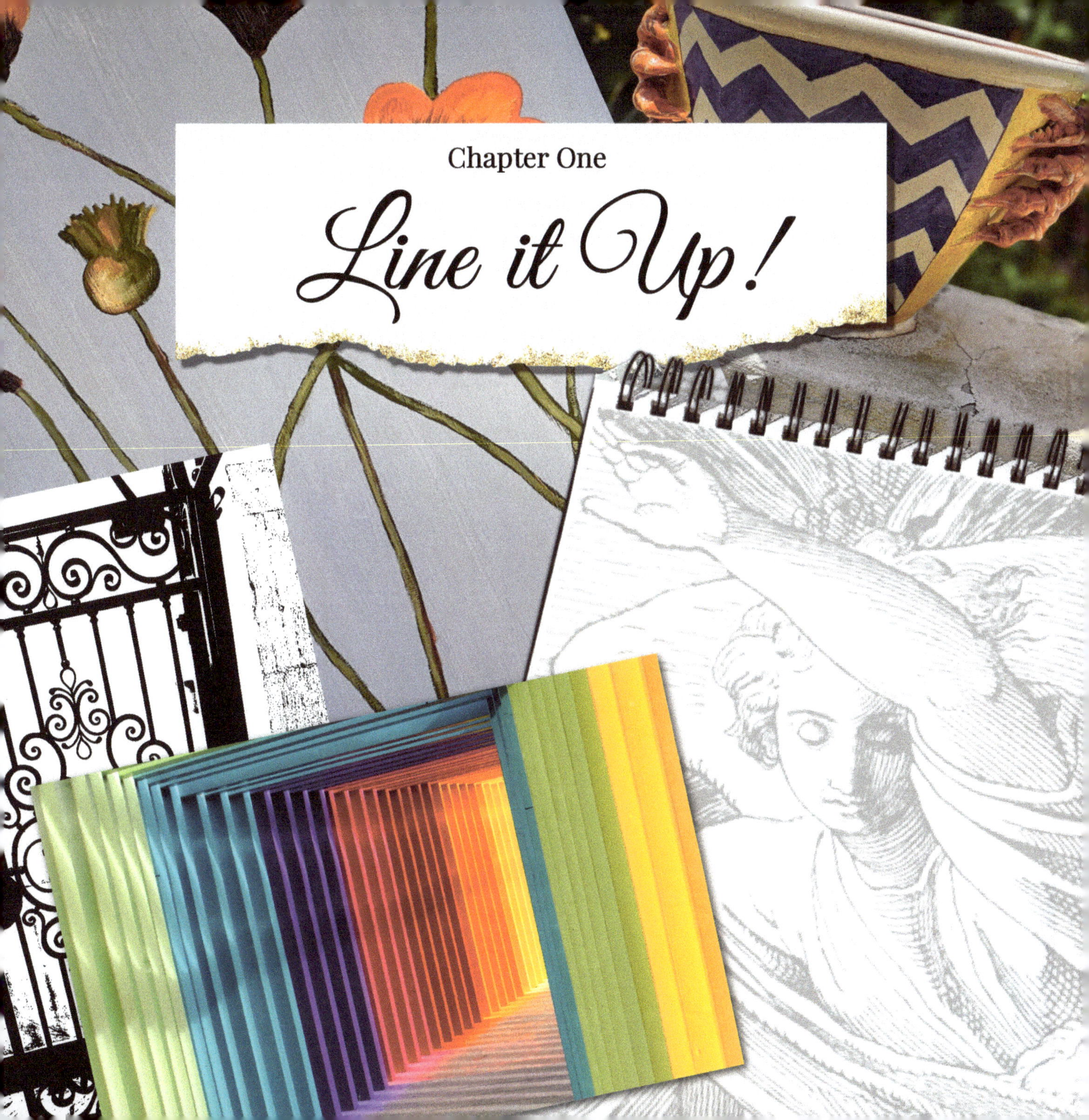

Chapter One
Line it Up!

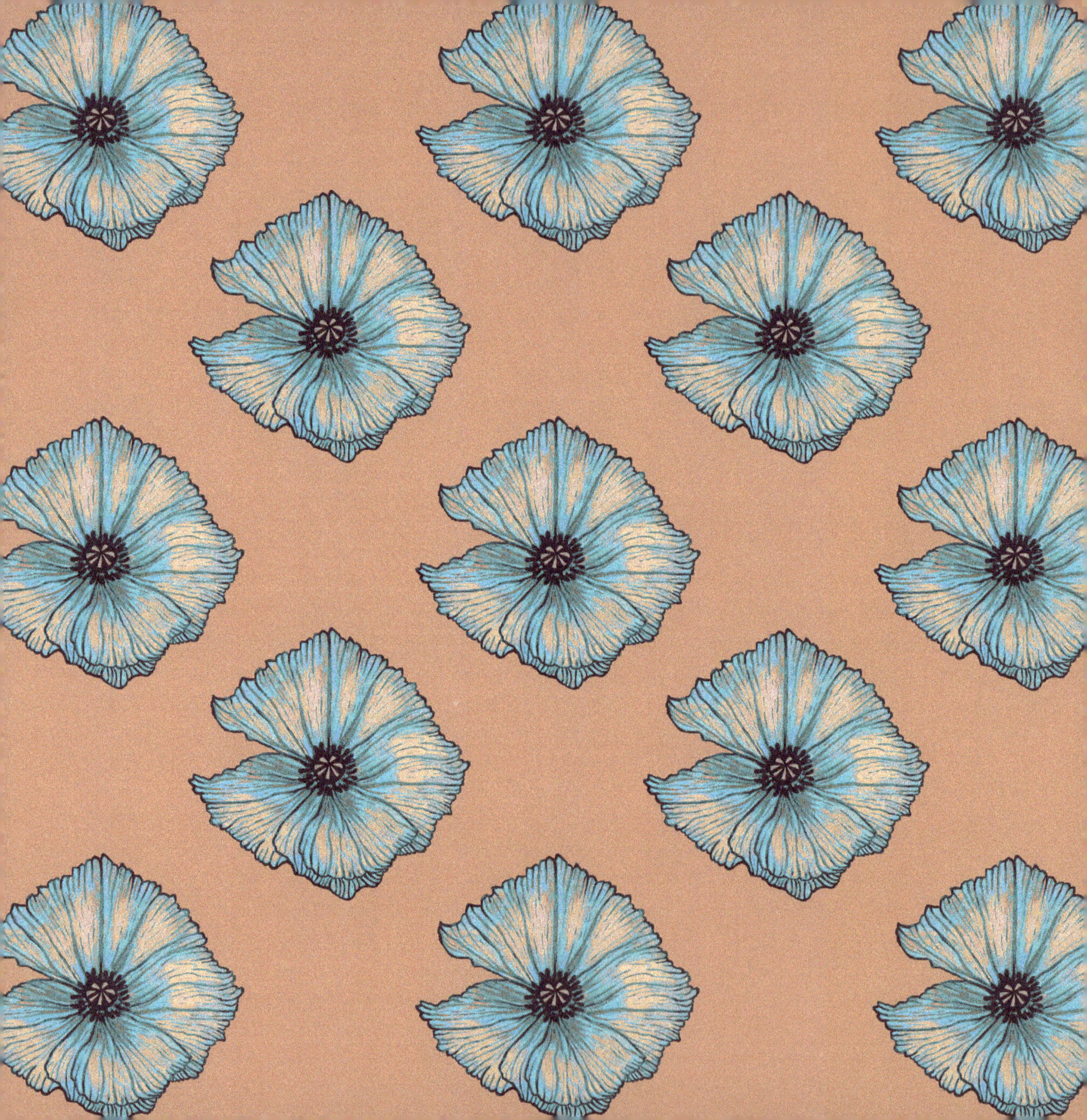

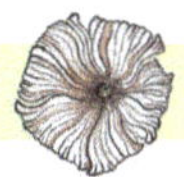

Chapter One

Line it Up!

So many lines, so little time! Lines wrap around our front doors to welcome us home. Some stretch across the horizon. Some curve in and out separating the ocean from the beach.

There are an infinite number of different types of lines. Some are short and some are long. Some are thin and some are thick. Some are perfectly straight, and others zig zag.

There's no end to the number of lines we see. Here, there, and everywhere, a line awaits us. Lines even lead us where we need to go. We see them on the road and on colorful street signs. This way and that way, they guide and outline. They tell us where to go and where to stay.

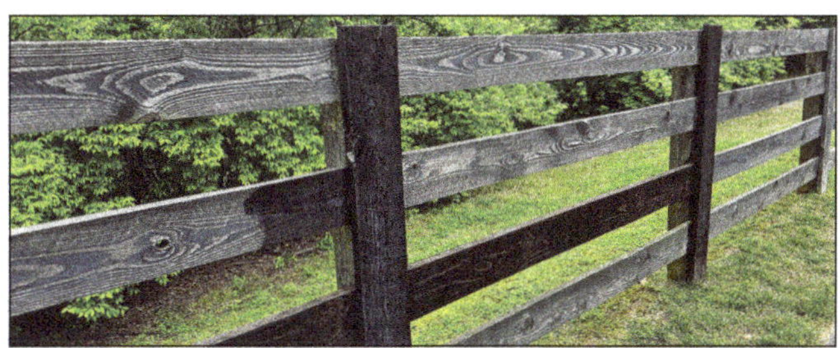

Property boundaries can be defined by fence lines.

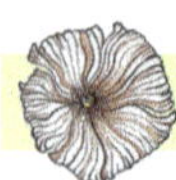

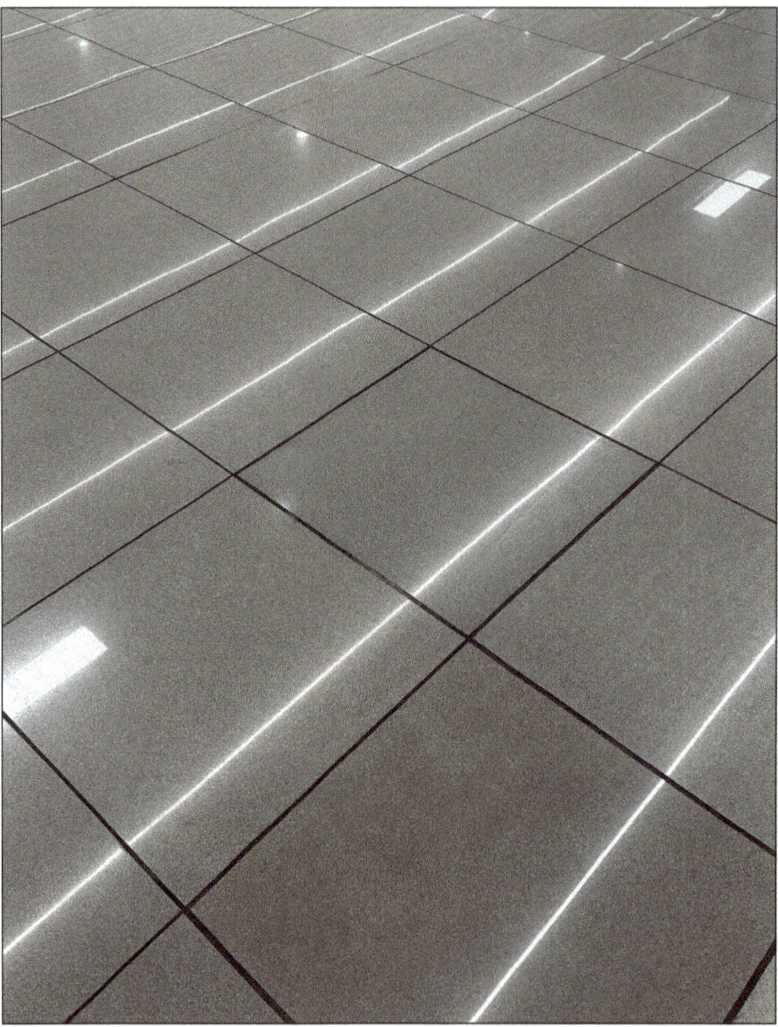

Reflected light lines on tile floor lines.

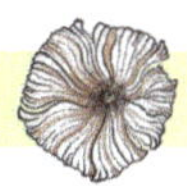

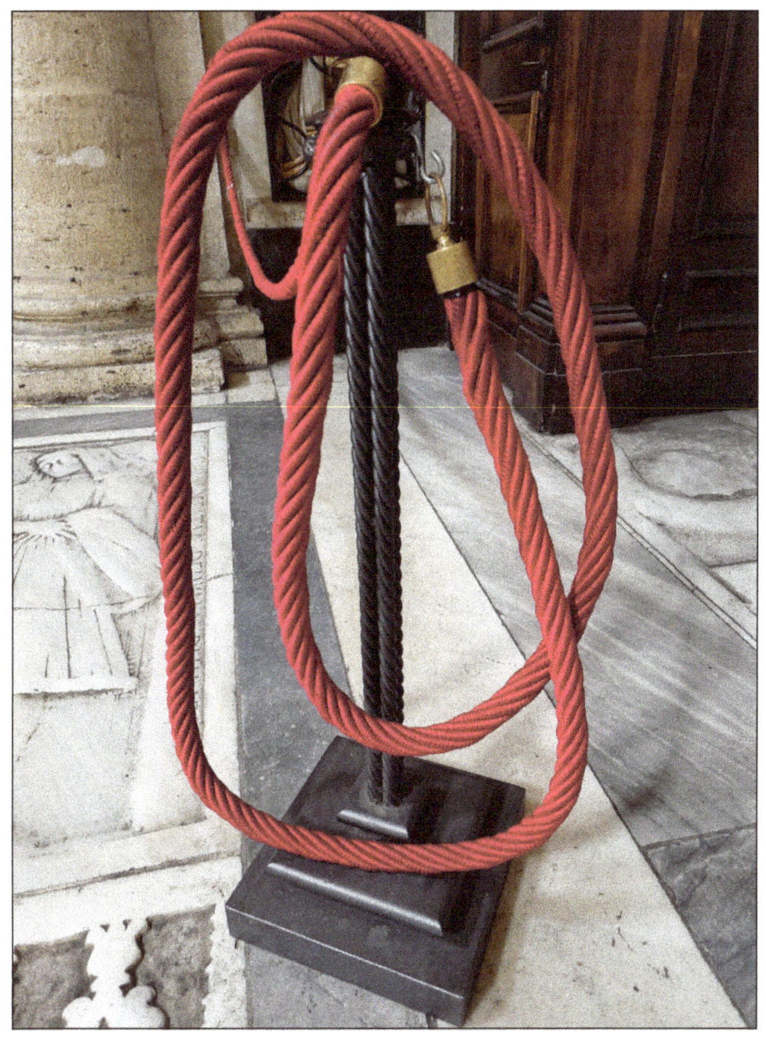

Curving red rope lines.

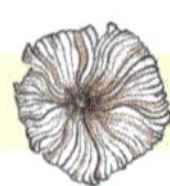

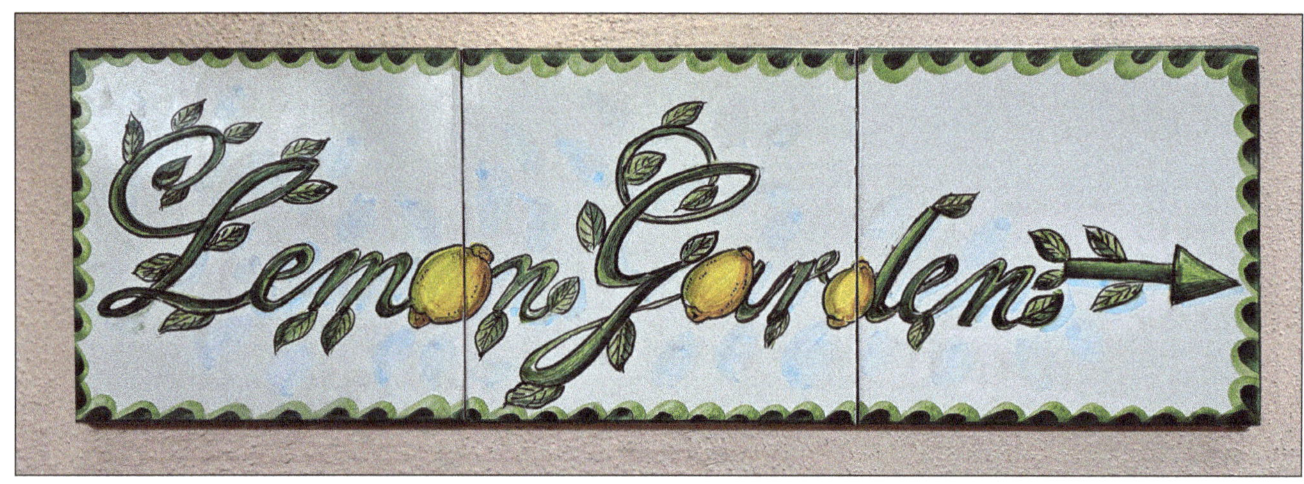

Whimsical and calligraphic garden sign lines.

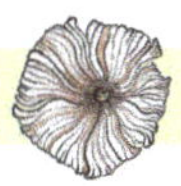

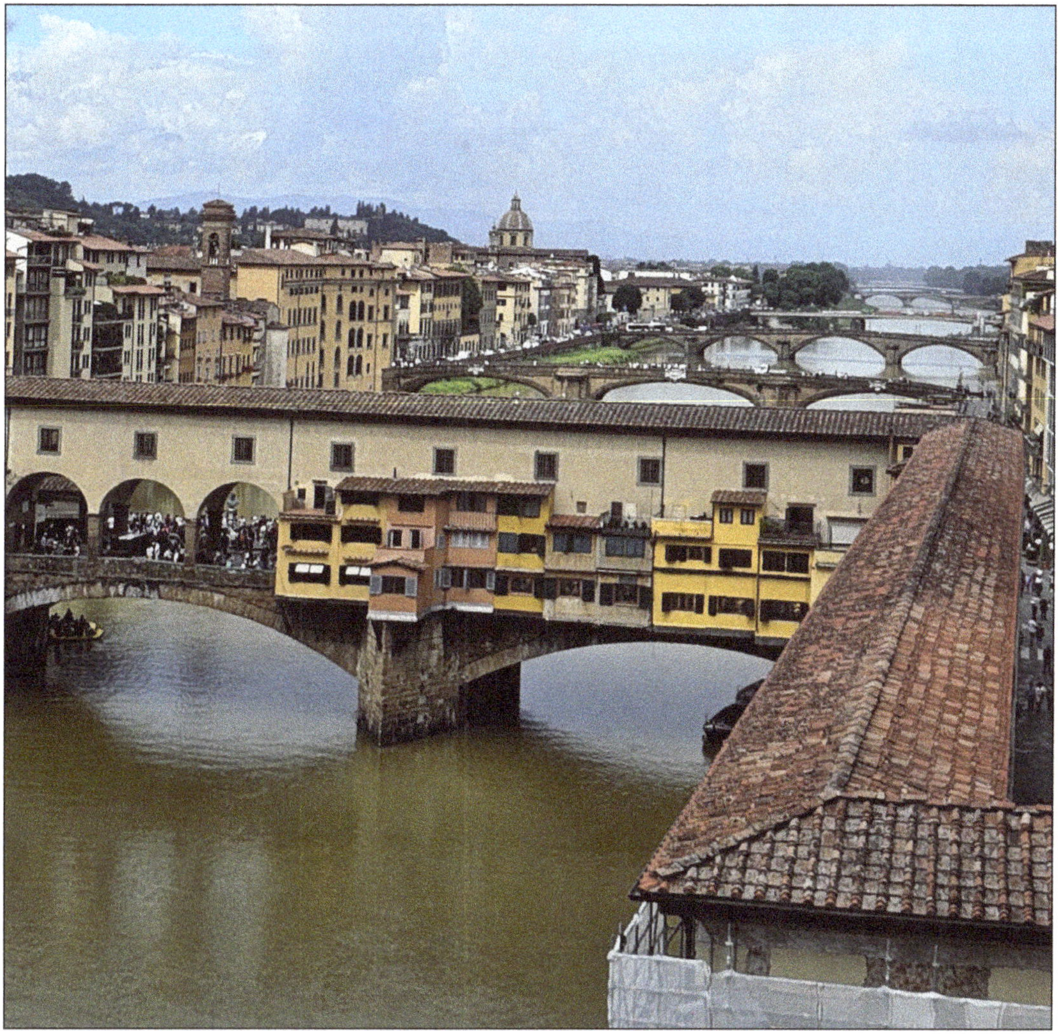

Rooftop and bridge lines.

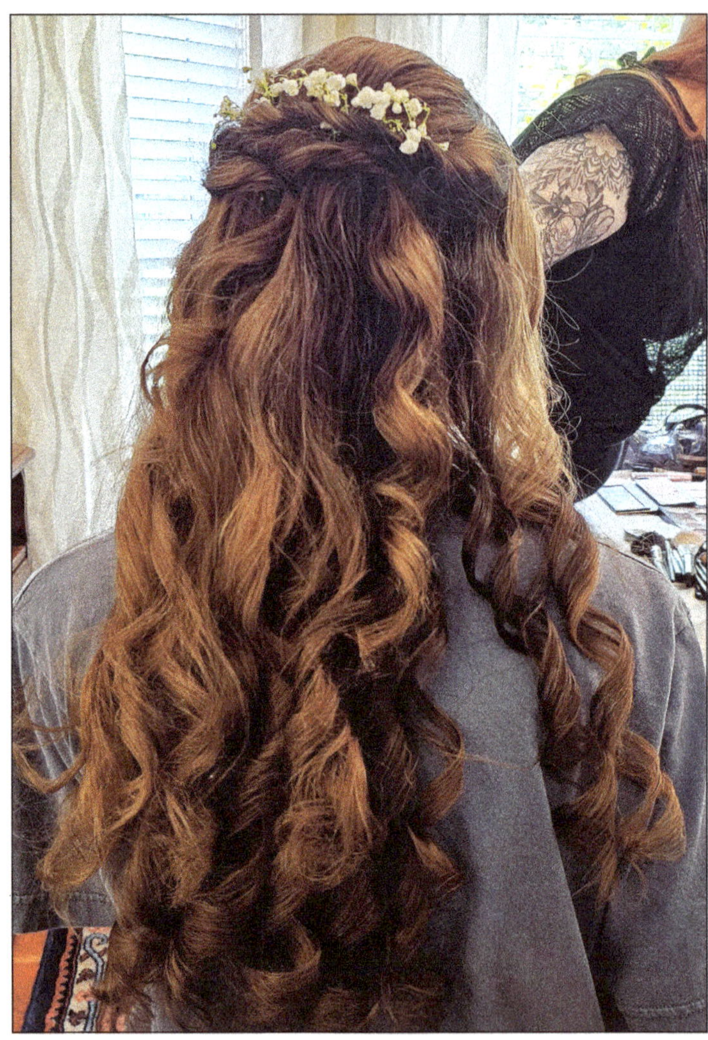

Curly hair lines.

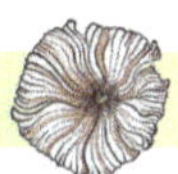

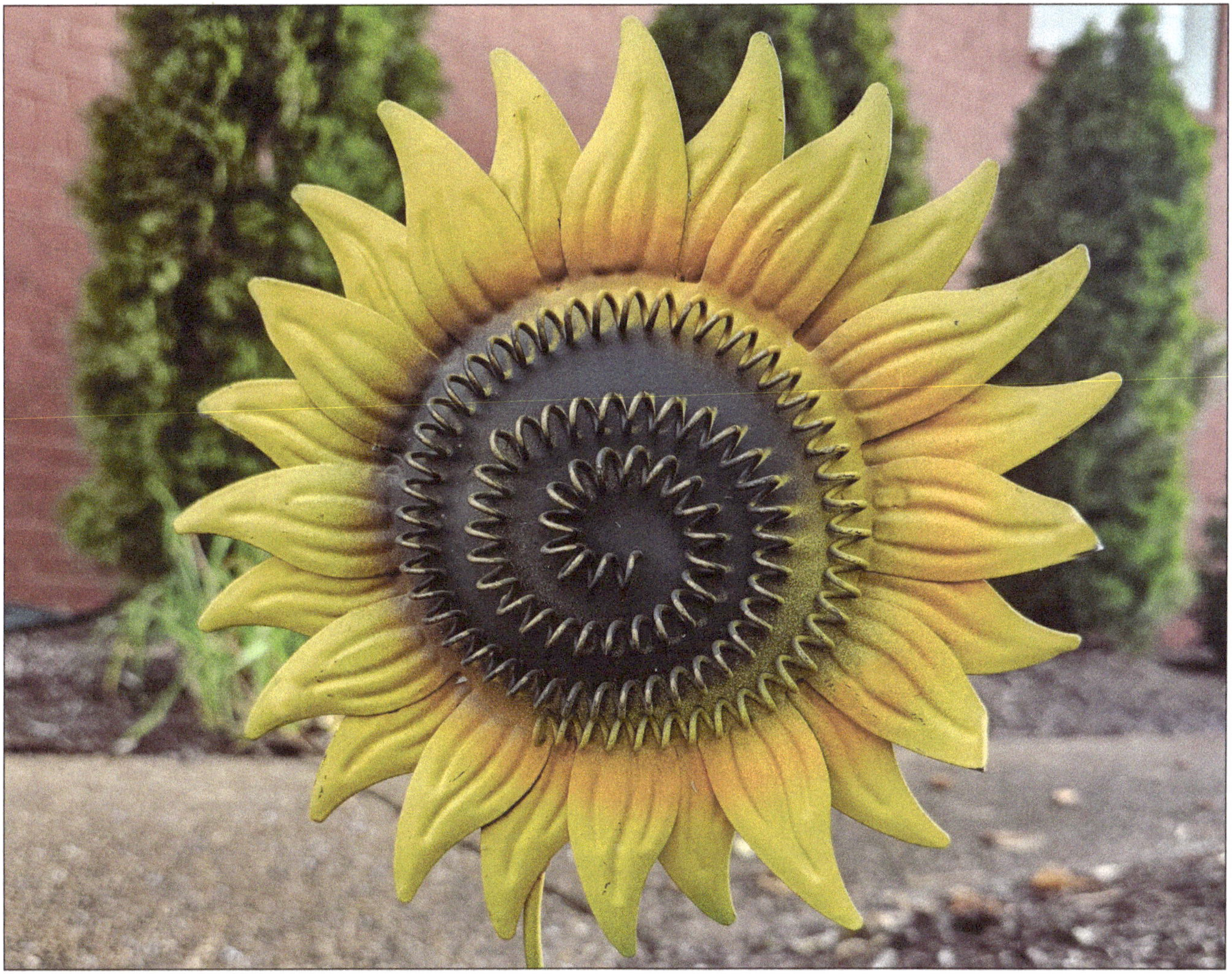

Squiggly sunflower garden décor lines.

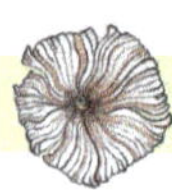

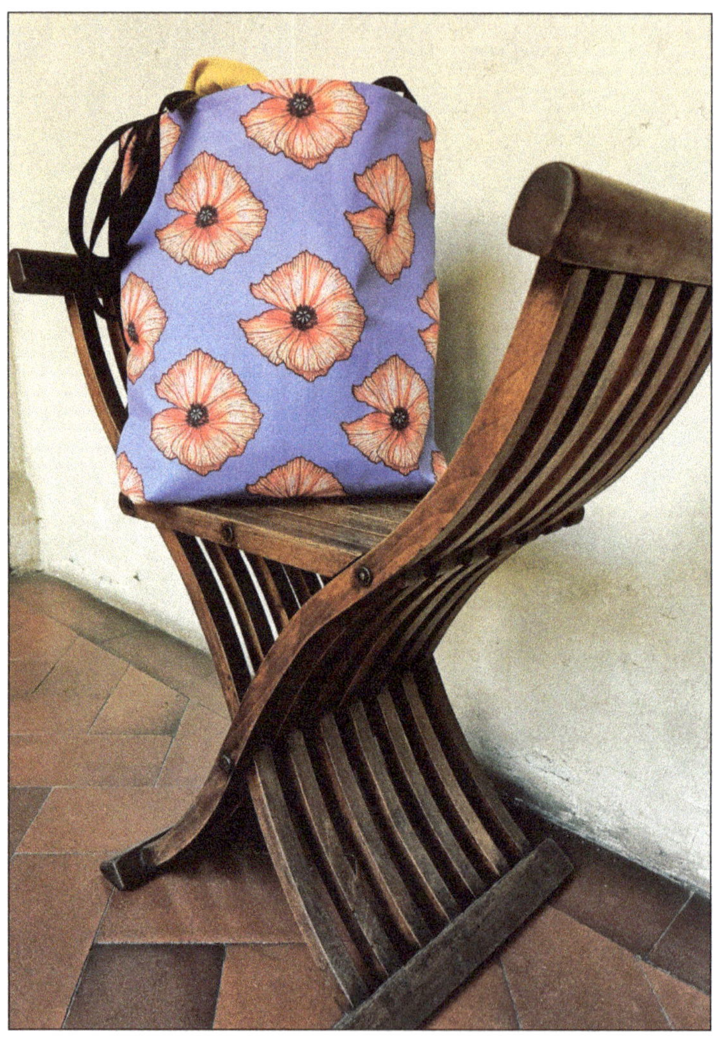

Graceful lines on a classic wooden chair.

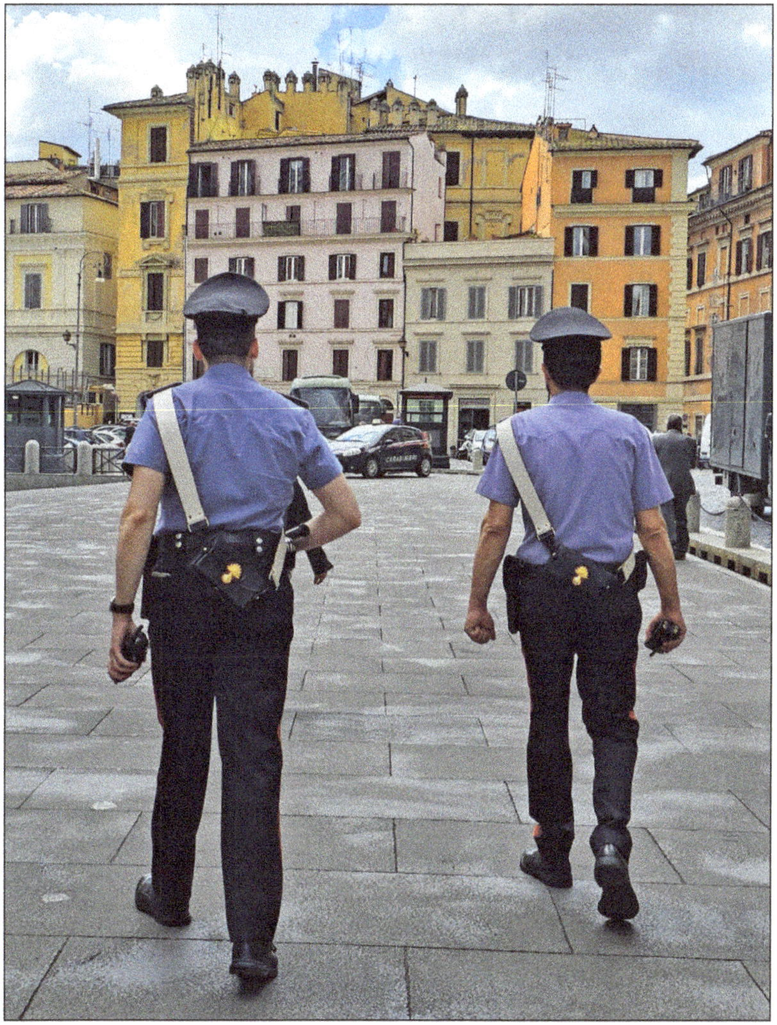

Diagonal lines of the officers' white straps.

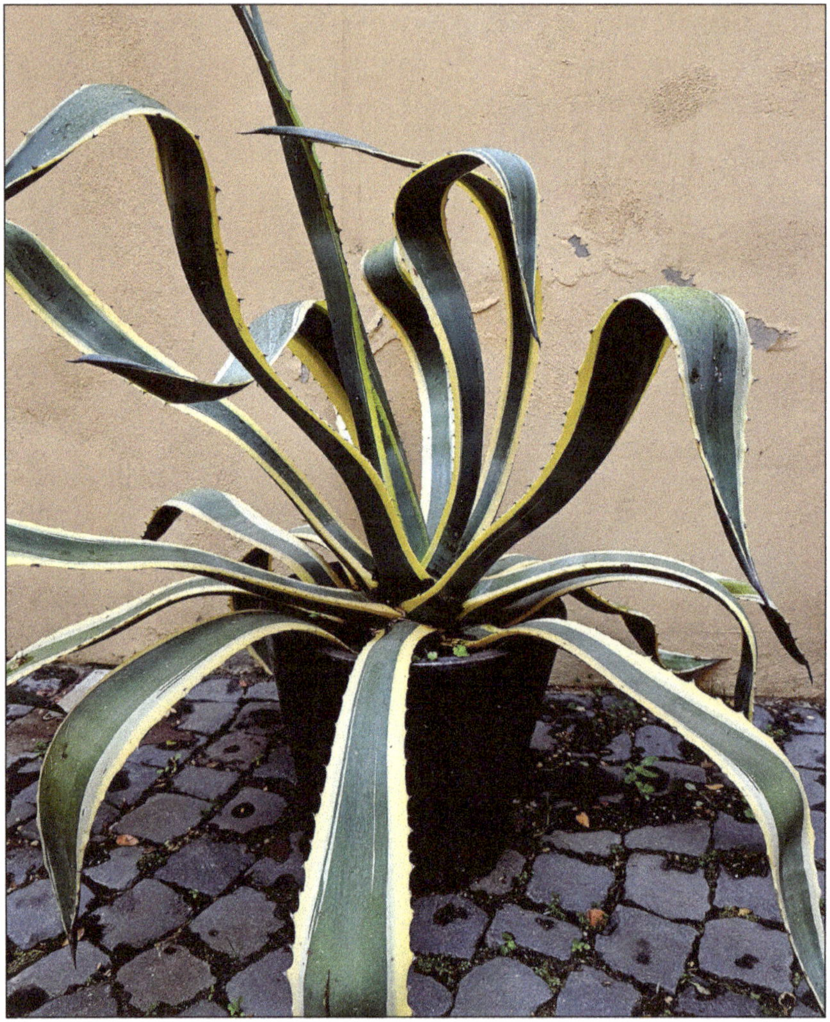

Organic lines of a potted plant.

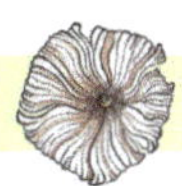

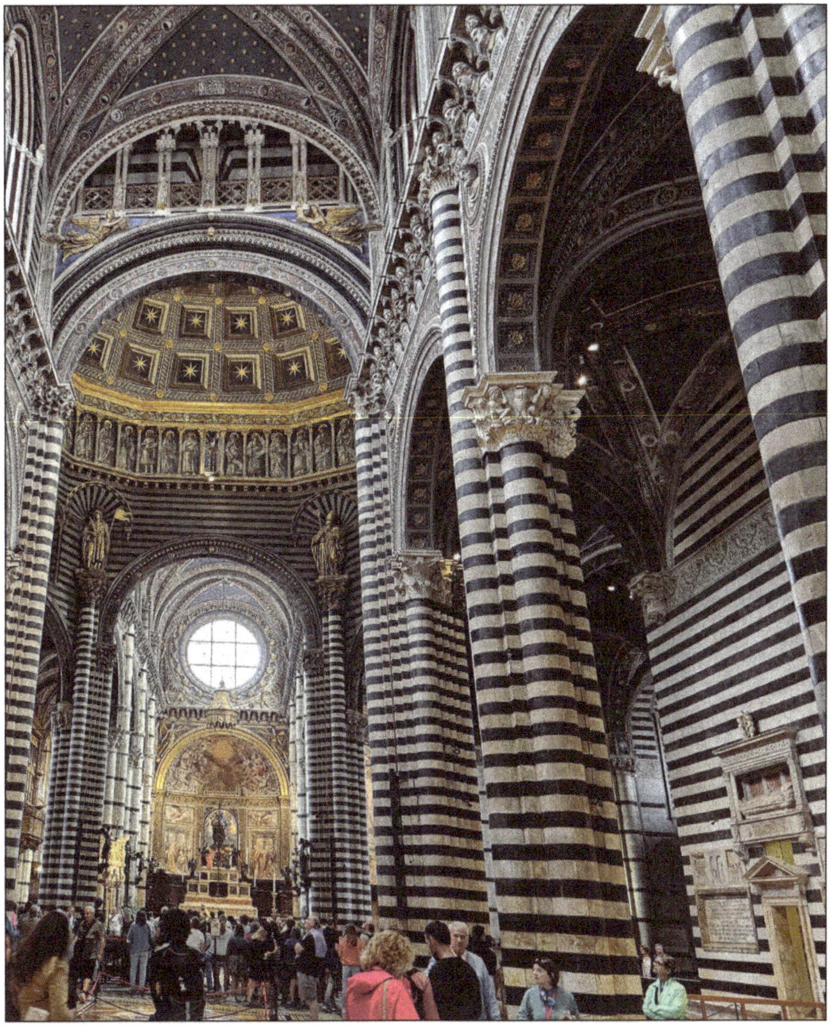

Architectural interior lines.

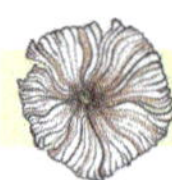

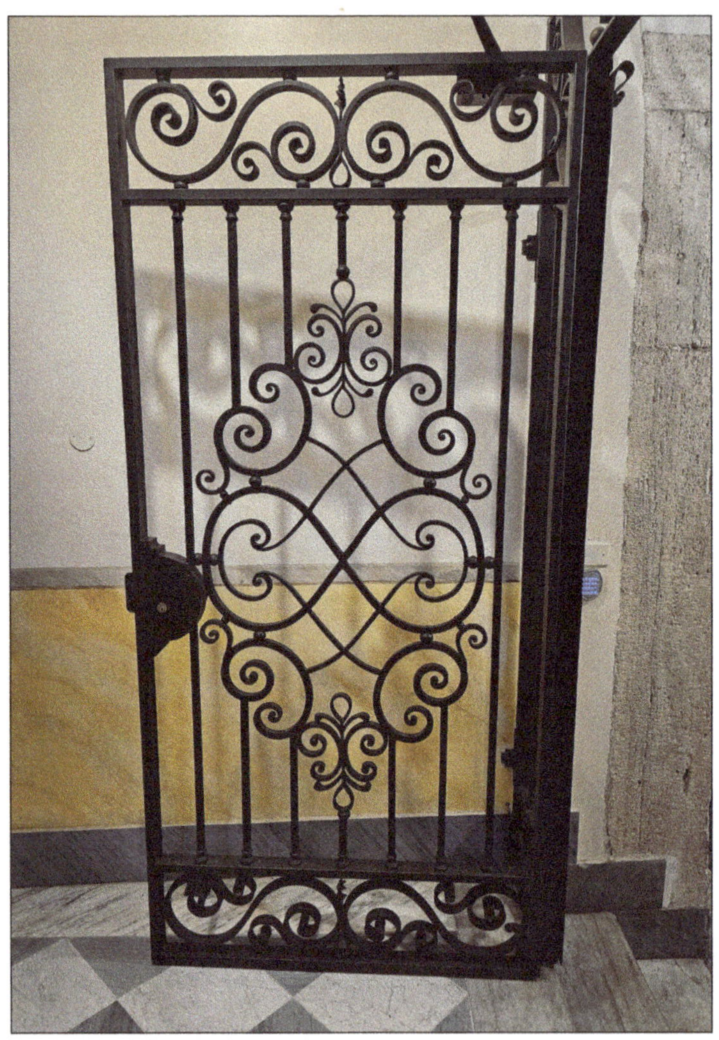

Curvy and straight door lines work together to welcome you in.

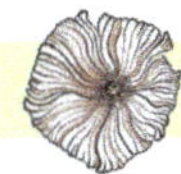

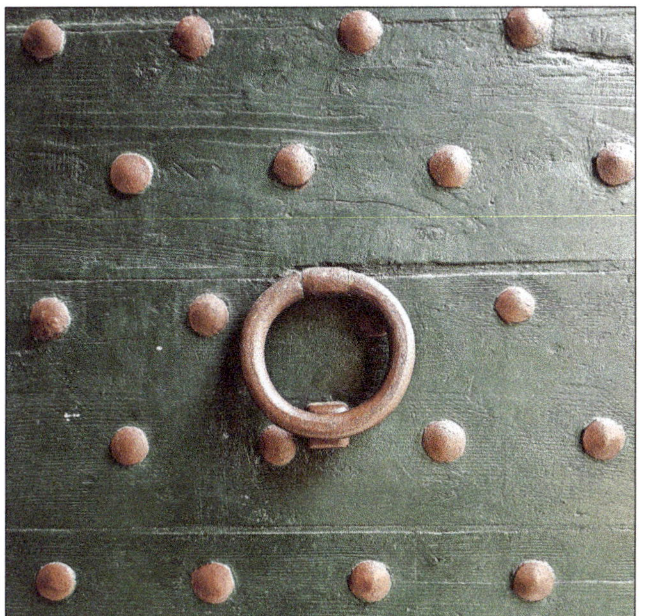 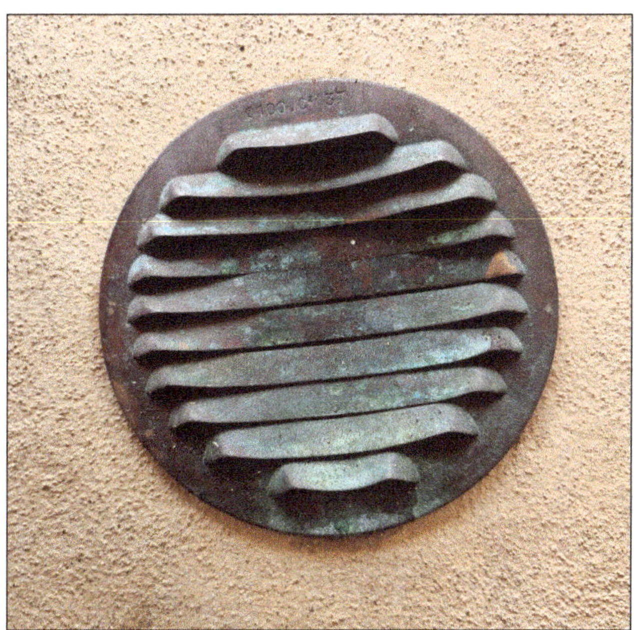

Dotted lines on a door and horizontal lines on a circular vent.

Compositional lines start out wide and eventually converge at a point on the horizon. Elegant calligraphic lines delight our senses. Power lines hold up birds as if they were musical notes. Roof lines lead our eyes around the town. Finish lines draw the runners to the end. Chalk lines inspire a children's game of hopscotch. Curly lines trace beautiful hair curls. And dotted lines beg us to draw a connection. The Swiss-born German artist **Paul Klee (1879-1940)** once said, "A line is a dot that went for a walk."

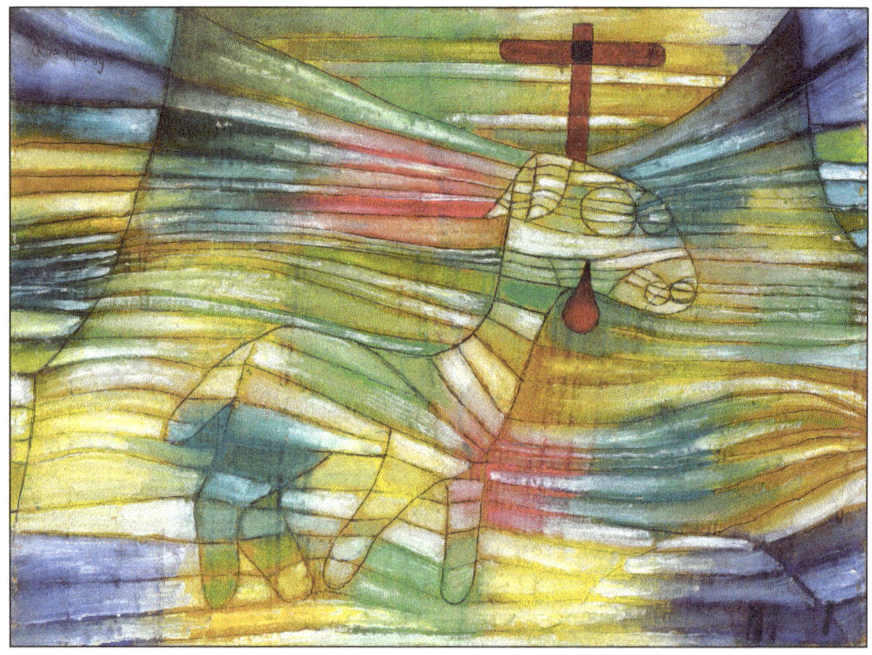

The medley of lines in a Paul Klee painting.

 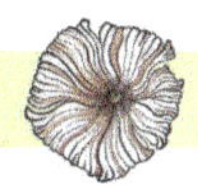

As we look around our everyday world, we can follow the squiggly, curvy, long, or short lines to help us see more beauty. **Don't forget to look for shadow lines, too!**

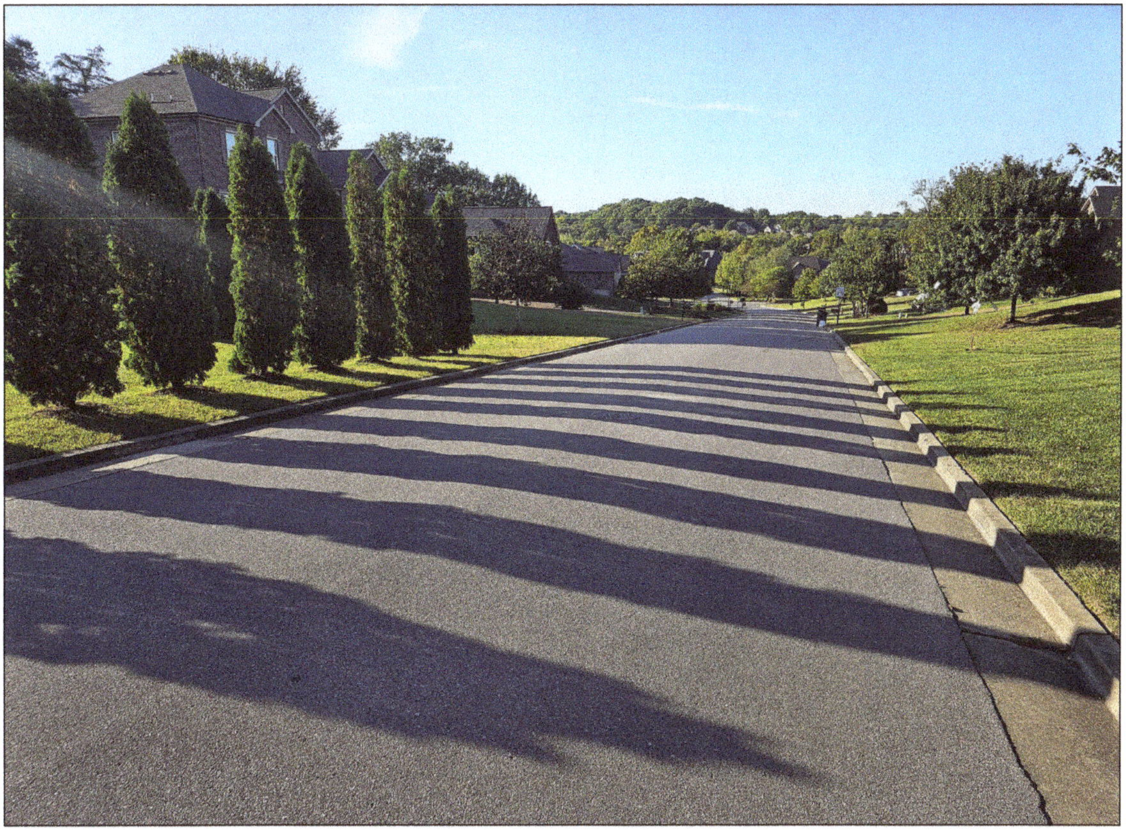

Shadow lines that remind us of piano keys.

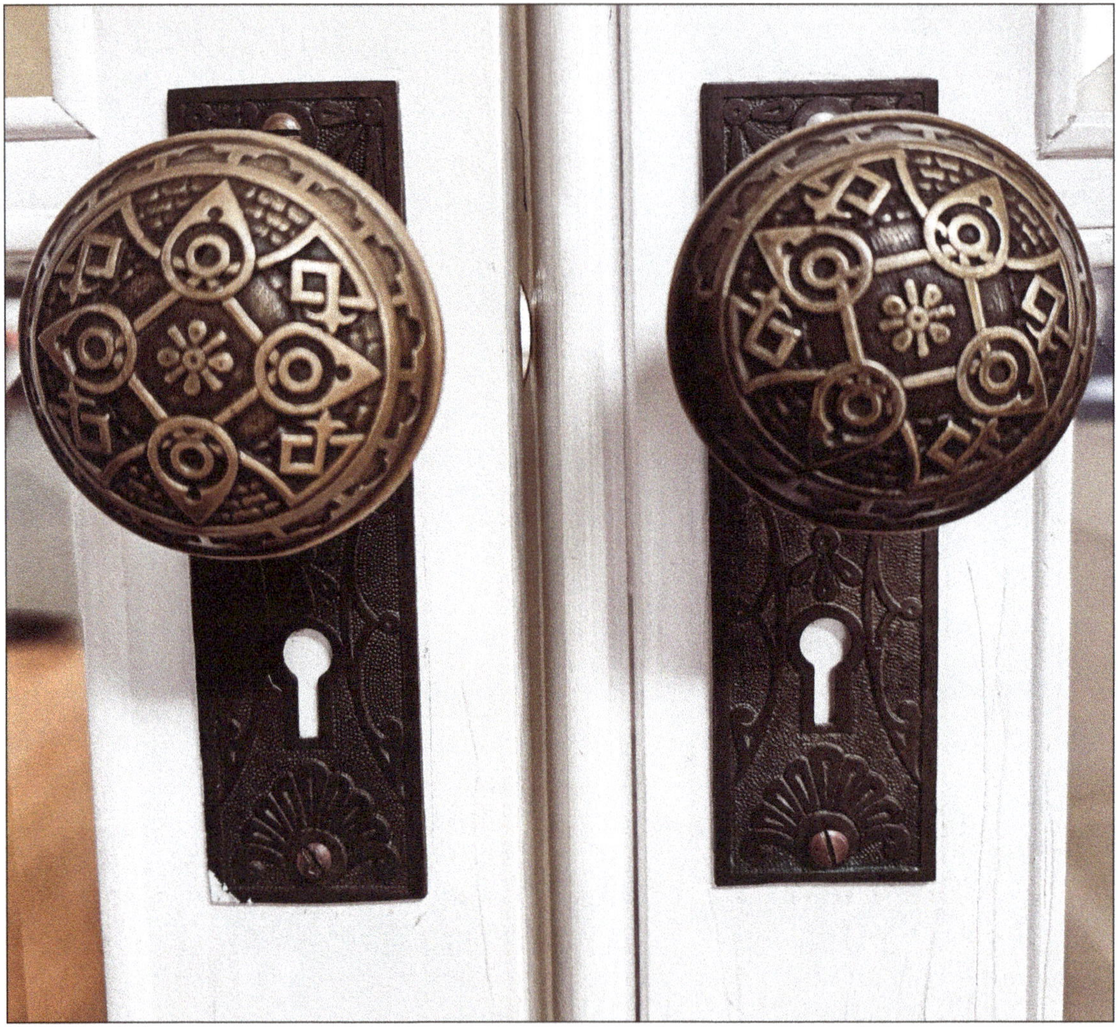

These beautiful door knobs are a symphony of expressive lines!

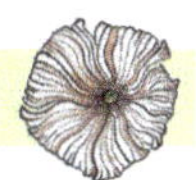

Now it's time to pick up a pencil and document the lines you encounter. Look around you. How do you describe the lines you see? Do they twist? Are they hairline lines, or thick lines? Do your eyes go up or down, or side to side? Would you say the lines you see are horizontal or vertical? Or, perhaps, diagonal or intersecting?

In the photo on the next page, a decorative line can be found at the bottom of the picture frame moulding. See how this line is drawn and documented. **On the next page, describe in words and draw four or more lines you see around you. Record your lines in the very same way.**

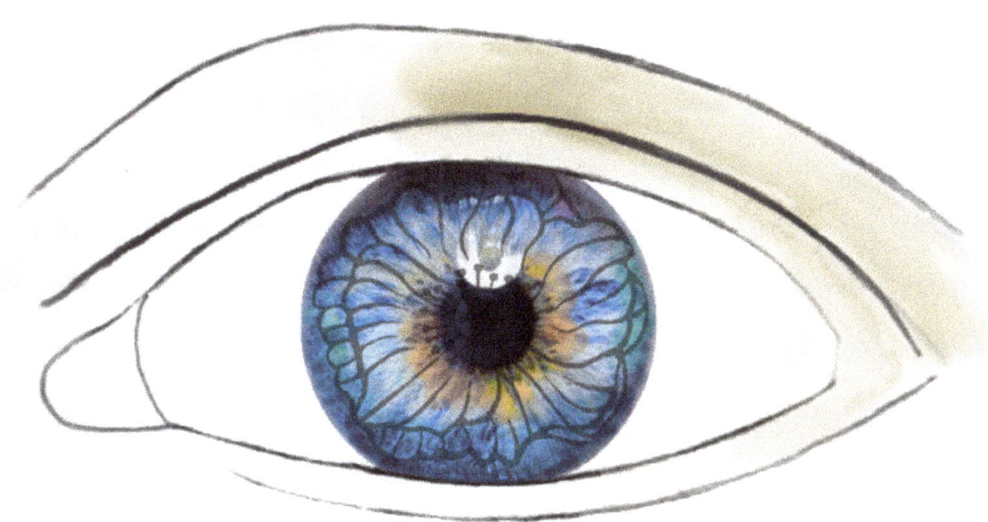

It's time to use your artist's eye to study lines!

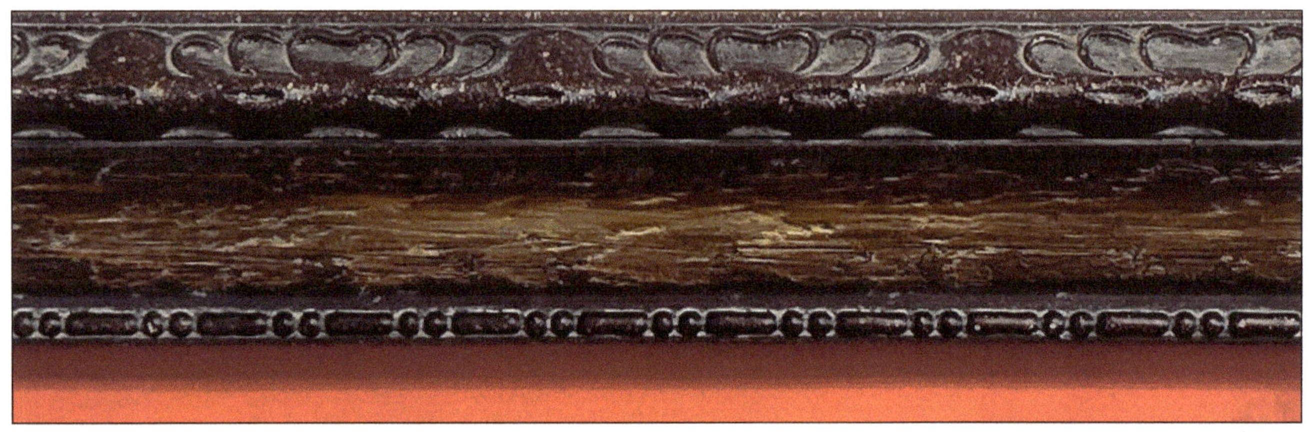

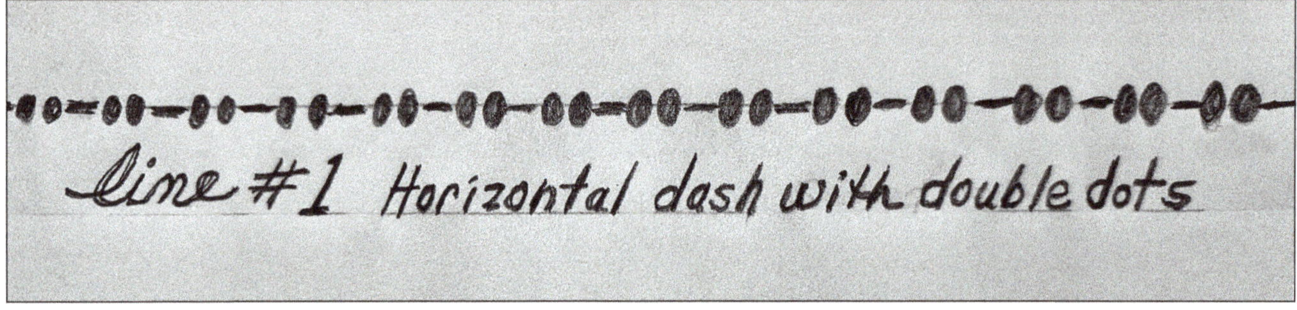

Study the picture frames in your home. Unique lines can be found everywhere.

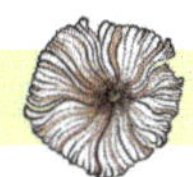

Record four different kinds of lines you see around you, using drawings and words.

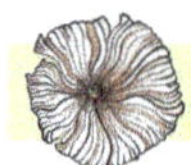

On the next two pages, draw the following two images using only lines. No color or shading. Only lines. First draw the willow branch with curvy, elegant lines. Next draw the poppy flower with short, choppy, dotted and irregular lines. This exercise helps you see how lines can influence the overall feel of any composition.

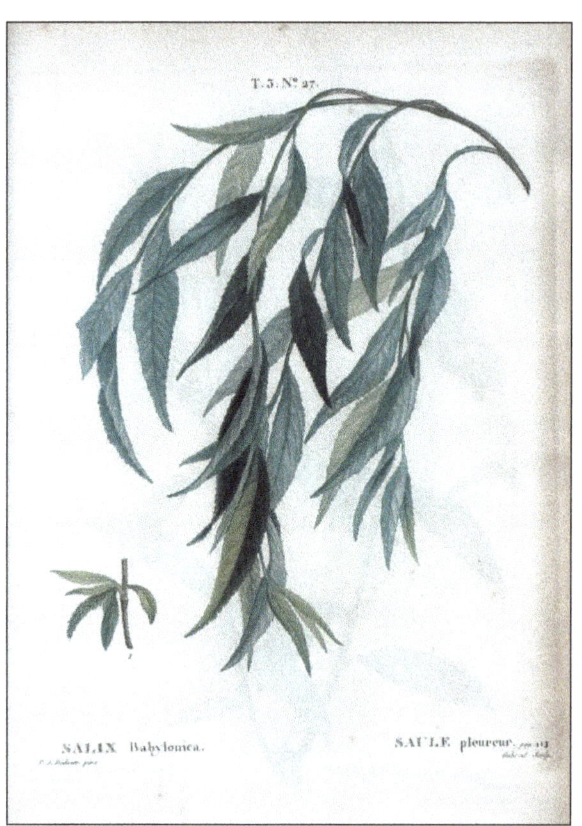

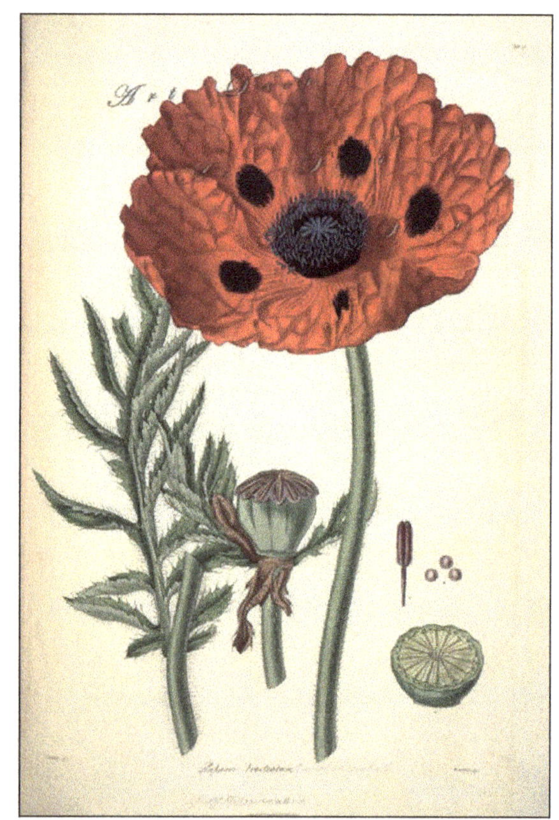

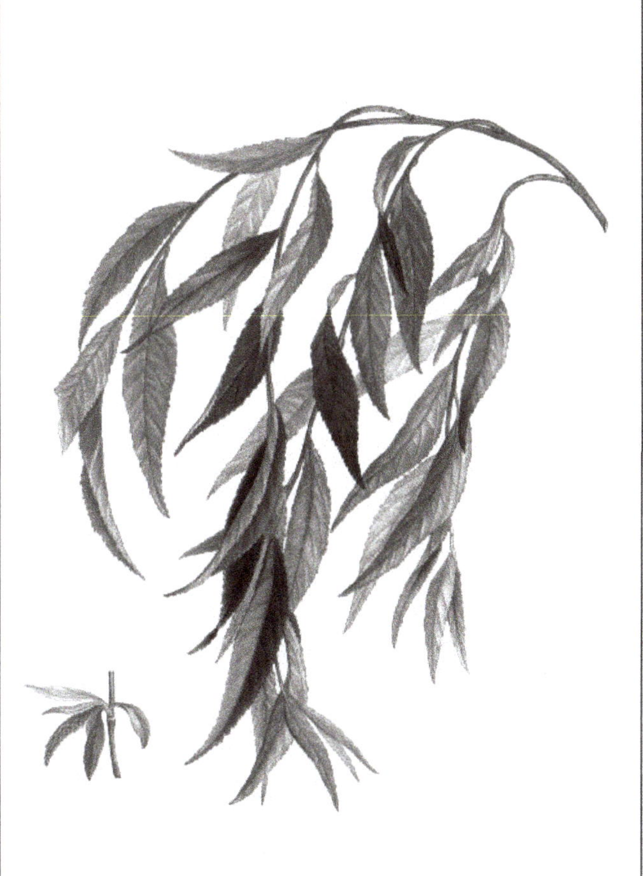

*Draw the willow branch with curvy, elegant lines.
Use your pencil (no color).*

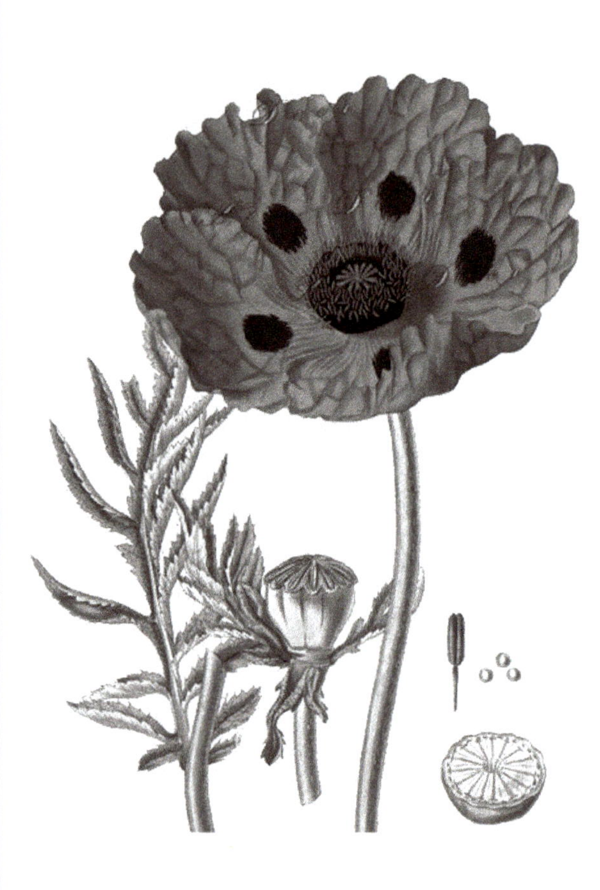

Draw the poppy with short, choppy, dotted, and irregular lines. Use your pencil (no color).

 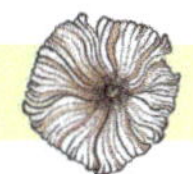

Do you like one of your line drawings more than the other? There is no right or wrong answer. Just observe what you feel. You are developing your vision and perceiving the world of lines around you. Take your time to carefully study as you add in each line. Remember some lines are thin and some are thick. Also observe how some lines end. Some end in a curl and some in a point.

Your very first drawings are done. Your eyes have been sharpened. You have begun searching for lines in the environment and translating them to paper. Your journey to seeing like an artist has now begun.

Keep seeing the beautiful variety of lines around you. They are out there waiting for you, *wherever you go*!

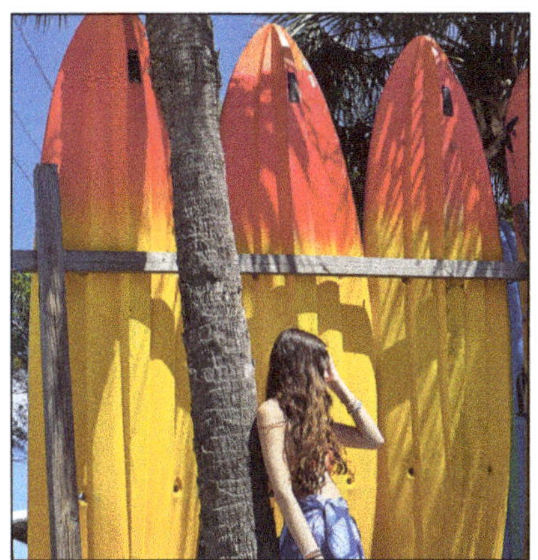

Vertical palm tree and kayak lines.

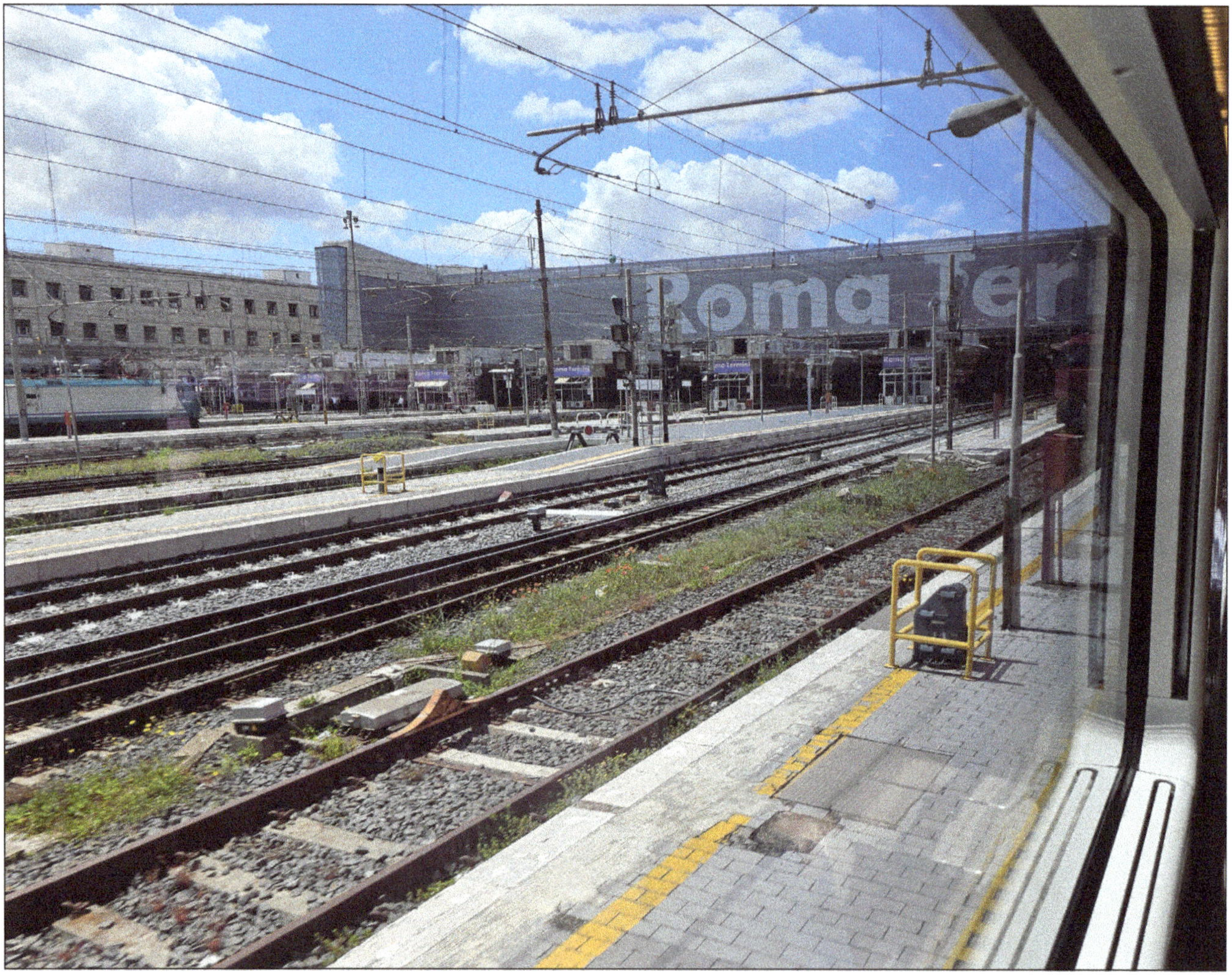

Train station lines.

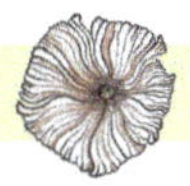

Chapter One Fun Fact

Line art is one of the most fundamental elements of art. Without line, the other elements couldn't exist. Line drawing has been around for ages. Ancient Egyptians were the most famous of early line artists. They masterfully incorporated line art into their ancient hieroglyphics and wall carvings.

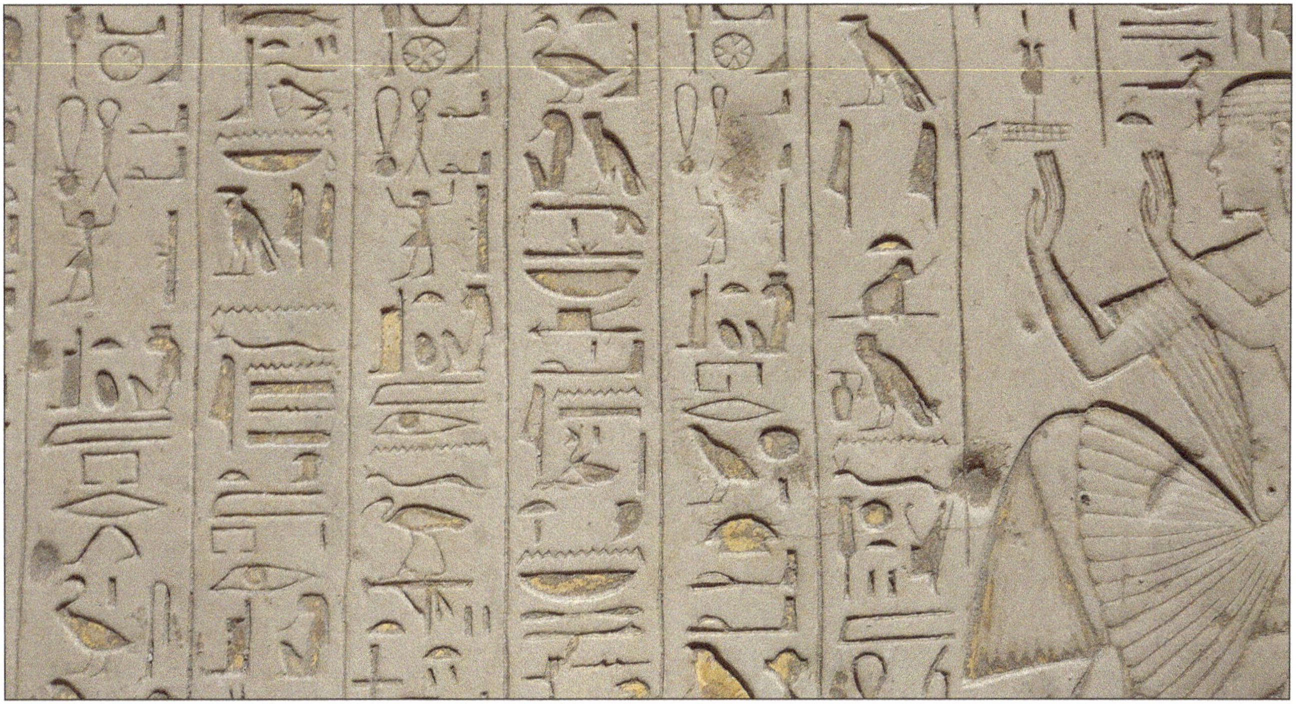

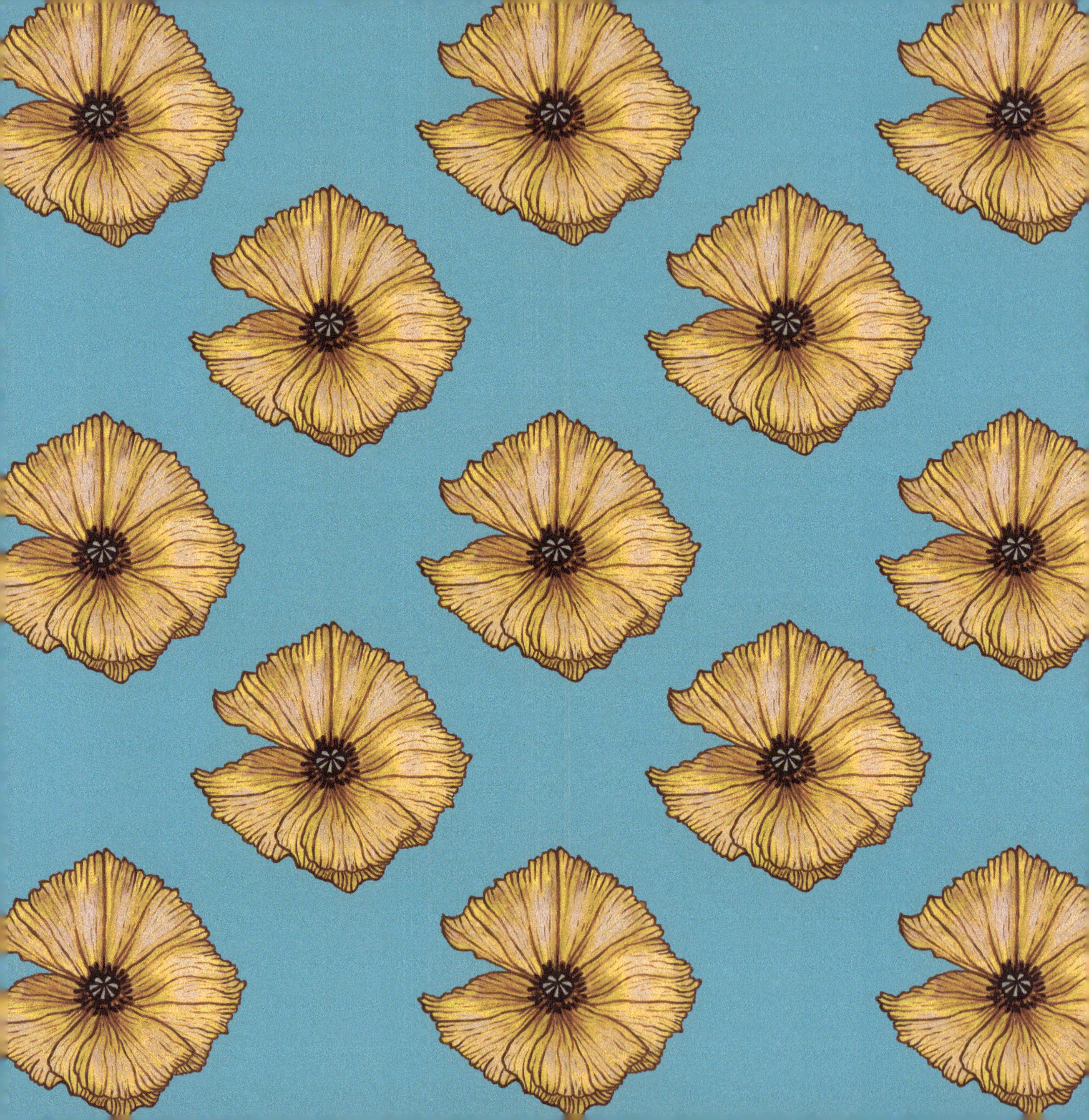

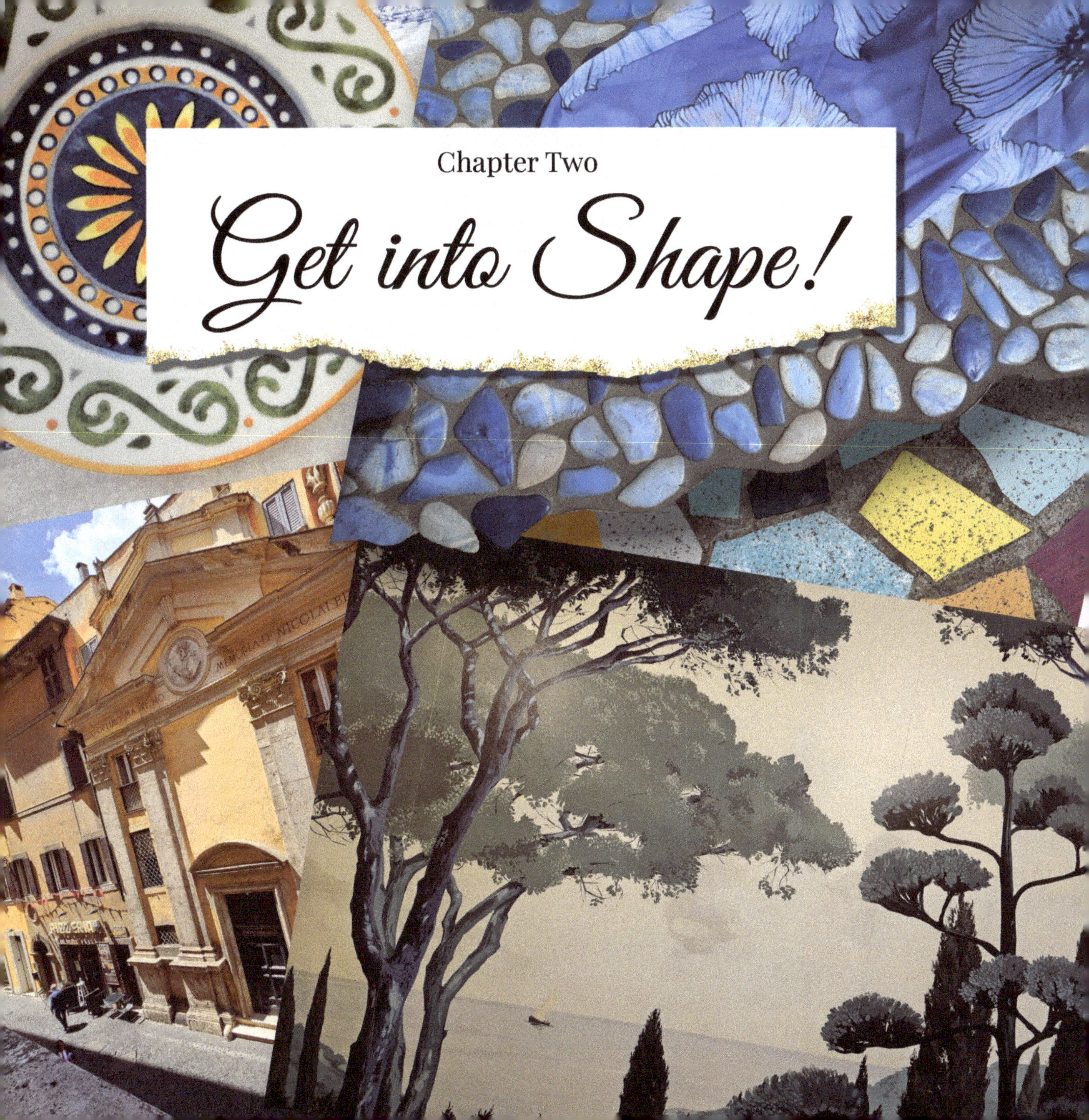
Chapter Two
Get into Shape!

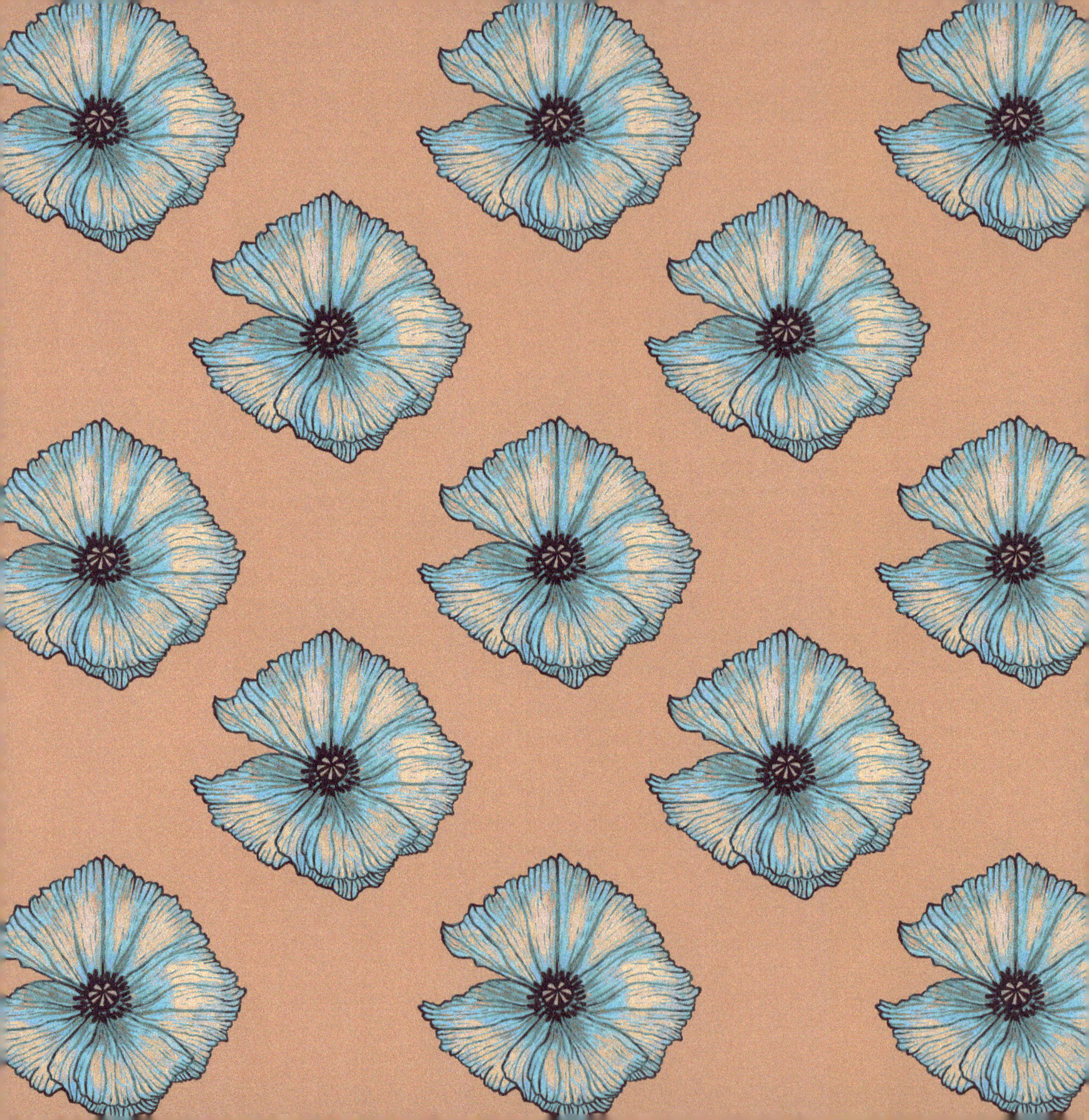

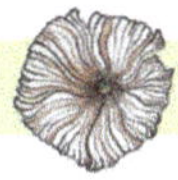

Chapter Two

Get into Shape!

Here, there, and everywhere, shapes outline our lives. Shapes speak to us. An arch invites us to enter. An X shape tells us railroad tracks are in front of us. A triangle tells us to yield. A red octagon tells us to stop.

From circles, rectangles, squares, octagons, and triangles to free-form outlines; lines meet up and become shapes. My art teacher used to say, when a line catches its tail, it forms a shape.

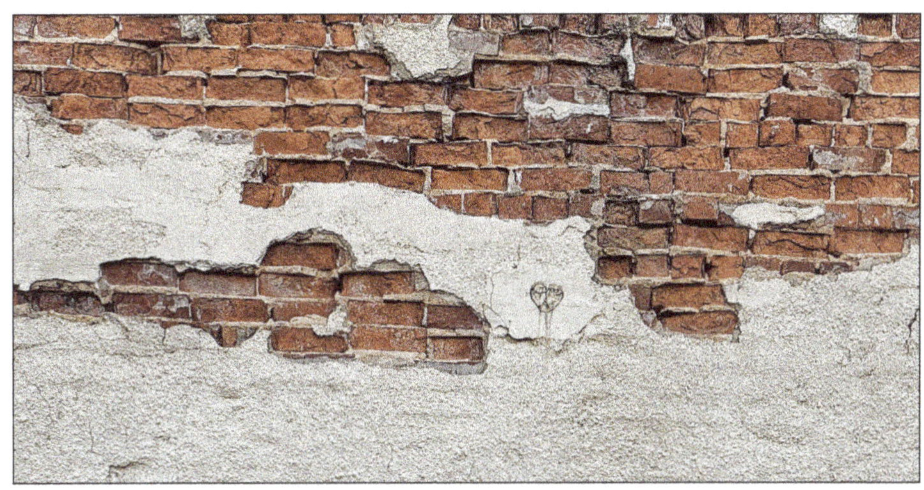

Rectangular brick shapes come together to form free-form shapes.

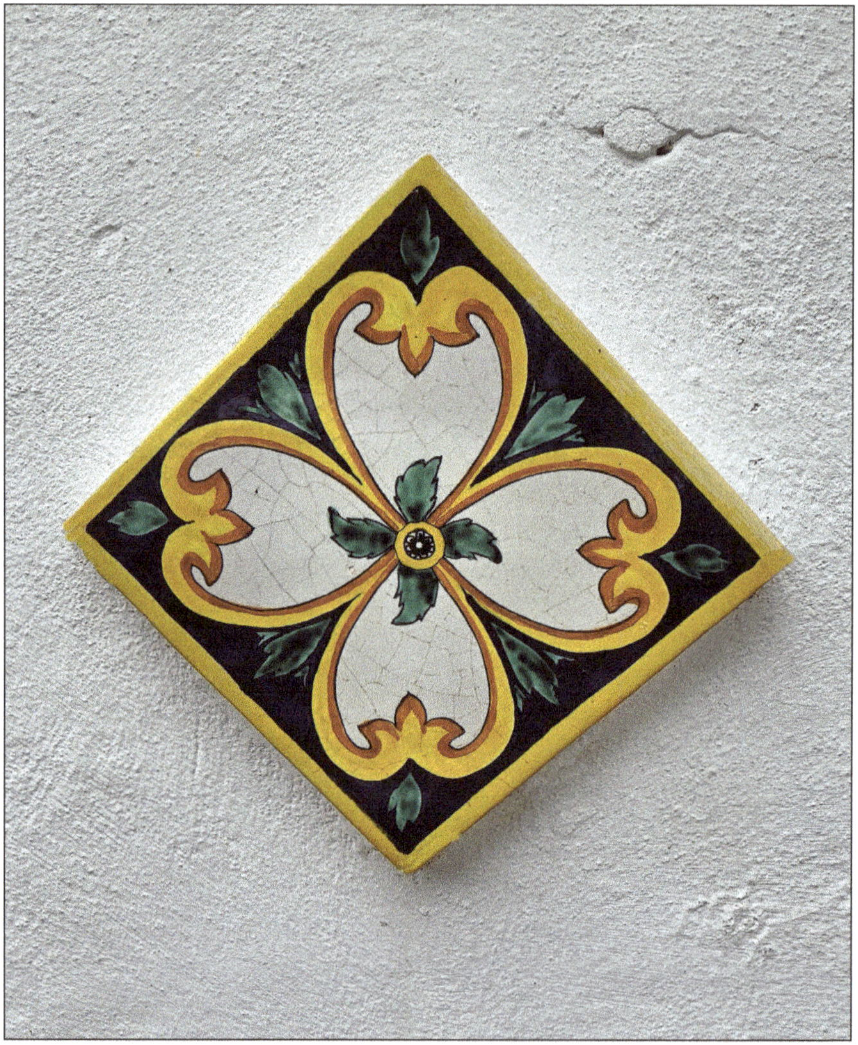

Diamond shape tile.

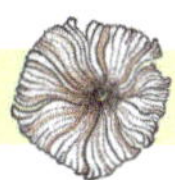

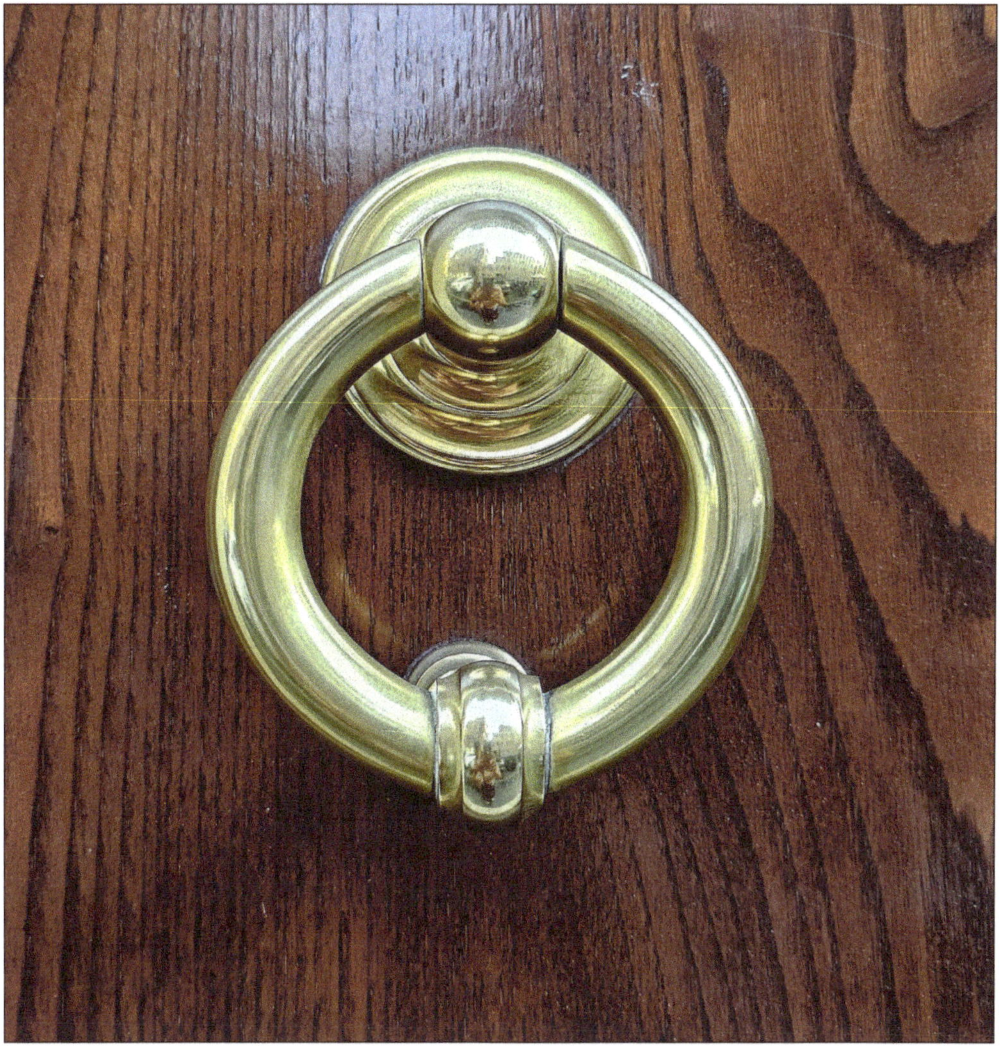

Circle shape door knocker.

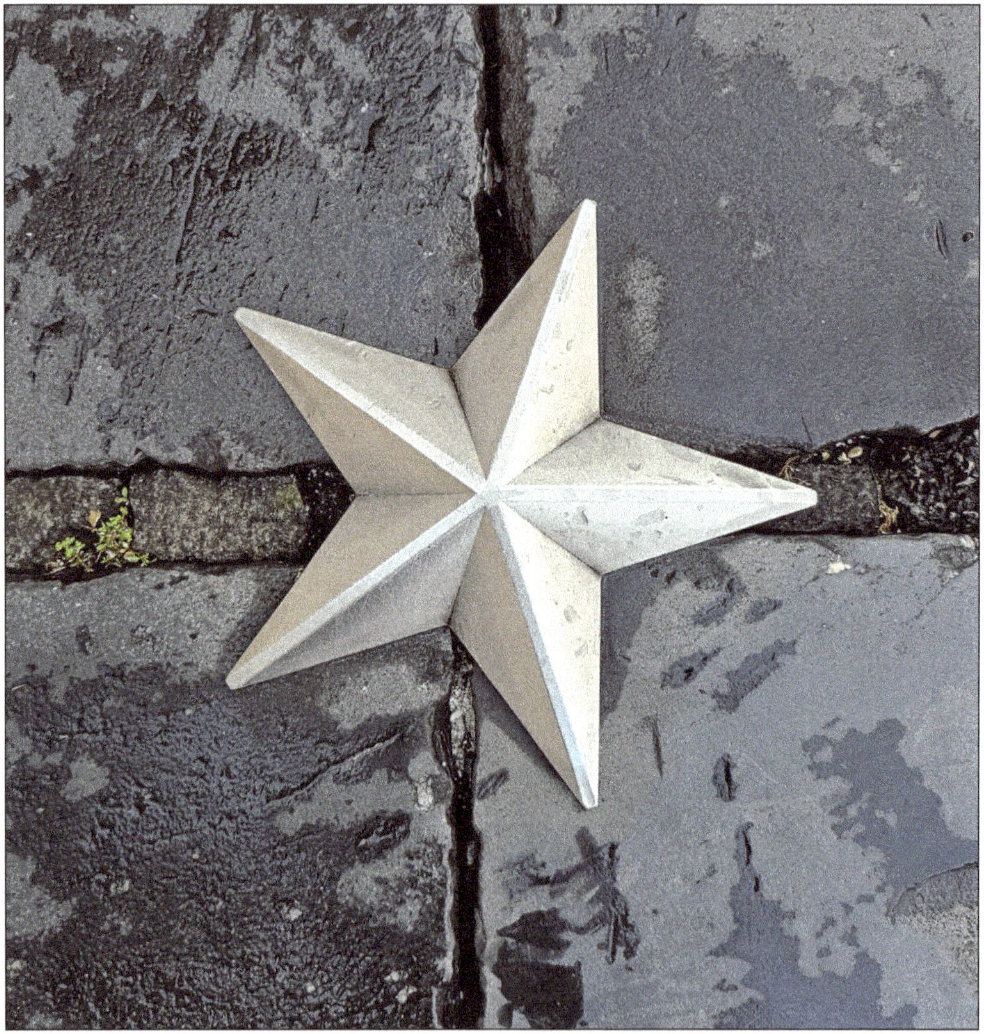

Star-shape pavement marker.

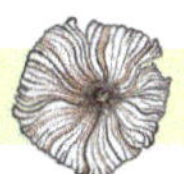

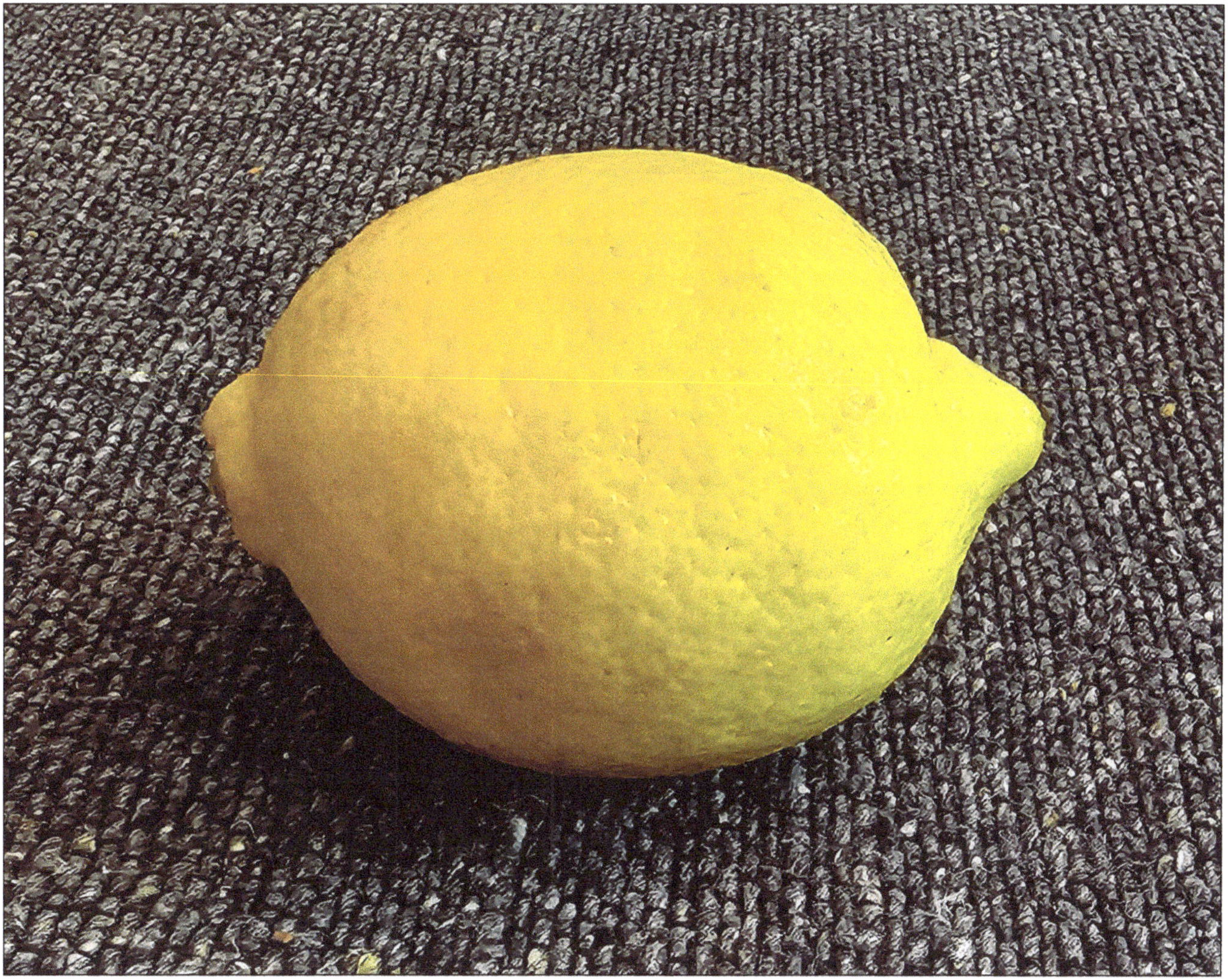

Organic shape of a lemon.

For many of us, the simplest language of shapes starts when we are kids drawing our first sun. We start with a big yellow circle and add yellow lines of radiating rays. Then we add blue lines outlining cloud shapes in the sky and a green line for the ground. In no time at all, we quickly learn to put two shapes together to depict something, as a home becomes a square and a triangle the roof. When our first outlines were finished, we grabbed our crayons to color our shapes.

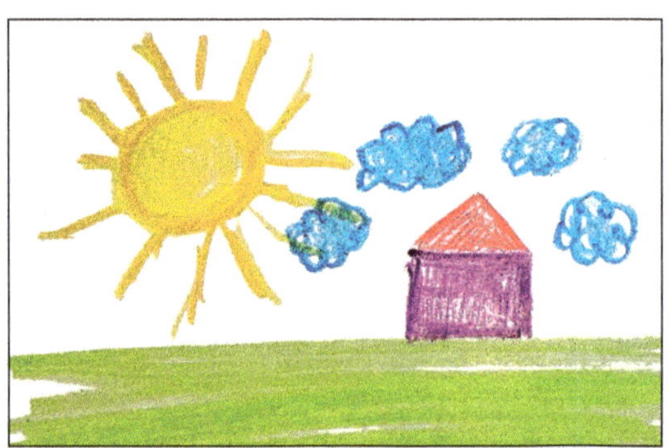

Shapes give us the building blocks to create anything. Shapes can be put together in any number of ways to visualize ideas. There are so many shapes to choose from. There are boat shapes and plane shapes, apple shapes and egg shapes and pear shapes. There are unusual shapes like the hexagon.

Shapes delight and inspire. Some love the heart and some love the diamond. We continue this affection for shapes when we grow up and even pick wallpaper and upholstery that reflect our shape preferences.

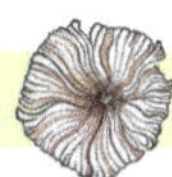

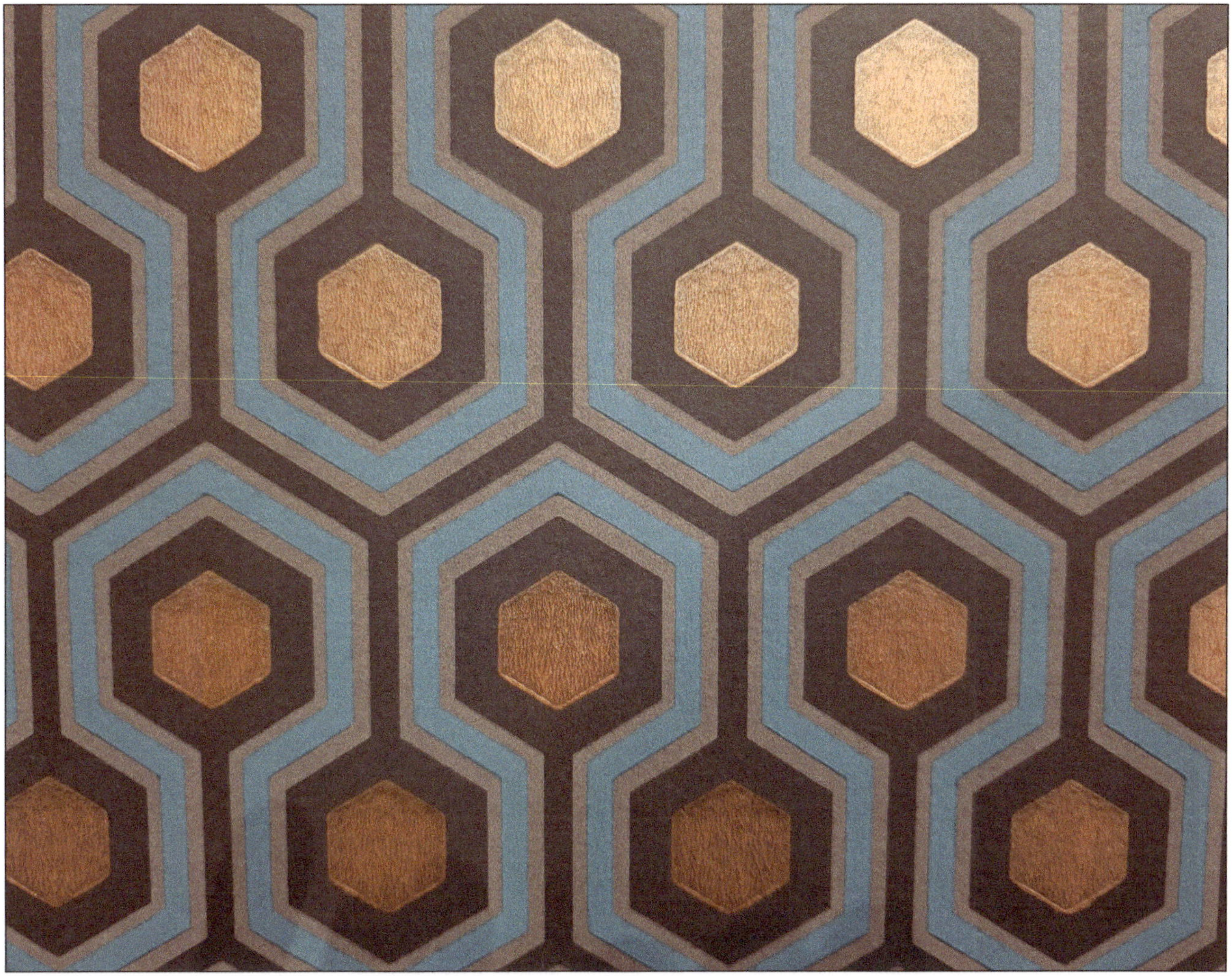

Hexagon–shape wallpaper.

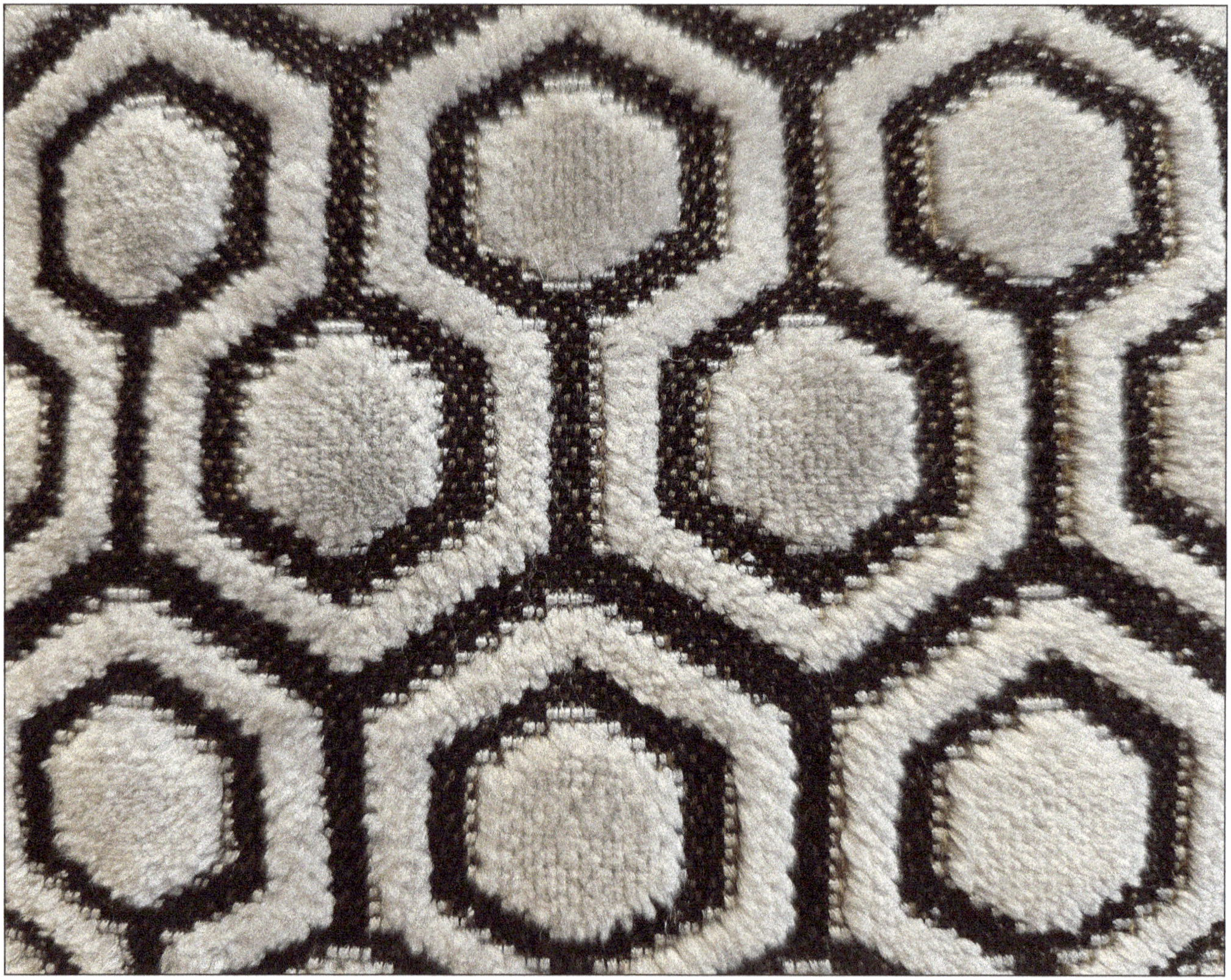

Hexagon–shape upholstery.

 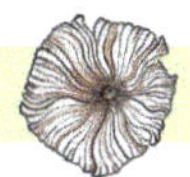

What shapes draw your attention? Grab your pencils and get ready to draw a variety of shapes on the next few pages. Start by drawing things that are easy to find. After you study your subject, you'll begin to outline it. Place the point of your pencil on your sketch paper. If you start at this point and do not lift your pencil off the page until the outline of your shape is complete, then you will have successfully created a ***contour line drawing***. This is your goal.

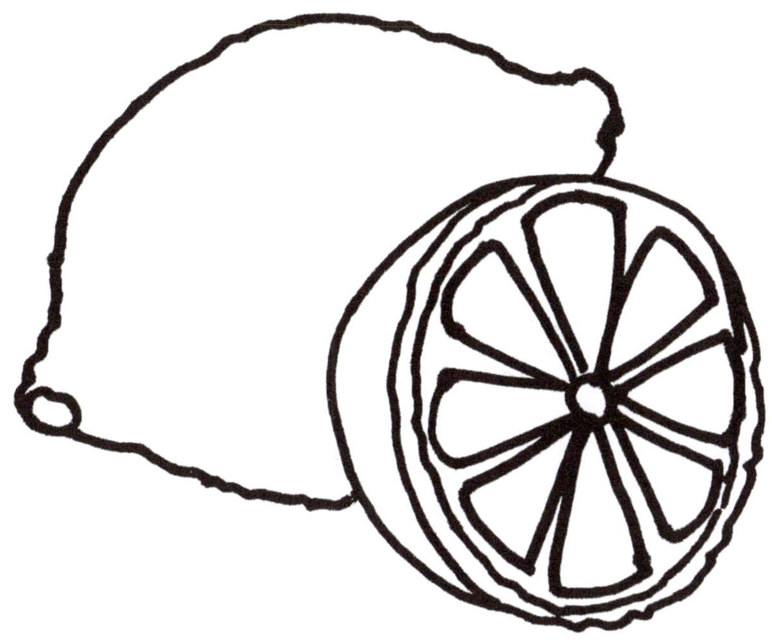

Contour line drawing of the outside and inside shape of a lemon.

For example, you might try a contour drawing of the shape of a piece of fruit. Grab a piece of fruit from your kitchen and begin! Go slowly and observe each organic curve of its surface as you get to know its shape.

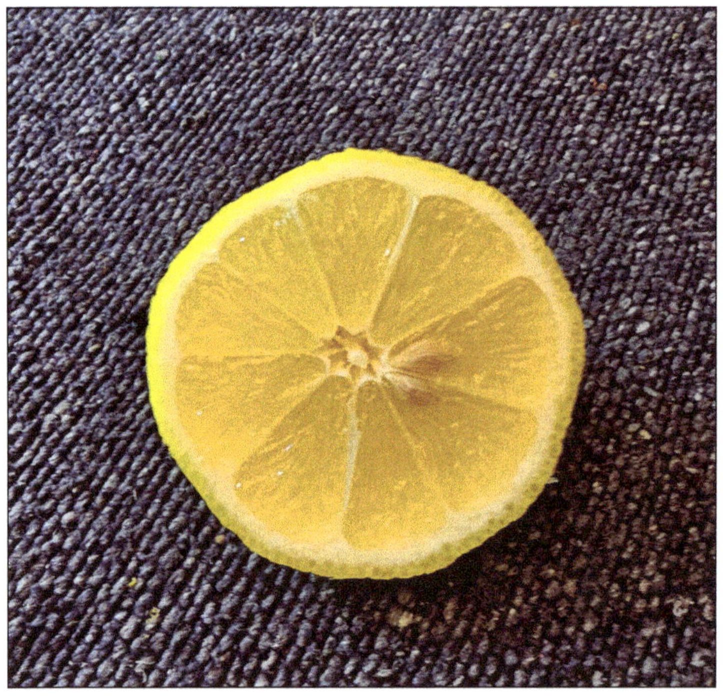

Then cut your piece of fruit in half and discover the lovely shapes inside that surprise your eyes! **After you draw the exterior and interior shapes, take a moment to finish your drawings with a little color!**

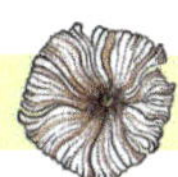

Contour line drawing of fruit of your choice here.

Now add color!

What we learn from this exercise is that shape is defined by lines and color. It is made of either one or both of these elements. When we examine our drawings, what we see before us is in *two dimensions*.

The next design element we'll review is exciting. We'll be introduced to a more detailed way of looking at the world around us. In the next chapter, we are going to add another dimension to what we've already seen!

Get ready, because a circle will become a sphere. And a square, a cube. These familiar two-dimensional shapes will be transformed into three-dimensional form!

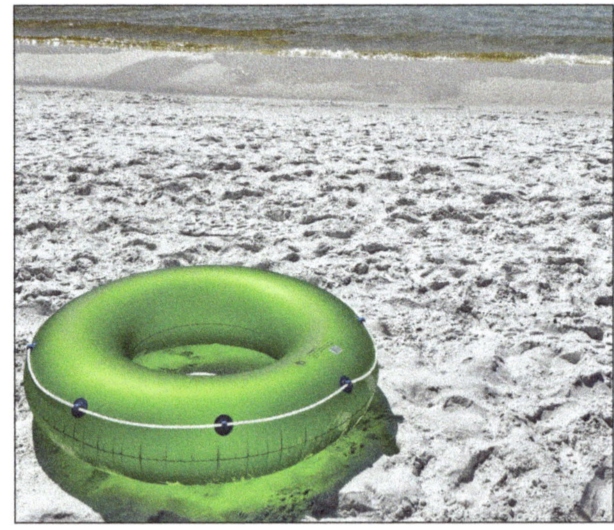

With a little air, your beach inner tube becomes a three-dimensional form.

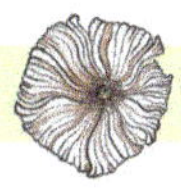

Chapter Two Fun Fact

Photographing shapes and colors that bring us joy is a great way to develop our artist eyes. **Edward Steichen (1879-1973)** was a well-known photographer who also painted. A man of many talents, he loved to garden so much so that he enthusiastically grew sunflowers and developed a new variety of delphinium flowers that he then also painted. Steichen's home in Voulangis, France, was his place of creative inspiration because of its beauty. His garden reminds me that each of us can also set up our own homes and gardens so that they support and reflect what inspires us. **Do you have a special space in *your* home to unleash your creativity? If not, make one!**

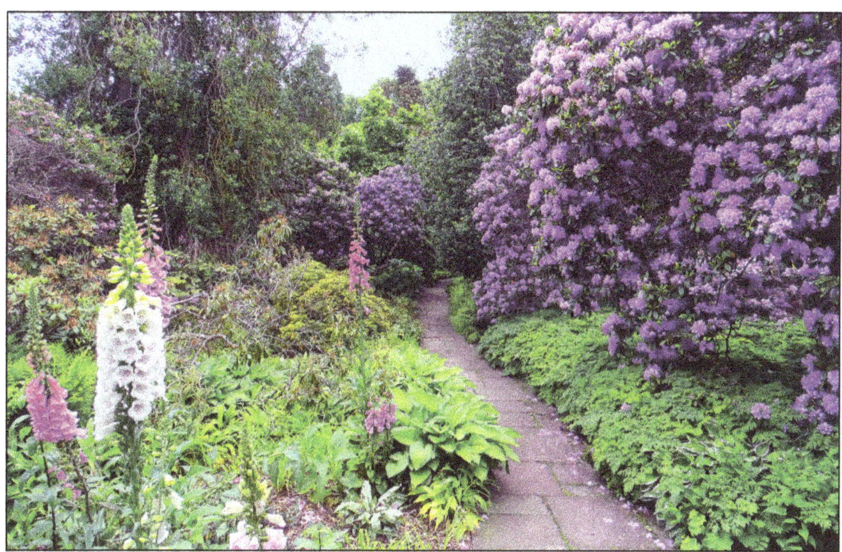

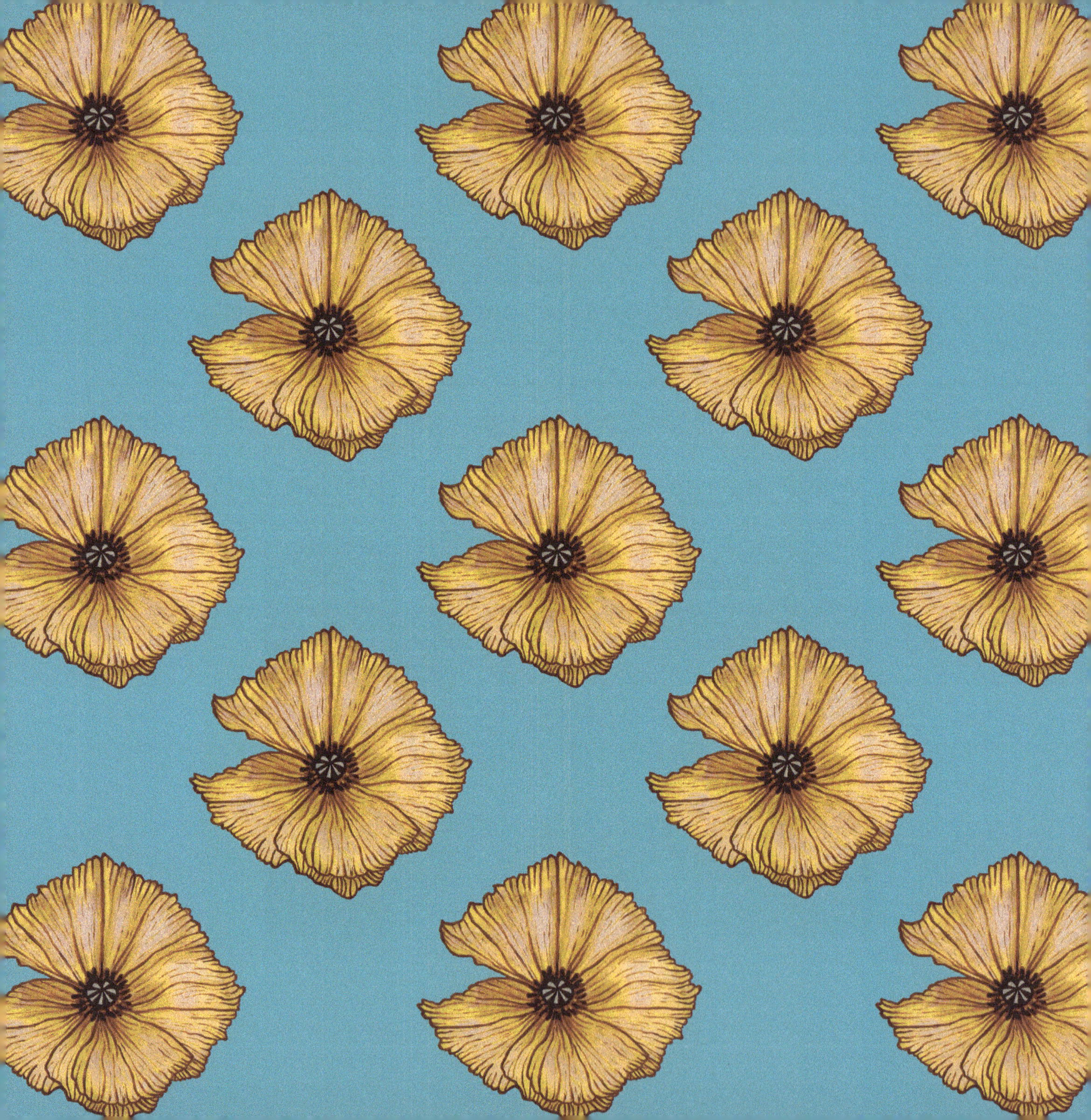

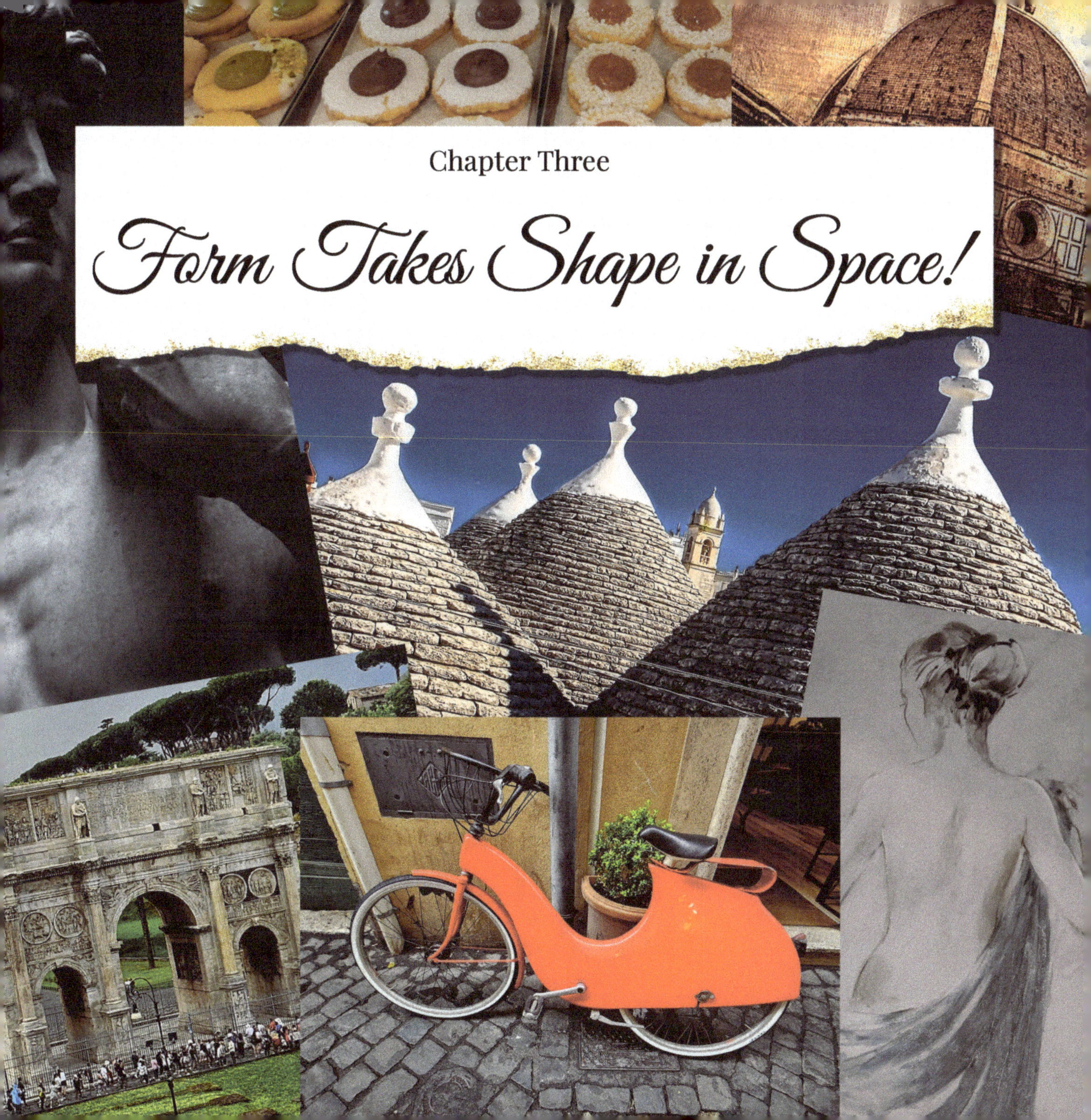

Form Takes Shape in Space!

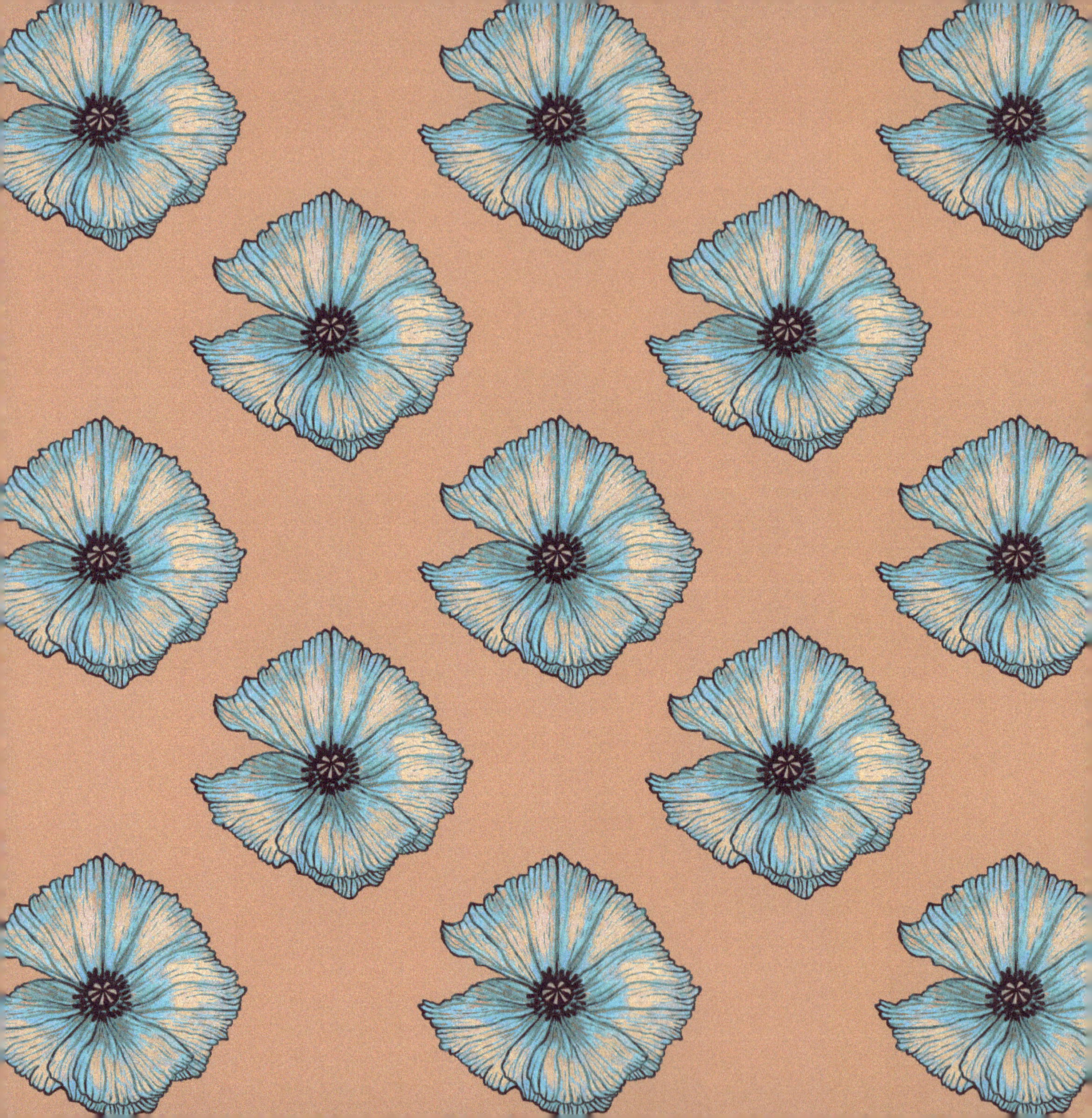

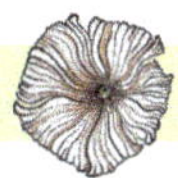

Chapter Three

Form Takes Shape in Space!

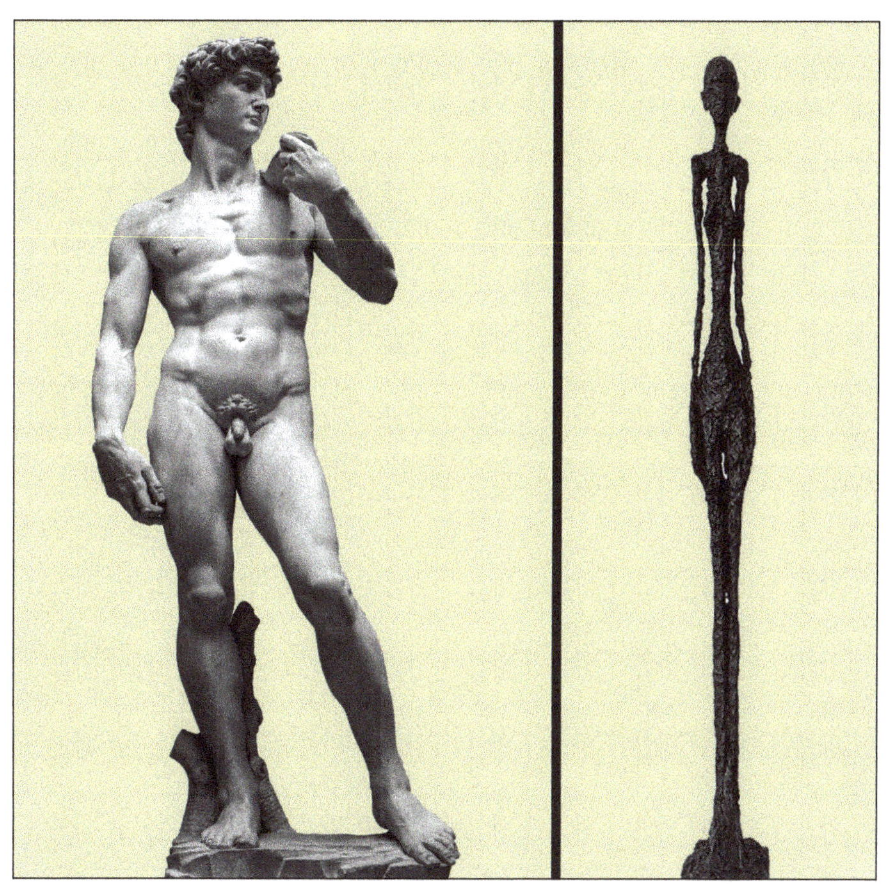

Different ways artists create forms: Michaelangelo (left) and Giacometti (right).

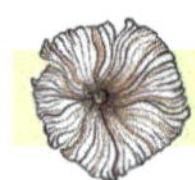

Height, width, and depth. It's time to see how form takes shape in three dimensions.

There are all sorts of ways shapes take form. Blow up a balloon. It changes form by taking in air. It goes from flat to round. Heat transforms tiny corn kernels into popcorn. Two pieces of bread become a sandwich when lunch meat comes between them.

Artists have been inventing new forms since the beginning of time. Italian Renaissance artist **Michelangelo (1475–1564)** found a masterpiece in a big rock. He saw his idea in the marble and freed it from its stone prison. All it takes is a little vision.

Another creative visionary was Swiss artist **Alberto Giacometti (1901–1966)**. He was fascinated by human form and its relationship to space. While carving away everything that was not part of the image he saw in his mind, he made his figures thinner and thinner until they almost disappeared. For him art was a way of understanding how he saw the outside world.

Giacometti was always starting over again and changing his forms as he worked. He gives us important advice when it comes to learning about form and space. He said, "If we master a bit of drawing everything else is possible." He also said, "The more you fail the more you succeed." His invaluable advice is important to remember as we begin to study and draw forms.

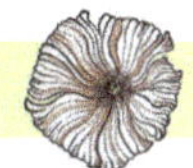

Form is divided into two categories. The first is *geometric* or precise mathematical shapes. This includes circles, squares, rectangles, pentagons and more.

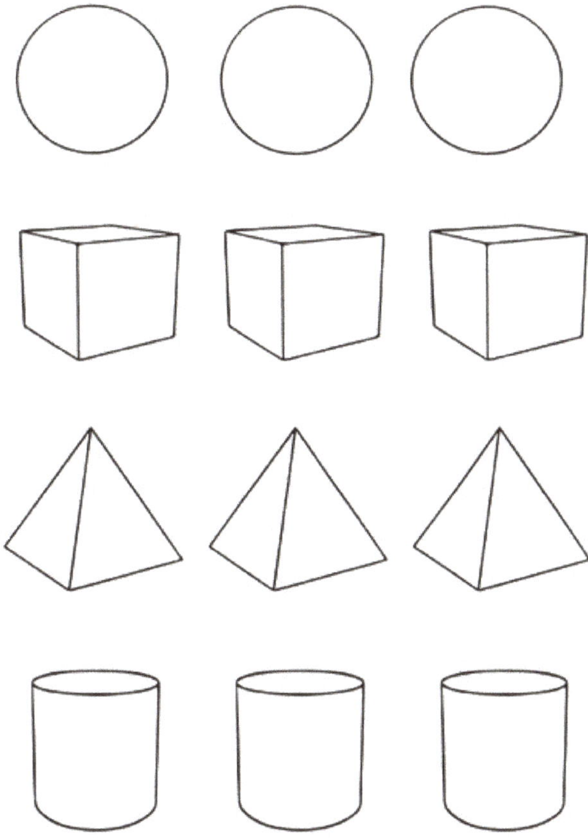

Outlines of Geometric Shapes.

The second is ***biomorphic*** or irregular organic shapes. This includes stones, seashells, trees, flowers, etc.

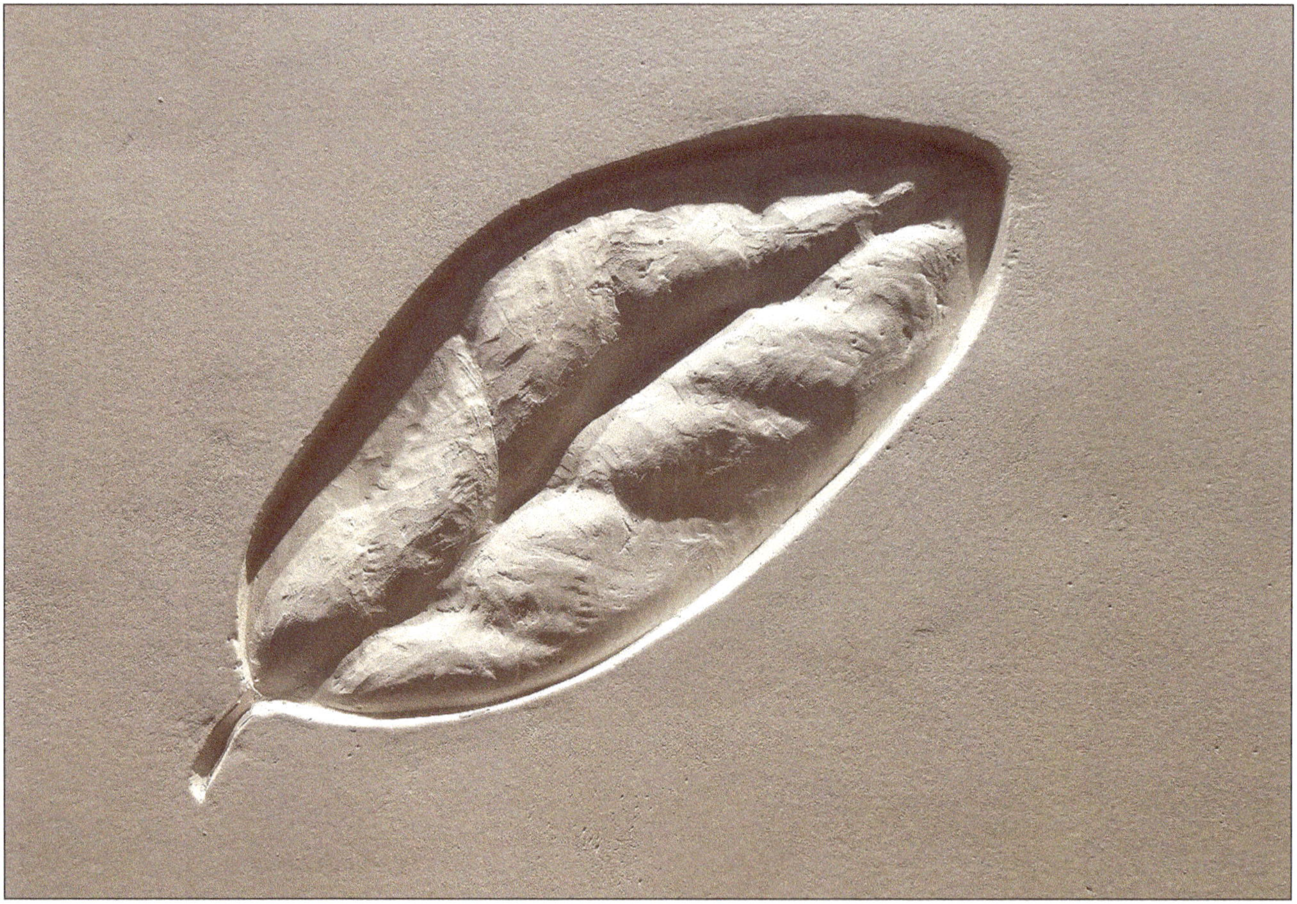

Biomorphic shape.

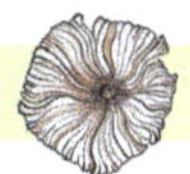

We see in architecture and sculpture that form is the shape, structure, and arrangement of height, width, and depth, resulting in a three-dimensional work. The architect and sculptor create form through physical shape.

On the other hand, painters create form through illusion. They approach a flat canvas and utilize light and shadow to create the illusion of a three-dimensional form. **Light and shadow bring forms to life.**

A quick way to practice creating a form is to add shading, which is also referred to as modeling. Modeling is the technique of creating the illusion of three-dimensionality by the use of gradations of value (the lightness or darkness of colors).

As you can see on the next few pages, it's easy to transform a circle into a sphere or an oval into a grape by simple modeling. **Light hits one side and dark models the other and the resulting shift in tonal values gives birth to *form*!**

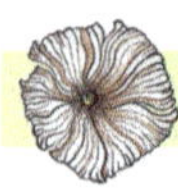

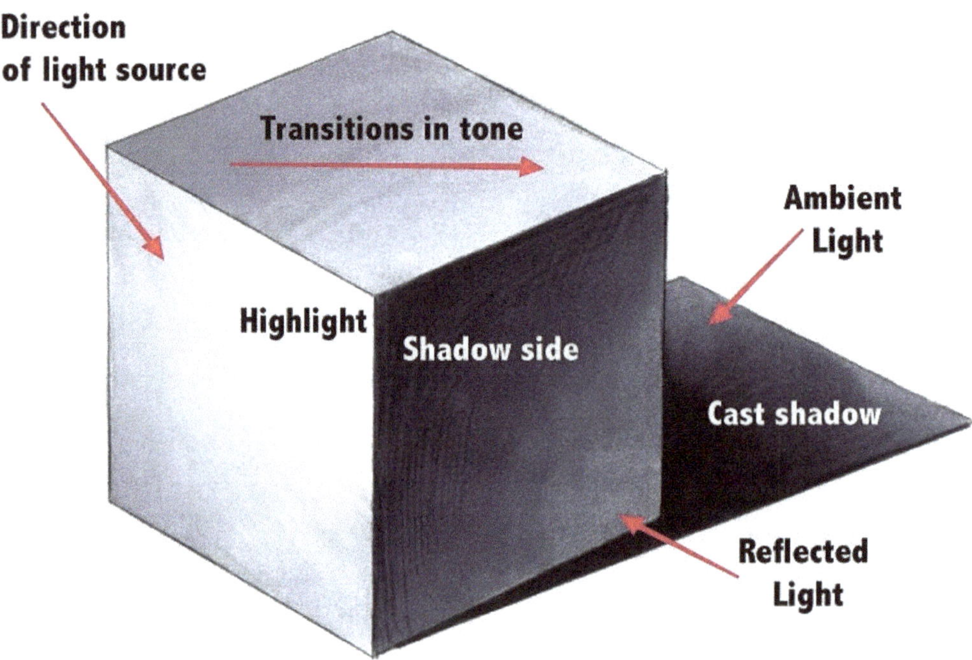

How light defines shape.

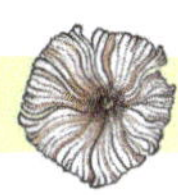

Hatching

Crosshatching

Stippling

Blending

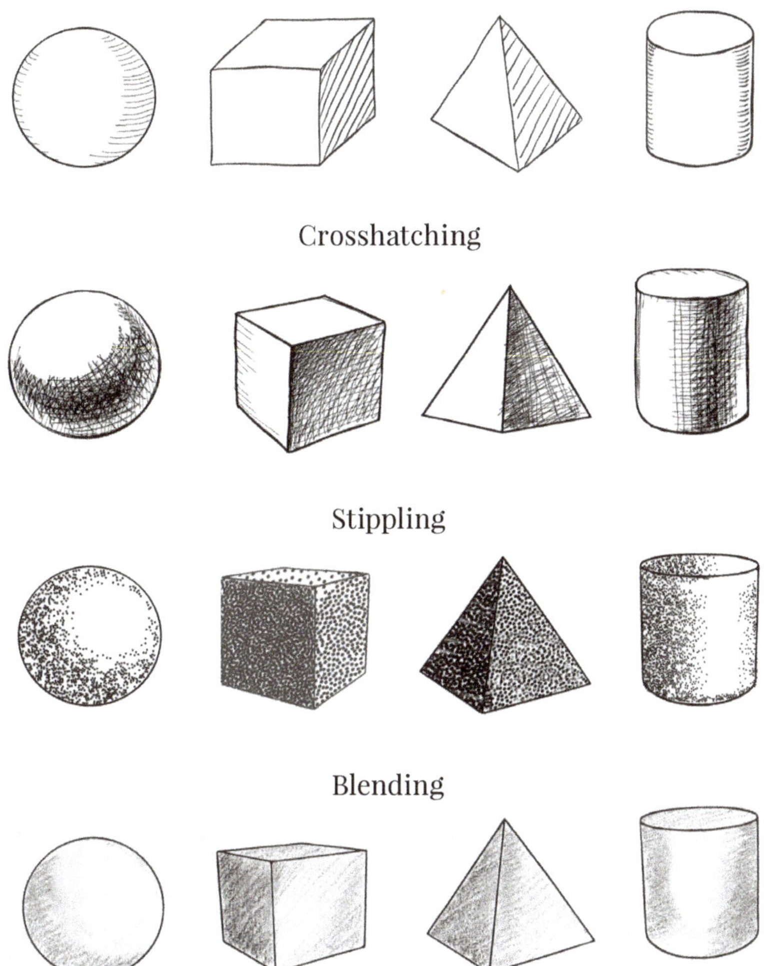

Types of shading to create form.

On the following pages, copy the sketches of the four shapes: the *sphere*, the *cube*, the *pyramid*, and the *cylinder*. Then use the variety of specific modeling techniques presented on each page to make the different shapes three-dimensional. This way, you will begin to understand how light and shade shape each form. This is a wonderful exercise to practice and repeat again and again with different shapes. Start with a row of hatching, then crosshatching, then stippling and finally blended shading. Use your drawing pencil first, then, after that, try your colored pencils.

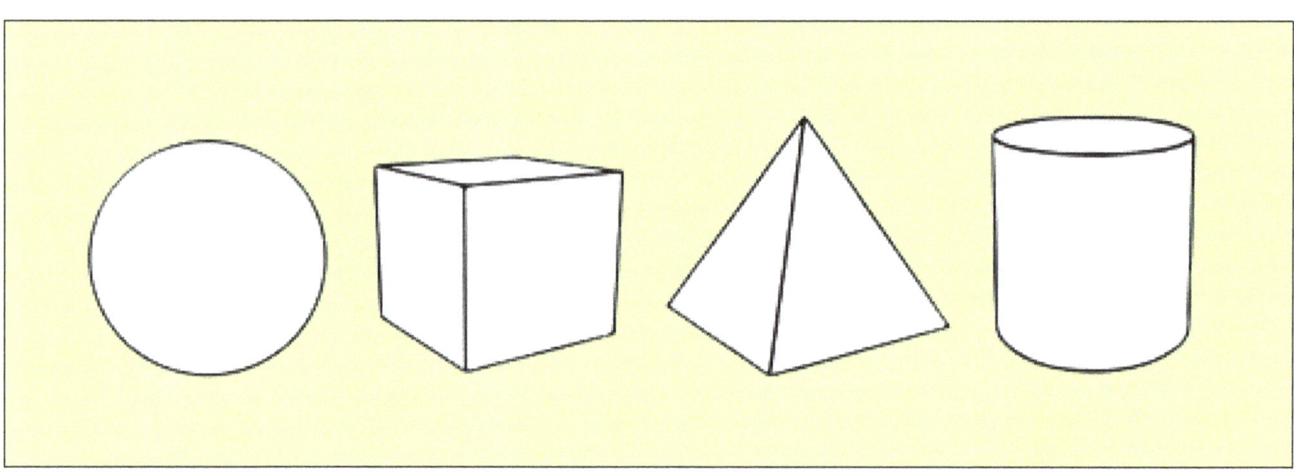

The following modeling techniques (hatching, crosshatching, stippling, blending) will bring these shapes to life on the next few pages.

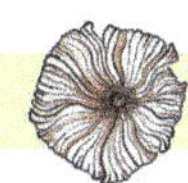

Hatching:

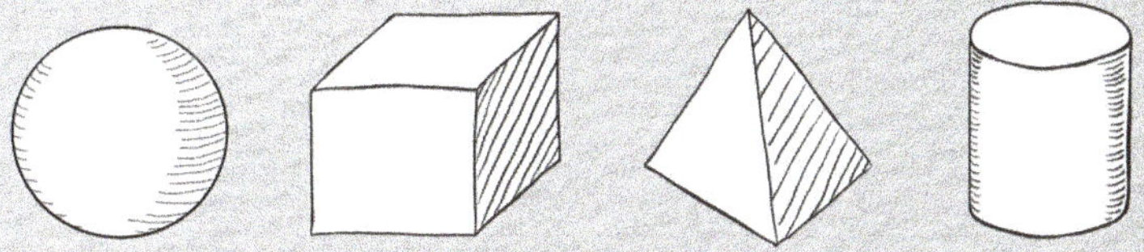

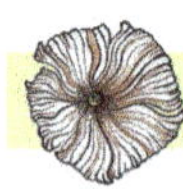

Crosshatching:

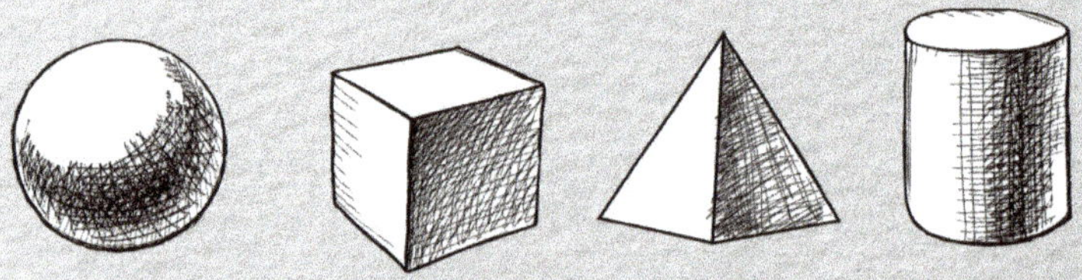

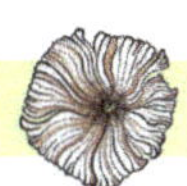

Stippling:

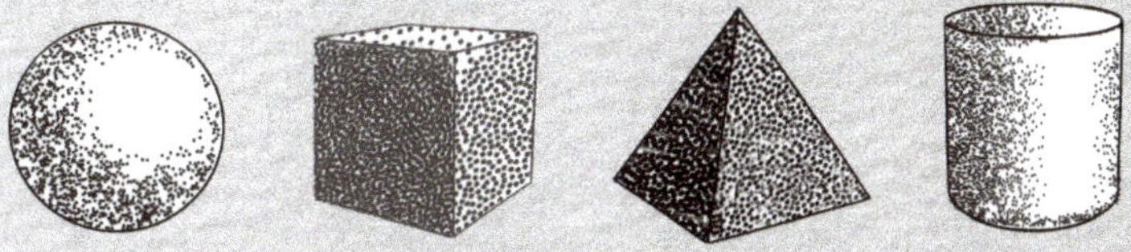

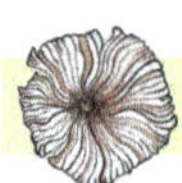

Blending:

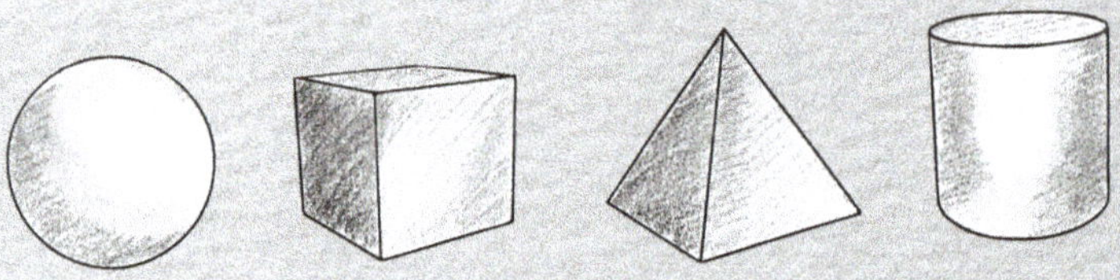

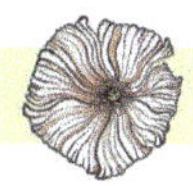

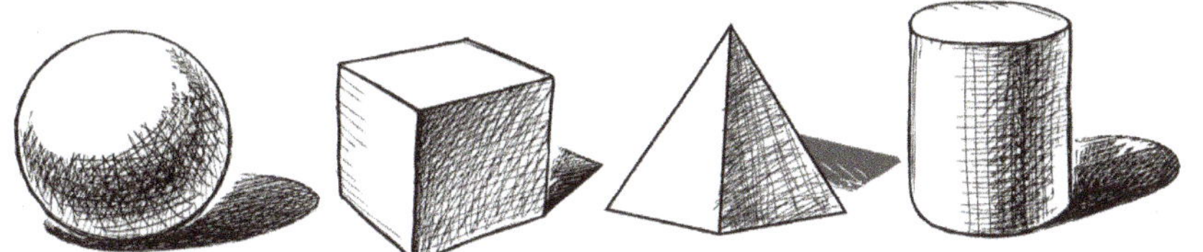

A simple cast shadow residing next to an object serves an important function. This shadow places the form firmly in its spot. Without this shadow, the form looks as if it's floating in space. Light and shade touch everything. They bring life to form and give it a place to reside.

Artist's eyes possess a heightened sense of visual intelligence. They can see the big picture. They discern the placement of three-dimensional forms in space with ease. However, artists not only depict three-dimensional objects with skill, but they also understand how the grand scheme of spatial relationships work.

Perspective is how we perceive the world around us. Many of us know that objects further away from us look smaller than ones that are near us. Some objects overlap each other. Others are adjacent. Objects in the distance are less detailed than those close by.

When we attempt to create the illusion of depth on a two-dimensional (flat plane) canvas we often get stuck. The good news is that anyone can learn to make space look real. There is a technique artists use called ***linear perspective*** that helps us see and understand spacial relationships.

One-point perspective is a mathematical system of drawing space and three-dimensional objects on a two-dimensional surface. Lines converge towards one or more distant vanishing points on the horizon line.

It's important to note that understanding perspective is much easier than you might imagine. **Beyond the mathematics of formal perspective, artists possess a natural or informal way of depicting perspective. *It is called sighting.*** The word means seeing. It's a special way the artist sees. Sighting is about comparison. It's all about seeing and drawing relationships. Sighting is all you really need to start learning basic drawing skills.

Let's begin with some useful vocabulary words that artists use to describe the basics of seeing forms in space. **Your artist's eyes will develop even more as you become familiar with these terms.**

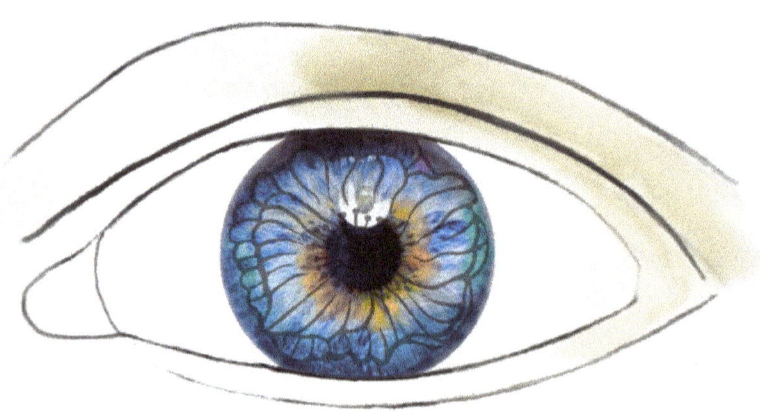

 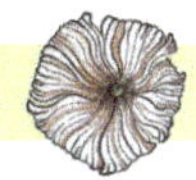

Form: A three-dimensional object which contains volume.

Horizontal Lines: Lines drawn from side to side. They will be parallel to the top and bottom edges of your paper.

Vertical Lines: Lines drawn up and down and should be parallel to the sides of your paper.

Diagonal Lines: These are slanted lines. They are neither horizontal nor vertical.

The Horizon Line: The horizon line is the horizontal line that represents eye level to the viewer.

The Vanishing Point: The vanishing point is located somewhere on the horizon line. It does not have to be in the middle of the horizon line.

Perspective Lines: Lines that meet at the vanishing point. They converge in one-point perspective drawing.

Perspective: Perspective is a word that comes from the Latin *prospectus*. Prospectus means to look forward. Perspective drawing in the field of art helps us recognize spatial relationships.

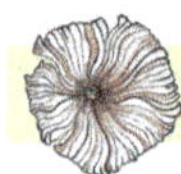

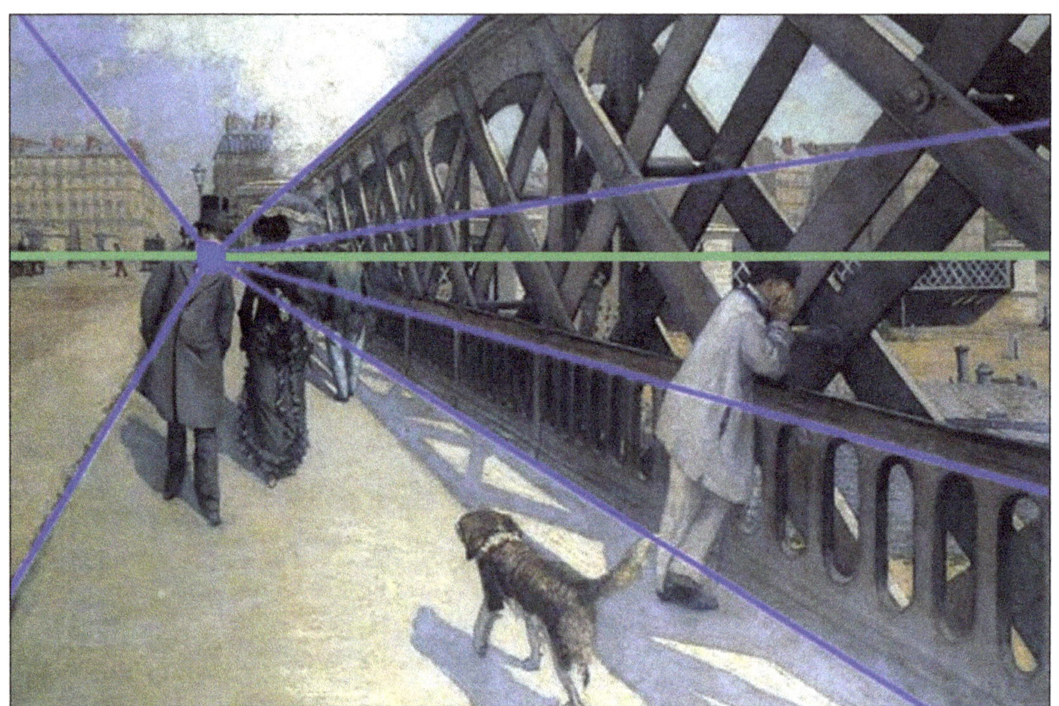

Le Pont L'Europe *by Gustave Caillebotte (1848-1894) is an example of one-point perspective.*

The image above is a perfect example of one-point perspective where lines converge at a vanishing point (the blue dot) on the horizon (the green horizontal line). On the following pages, you will see an example of one-point perspective in an indoor scene and an outdoor scene.

We encounter perspective scenes like these in our everyday lives. **Strive to see like an artist and be on the lookout for more examples.**

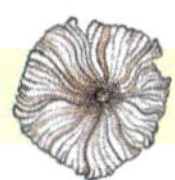

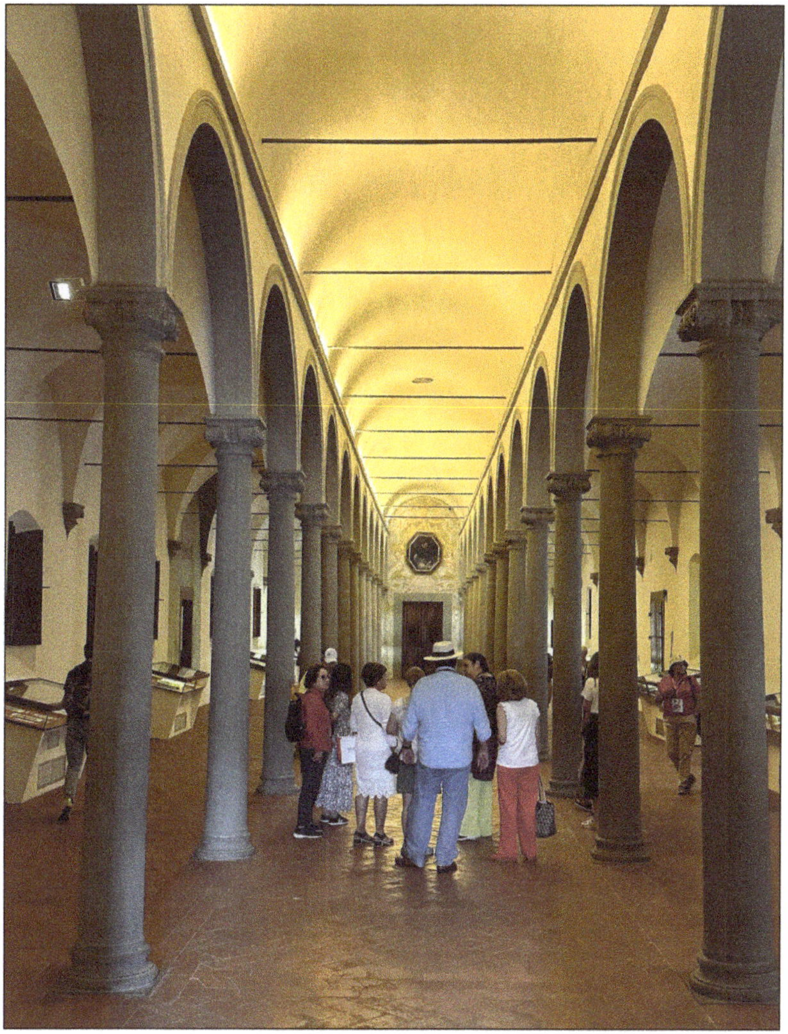

One-point perspective inside a building.

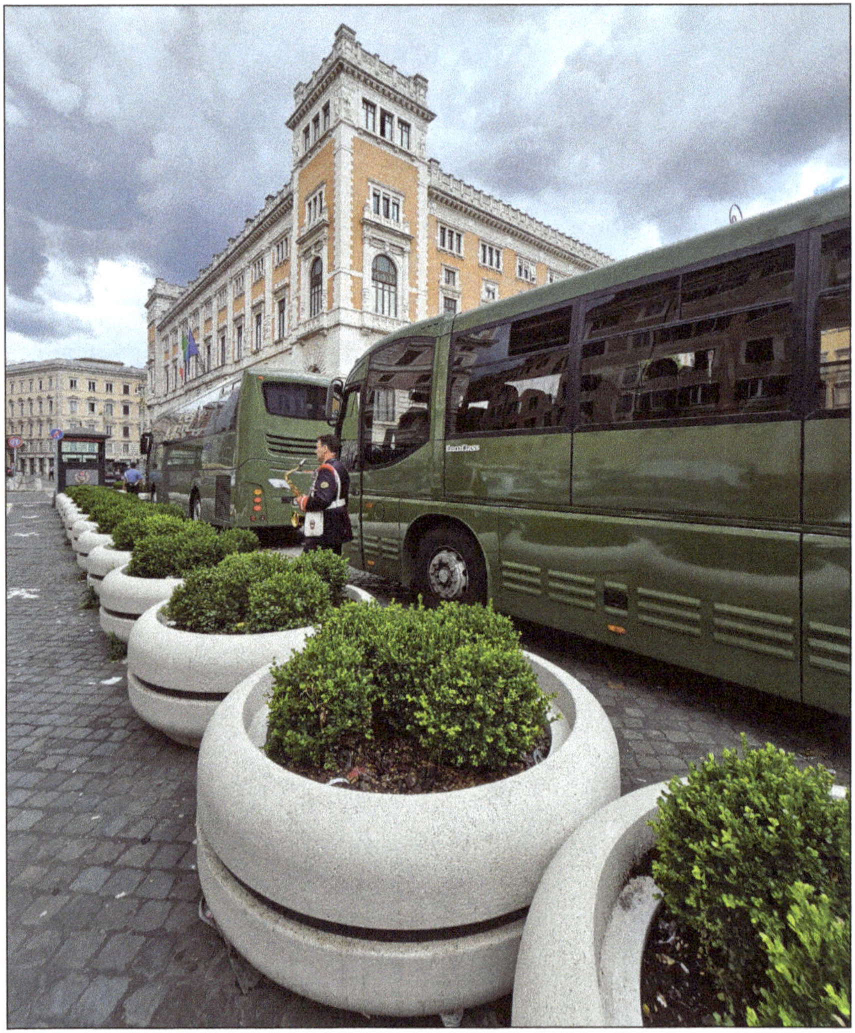

One-point perspective outside.

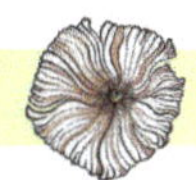

What is important for us as we strive to see like an artist is beginning to notice perspective and proportions *wherever we are.* The more we practice looking, the more we refine our sight. It really helps us to see spatial relationships when we focus in and study an isolated area. Grab a toilet paper tube, or roll up a piece of paper, and look through it at a specific area near you. Perhaps you see a chair close to you and another chair in the distance. Notice the difference in size between the chairs. Then look through your tube and focus on studying the arrangement of some other objects in your home. See how they ***overlap*** and study their ***contrasting sizes***.

Now try another compare-and-contrast exercise. Find a small and large vase. Then pick up your drawing pencil. We will use it as a measuring tool. Hold it up vertically at arm's length. **Close one eye and align the tip of your pencil to the top of the smaller vase. Then slide your thumb to mark the bottom of this vase.**

You have just measured how high the small vase is.

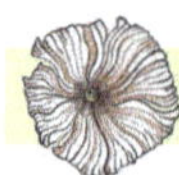

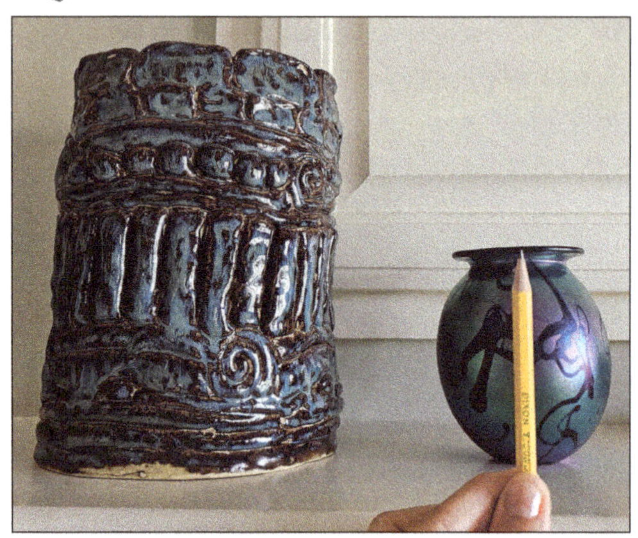 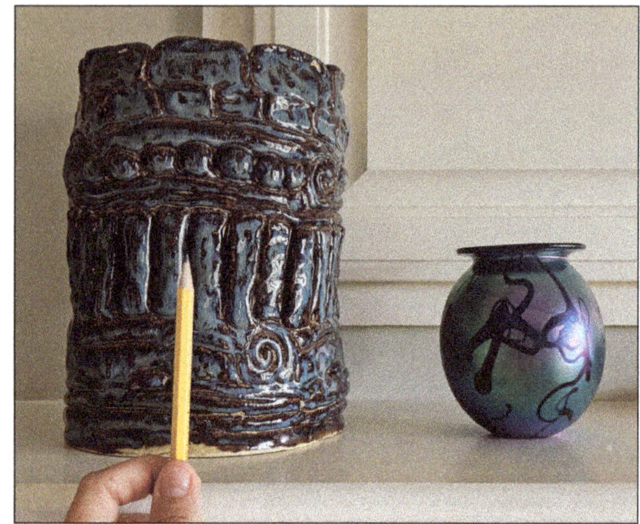

Without moving your thumb from its pencil position, align it with the bottom of the large vase. Now look at where the tip of the pencil falls. **How much higher does the large vase appear than the small?** In the above photo it appears to be half the height of the large vase. How do your vases size up? This is an easy exercise to help you figure out the relative heights of two objects.

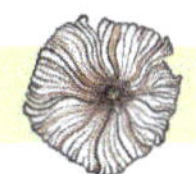

Take your pencil outside and repeat this exercise. Compare the sizes of people to buildings or people to trees. Branch out and compare and contrast the space between objects. You can also use this simple technique to compare the various distances between objects.

It's easy to practice this anywhere. All you need is a pencil. Use this exercise to sharpen your ability to discern size and space. The good news is you don't need to know the exact inches or centimeters to see like an artist. It's amazing how a simple exercise like this can teach us how to begin to see a world of correct proportions.

You can try another sighting exercise by scattering some fruit on a table. Grab a picture frame and hold the frame before you. Look through the frame and what you see is your next sketch project. Draw the still-life scene you see by looking through this frame. Be sure to note the size differences of each piece of fruit in your picture plane. Do some appear bigger or smaller than others?

Practice comparing sizes using your picture frame and then sketch your tabletop fruit-frame composition on the following page.

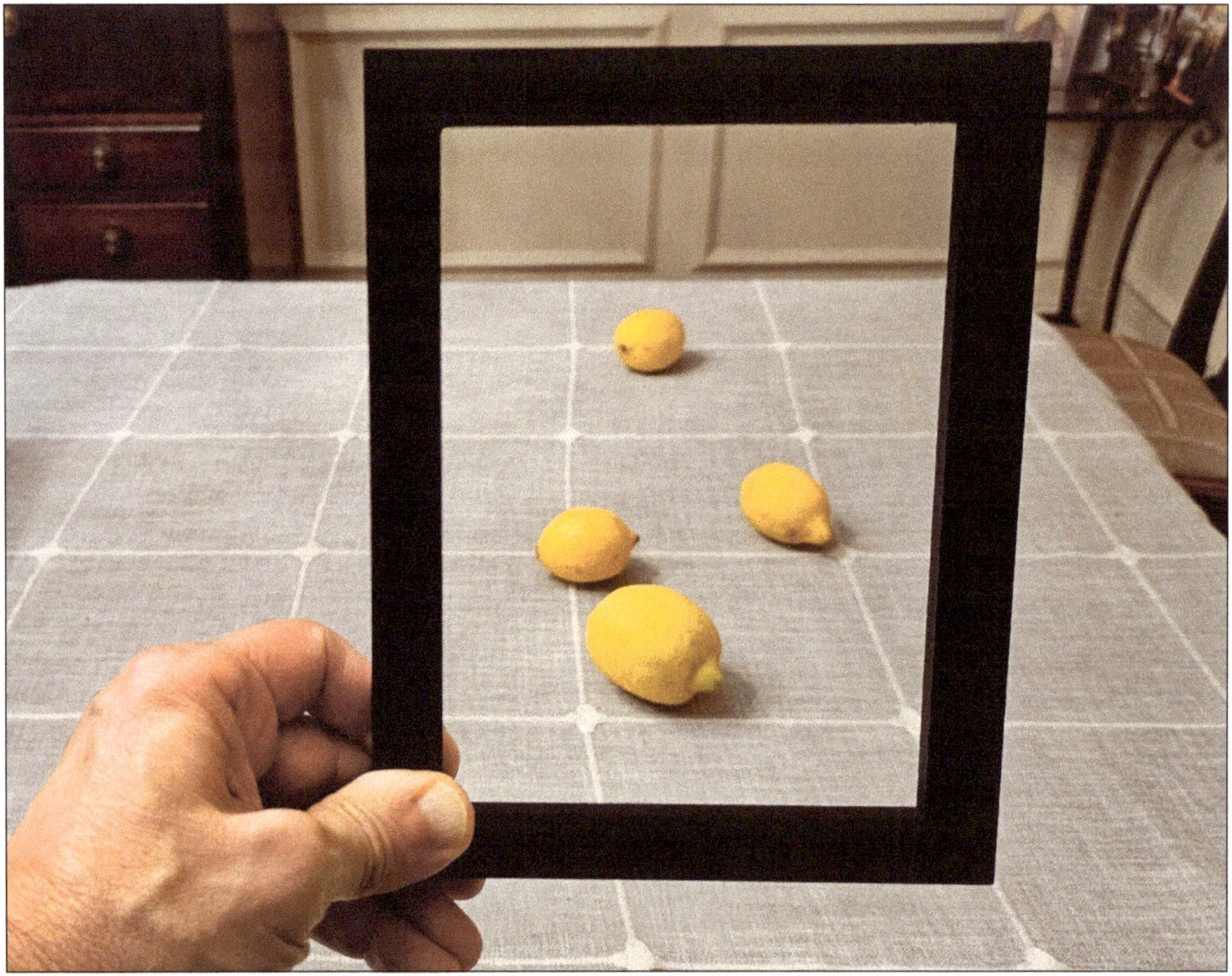

Drawing Tip: Remember to add cast shadows to your fruit-in-frame sighting exercise.

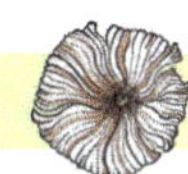

Fruit-in-frame sighting exercise.

Once you finish the previous sketch, use the very same frame for your next one. Lay out some books of different sizes and place them in different directions on your table. This is your picture plane. Once again hold up your frame and look through it and draw the books as they appear. Compare the vertical lines to the horizontal and diagonal lines. Extend your lines even longer than needed so the form of each book begins to appear within the elongated lines. ***You can always erase your extra extended lines later.*** After your shapes are completed, color them to see what your lines have formed.

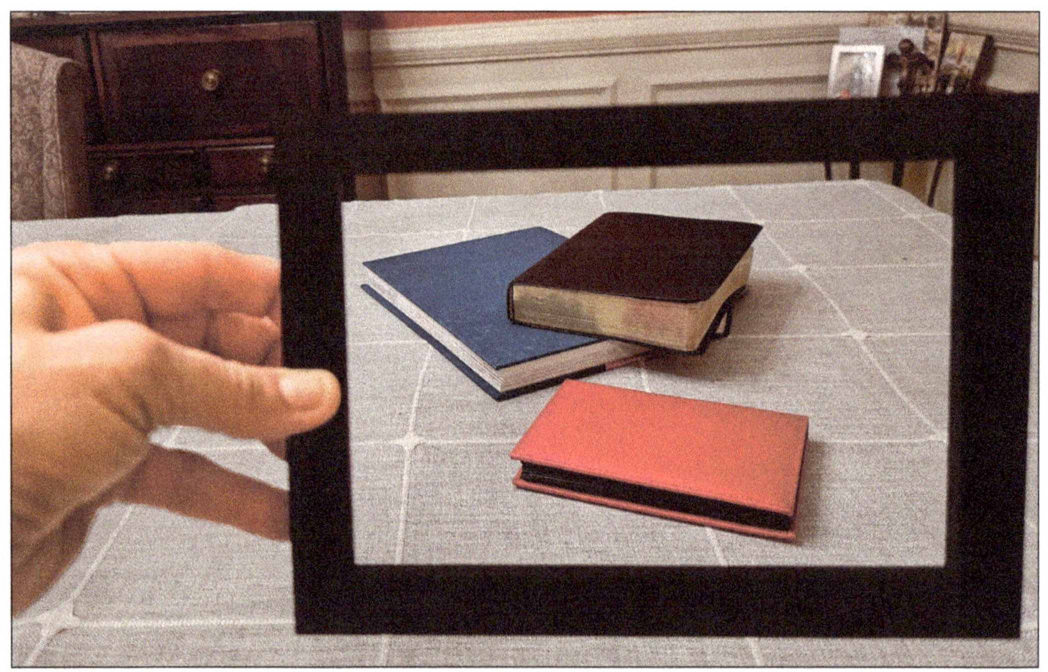

 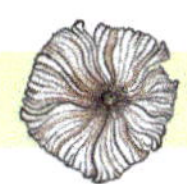

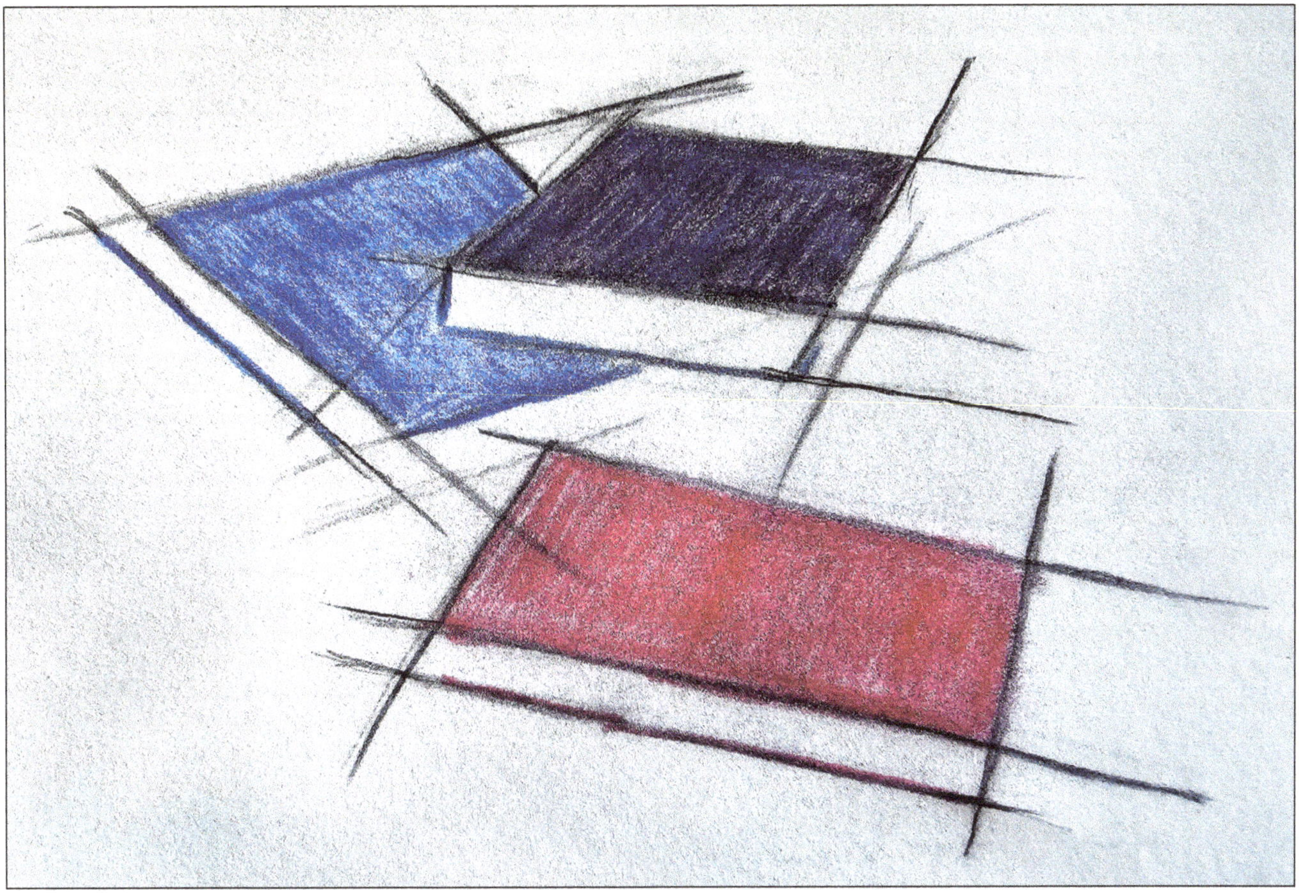

While you draw, try not to focus on the specifics of what you are drawing, instead strive to see the lines and shapes. Erase extended lines later.

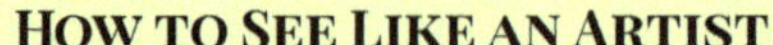

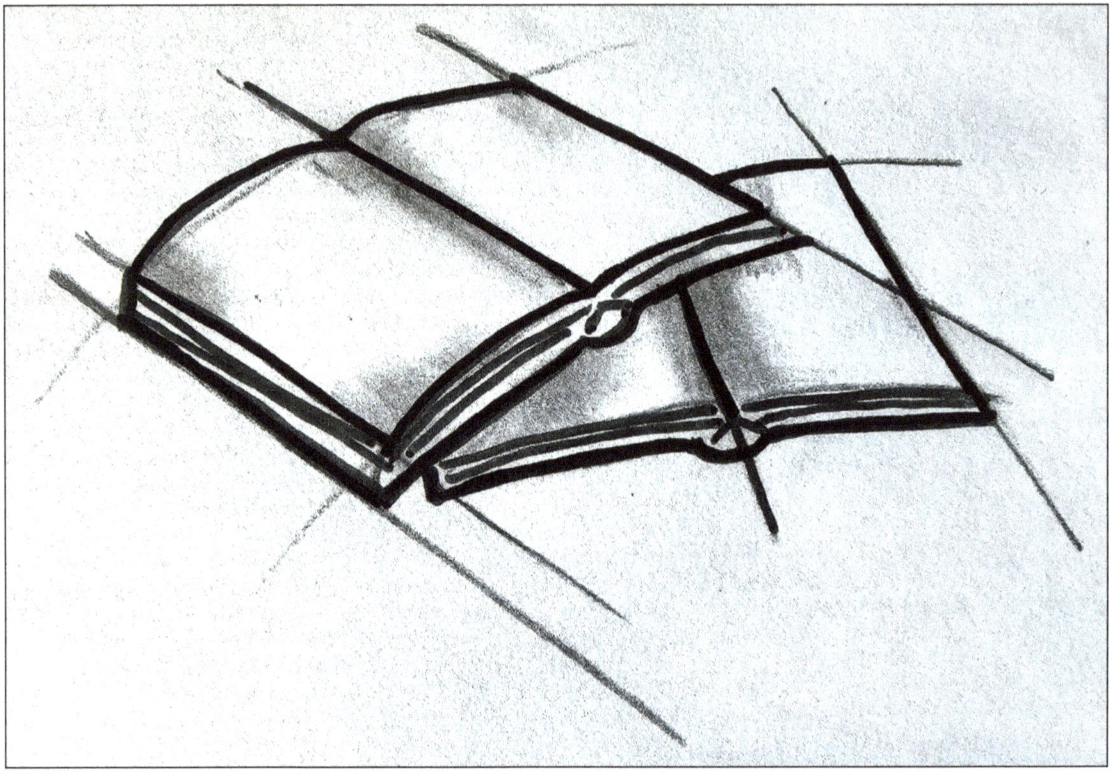

Look for the lines, lights, and shadows. Compare and contrast spaces between objects. **See with your eyes and not your mind.** *Forget the fact you are drawing books.* This way you are studying your subject exactly as an artist does. **Sometimes, artists even turn things *upside down* to draw them, so they only see shapes and forms, and don't recognize the subject matter they are copying.**

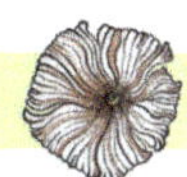

Books-in-frame sighting exercise.

Line, **shape**, **form**, **perspective**, **color**, **texture**, and **composition** are indispensable tools the artist uses. These basic design elements and the ways they relate to each other are the key to seeing beauty. Your picture plane comes to life once you get to know each of these art elements.

Save your frame for a new sketch. Put your pencil down. Walk around your home and observe objects and their special relationships. Where do the shadows fall?

Now it's *your turn* to set up another still life. Think of an everyday object you might like to draw. The more you study it, the more you'll see. Change the layout of your objects and draw the same thing again and again. **Use your frame and continue to draw new compositional arrangements.**

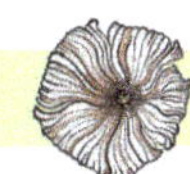

Everyday object still-life sighting exercise.

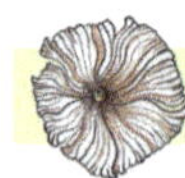

You can even use a frame to practice drawing people! **On the next page, practice sighting and drawing a portrait of someone you know.**

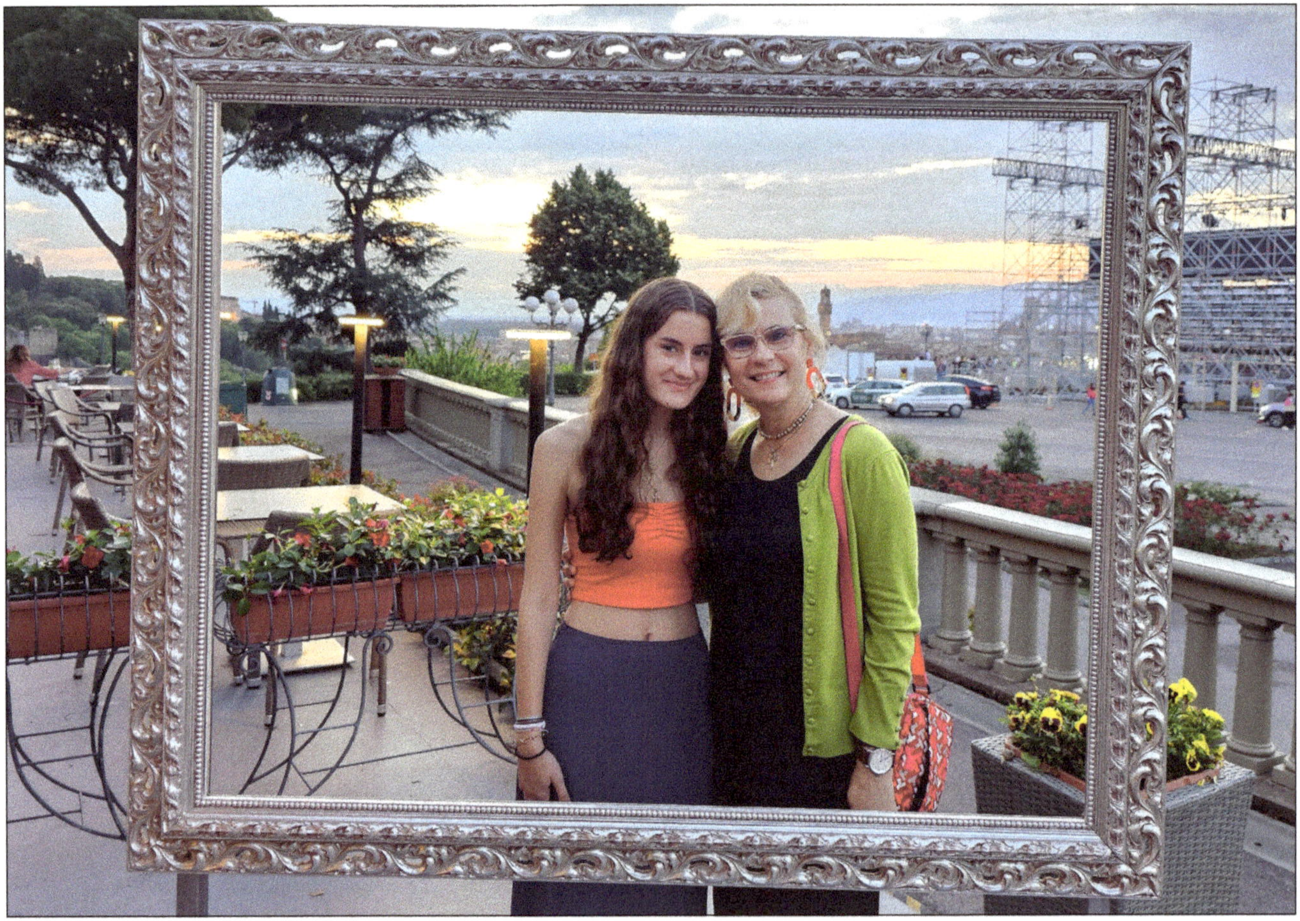

A frame helps the artist focus on the main subject matter.

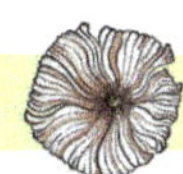

Portrait sighting exercise.

If you get discouraged, don't give up! You can take a picture of your still life and print it out. Then use tracing paper to get to know the lines and shapes. After this, try freehand drawing a few times, again using sighting techniques. Remember what Giacometti said. *Keep practicing and eventually you will find success*.

The main thing is to express yourself. You are learning a new visual language. It takes time, effort, and, most of all, *practice*!

Keep looking around your world. Save swatches of colors you love. Save quotes that inspire you. Make notes of artists you admire. Copy their work. Save pictures of special places and people you find beautiful. Find beauty you love on your doorstep and document it. **This is your time to experiment and collect information on each of the elements of art we cover in this book.**

As you refine and develop your artist's eyes, the surprises will begin. A little confidence in your artistic perception will go a long way towards lighting that unique spark of creativity from within that only you can express.

In the next chapter, we will have fun discussing my all-time favorite design element, color!

 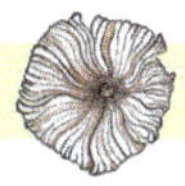

Chapter Three Fun Fact

Ancient Greeks and Romans attempted to explore and create spatial depth in art. However, it was the Florentine Renaissance artist and architect **Filippo Brunelleschi (1377-1446)** who made the first drawing using linear perspective. His discovery had a great impact on the history of art. **Look him up and study his life's work.**

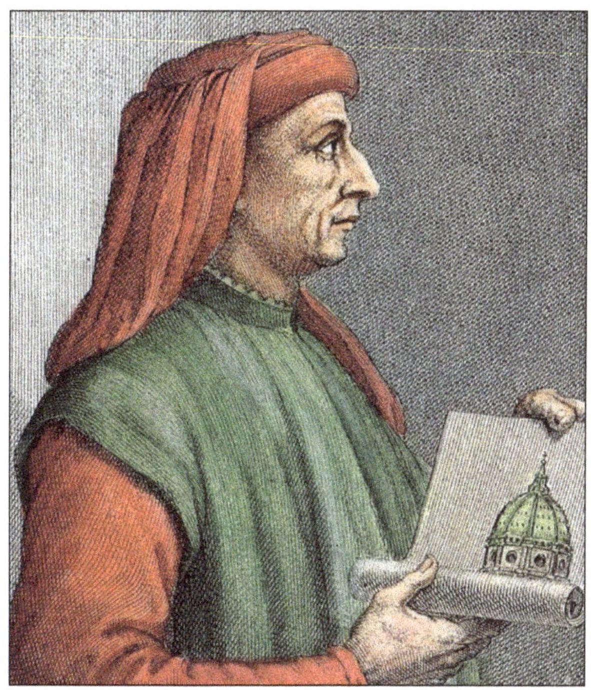

Filippo Brunelleschi

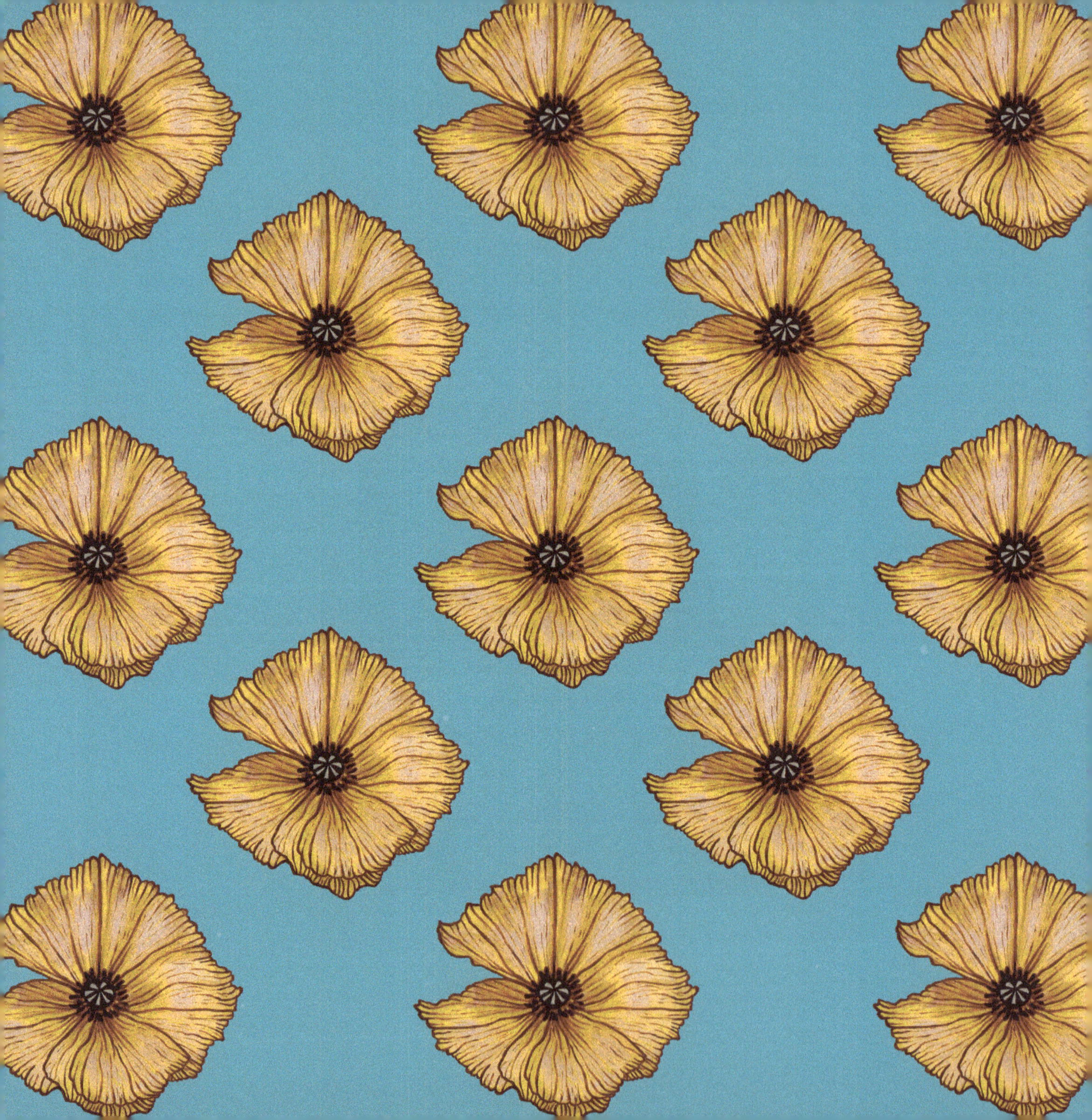

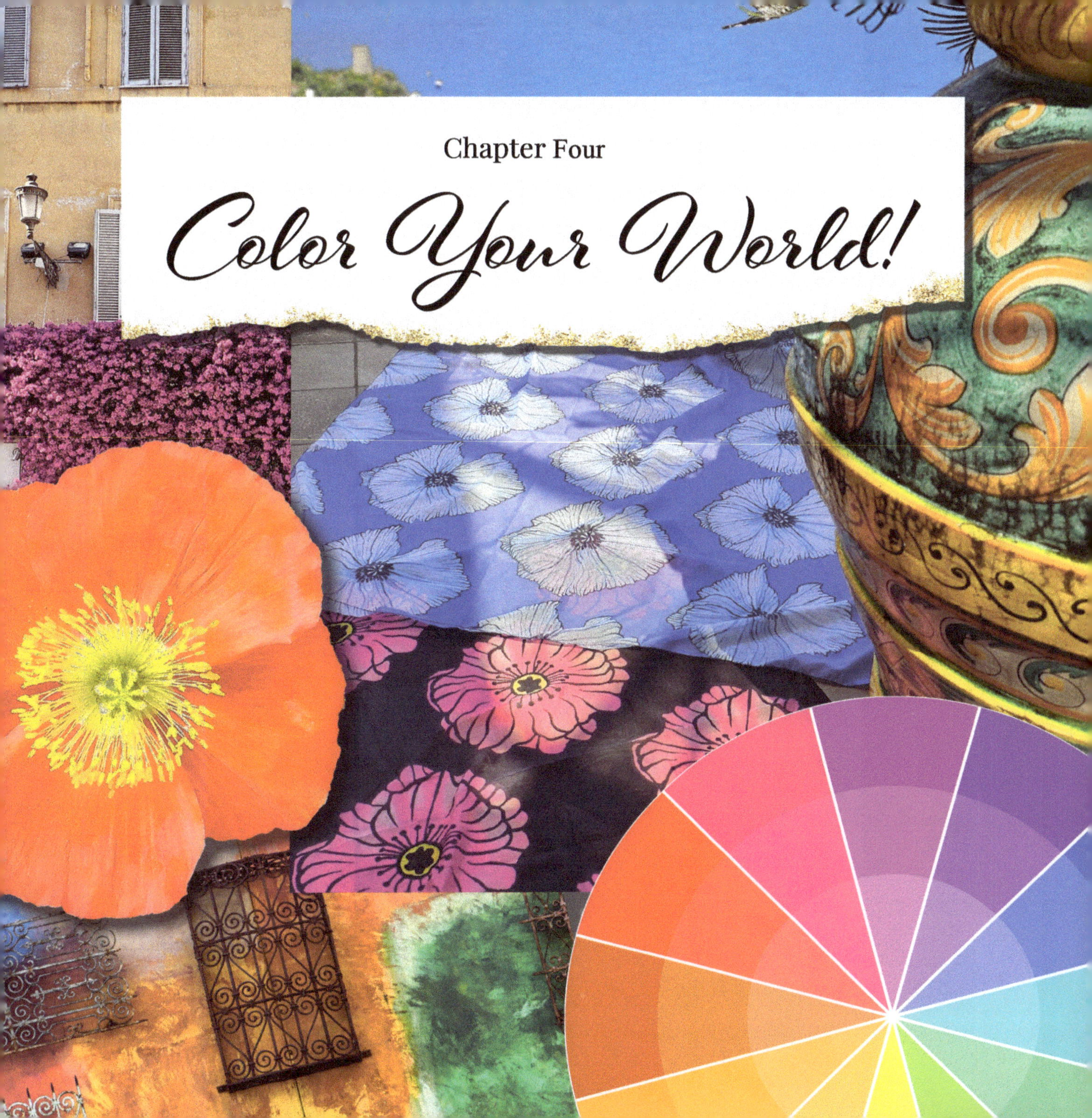

Chapter Four
Color Your World!

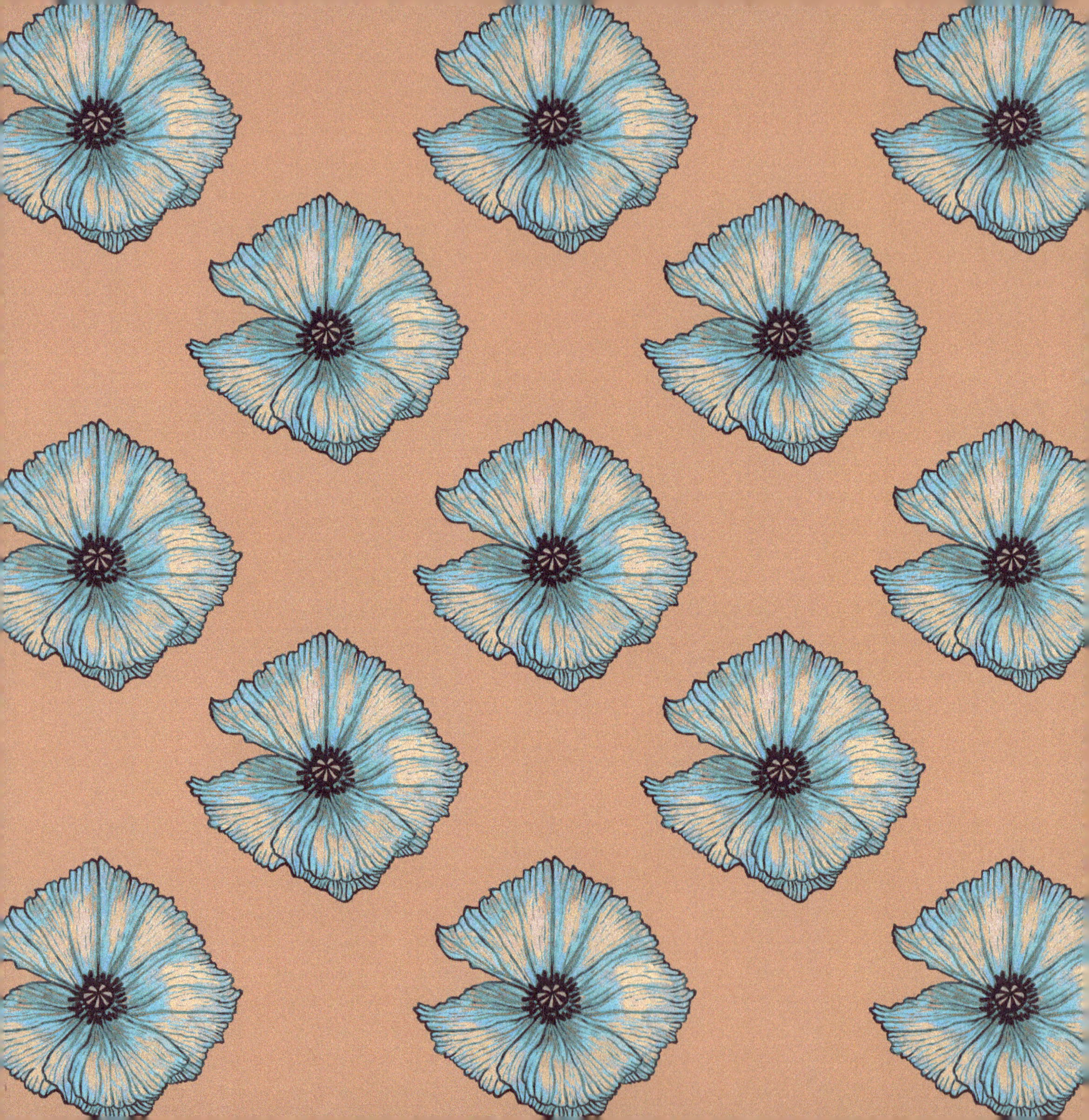

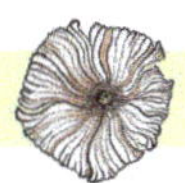

Chapter Four

Color Your World!

A world of beautiful colors exists to greet us every day. Some are lemon yellow, others emerald green, cobalt blue, or crimson red, and the list goes on. We all have favorite colors that bring us joy and ignite our imaginations. Purple is my favorite but there are many others that speak to my heart. It is hard to pick just one. Experts say the human eye can perceive up to ten million different colors.

From colorful flowers to colorful people, it's important to remember one word when it comes to color, *light*. Color is all about light. Light is made up of many different wavelengths of energy. Our eyes see this energy as different colors. So, when light hits an object the colored light that reflects off the object is what we see as its color.

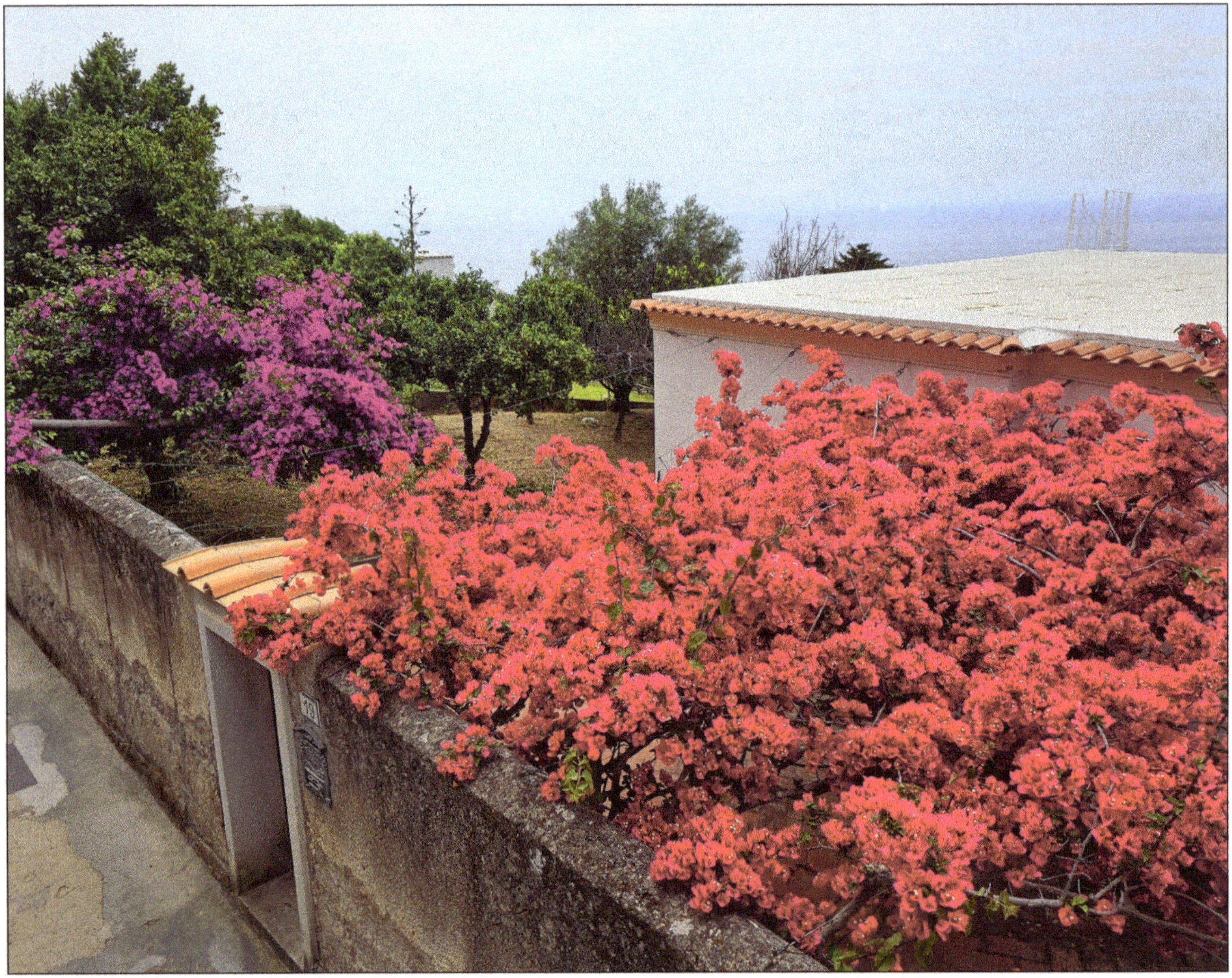

An explosion of color! Vibrant Bougainvillea on the Amalfi Coast.

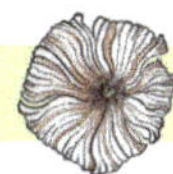

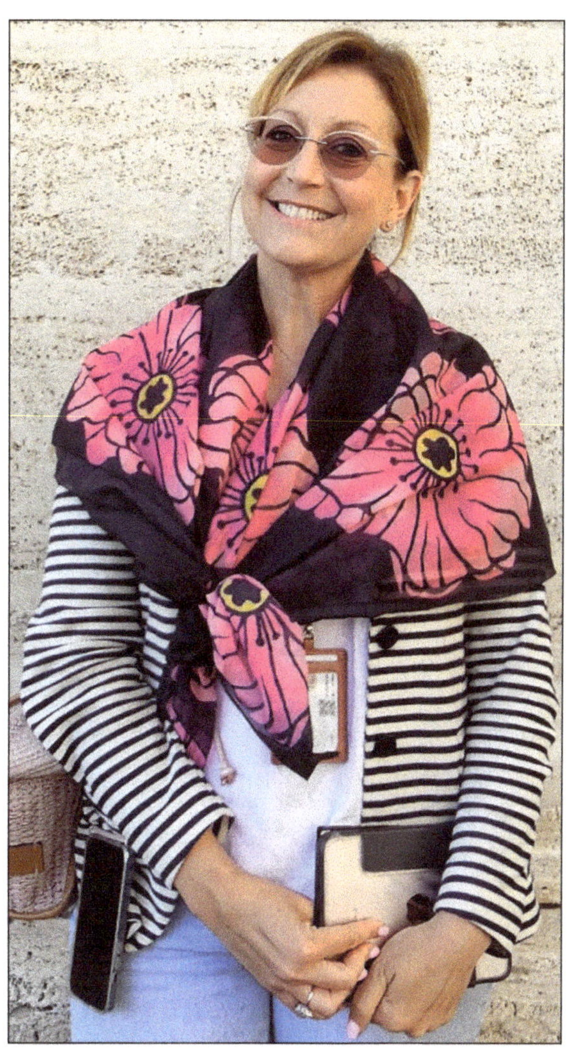

Lines and color! Our beautiful Roman tour guide.

The primary colors are *red*, *yellow*, and *blue*. These three colors mix together to make many other wonderful colors. When you mix primary colors together, you get what is called secondary colors. Blue and yellow make the secondary color of green. Red and yellow make the secondary color of orange. Red and blue make the secondary color of purple.

This Color Wheel includes primary, secondary, and tertiary colors.

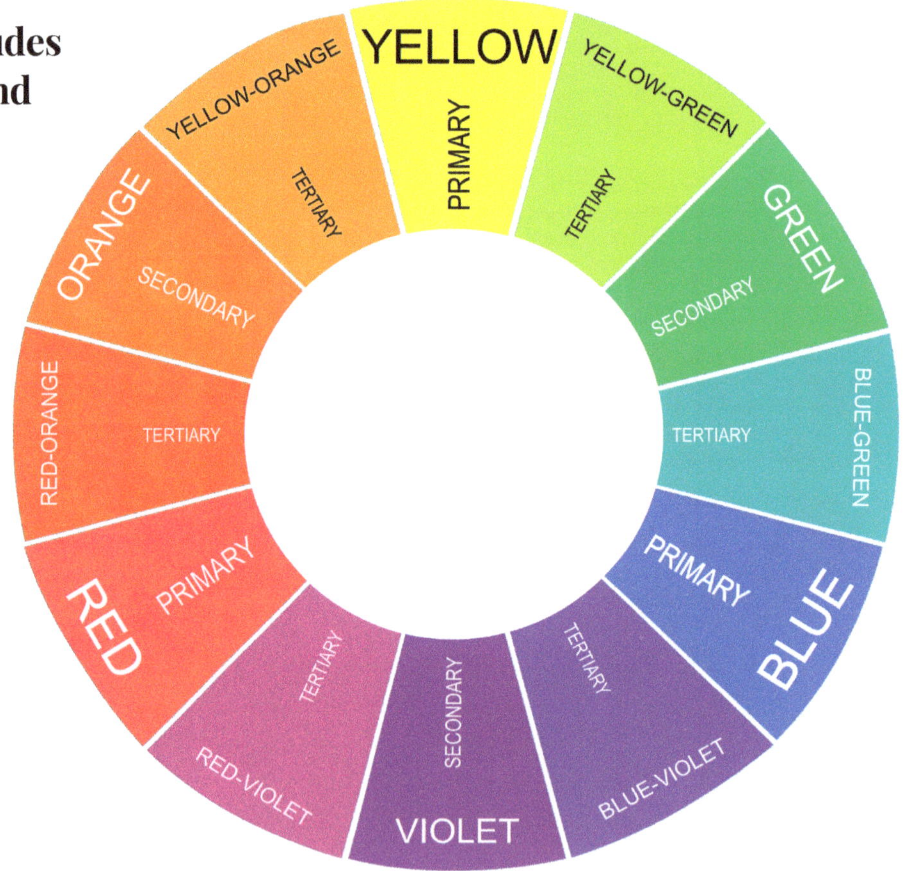

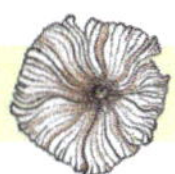

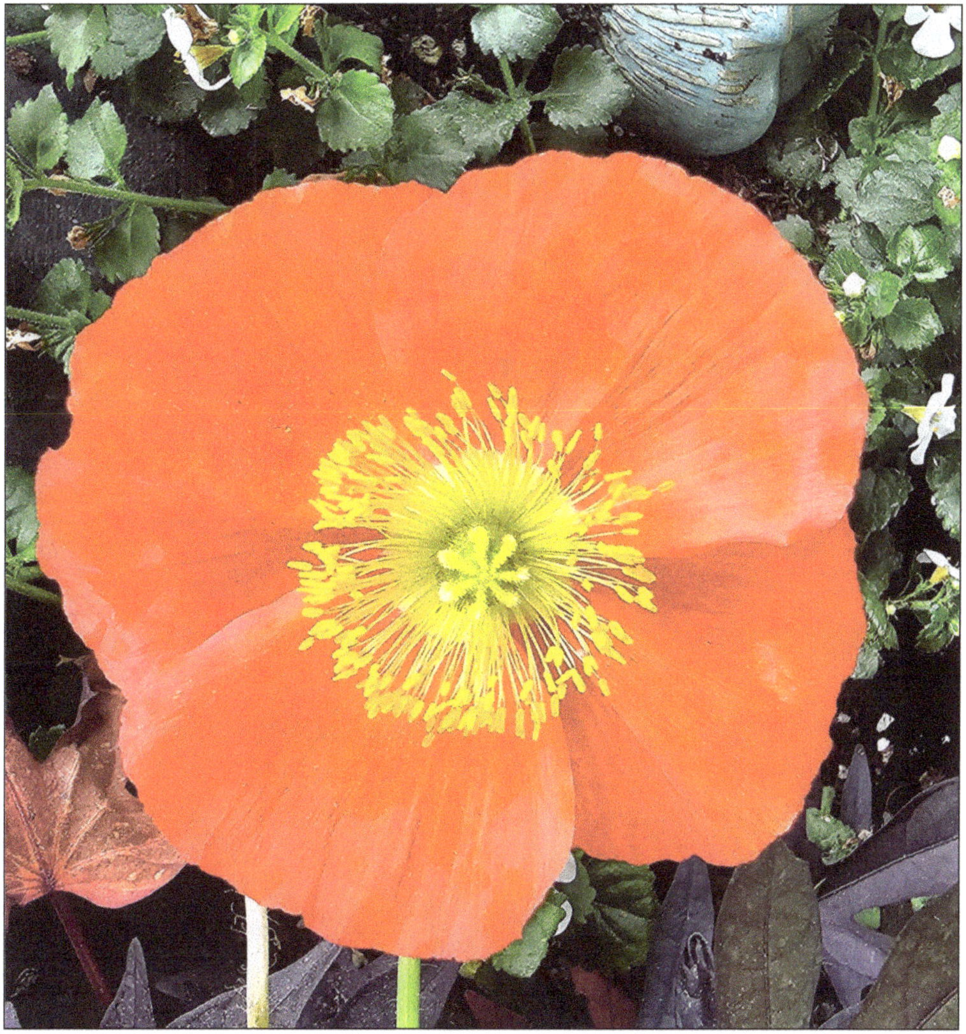

A gorgeous orange poppy growing in Highlands, North Carolina.

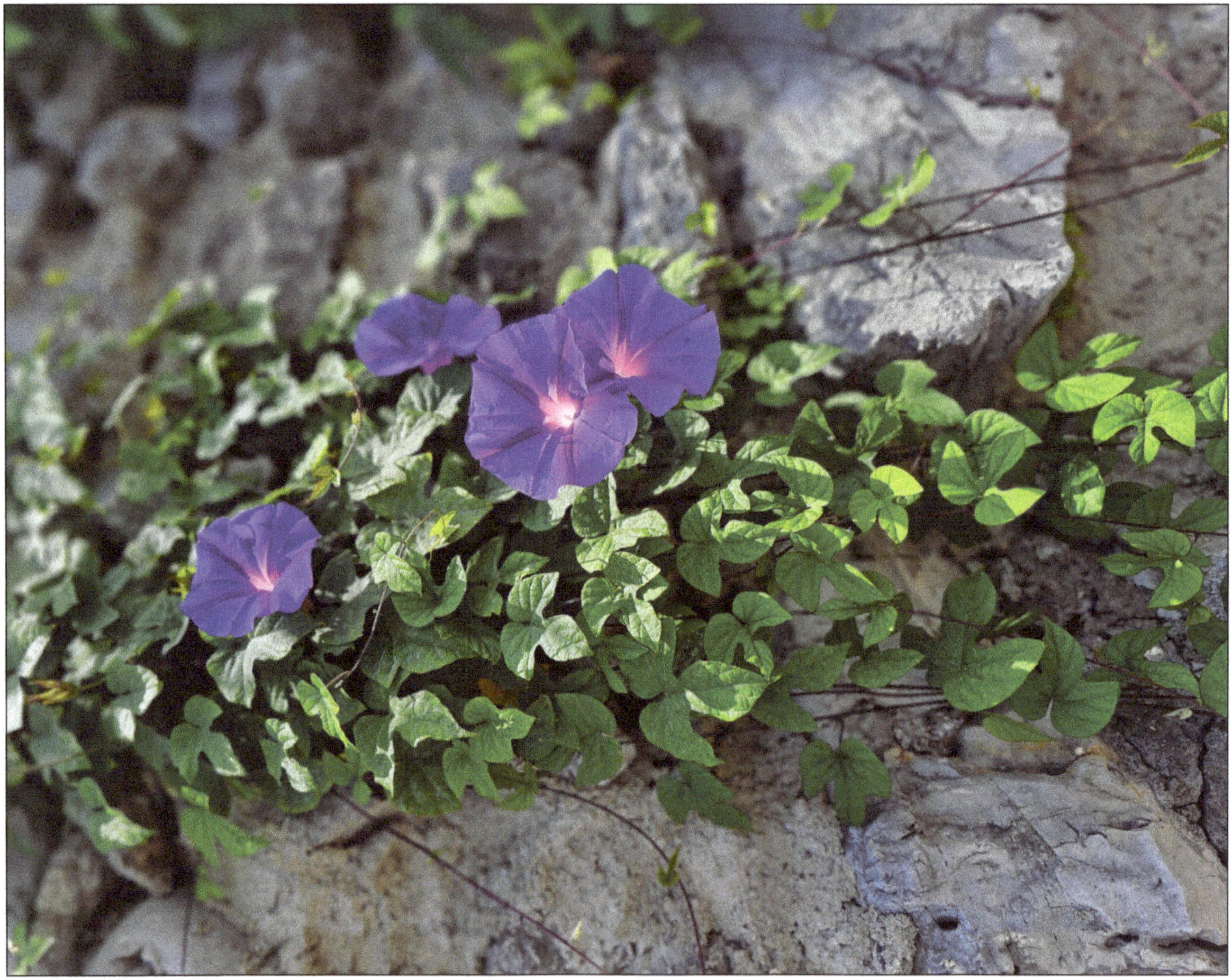

A touch of color always brings joy.

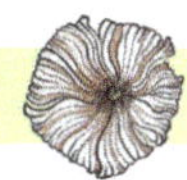

Artists see colors across from each other on the color wheel as complementary colors. For example, my favorite pair is blue and orange. Whenever I see these colors together, I immediately feel happiness. **We all have our favorite color combinations.**

A few other fun complementary colors are yellow and purple and red and green. When these colors match up, they come together to create unforgettable pairs. They are almost more beautiful together than apart!

The primary colors of red, blue and yellow cannot be made by mixing other colors. Secondary colors like purple, orange, and green can be made by mixing two primary colors together in equal amounts. We can even go one step further to broaden our color horizon. Tertiary colors are made by mixing a primary and a secondary color together.

For example, if we combine violet (secondary) and red (primary), we discover a tertiary color that is a warmer shade. It is found between red and violet. It's also referred by some as magenta. On the cool end of colors, if we mix blue (primary) and green (secondary) together, we discover a color we know as teal, located between these two colors on the color wheel.

Color theory can be tricky but knowing a bit about it helps introduce our eyes to the infinite subtleties of color. It inspires us to notice unique color variations in our world.

When we travel, we love to sightsee and take in all the colors around us. One delightful way to observe color is to watch people. See what they wear. Do some window shopping. **Observe how people put colors together. *Colors we wear influence how we feel.*** They also say so much about how we see ourselves. A new color combination in our wardrobe can give us a boost of confidence when we make a new start in life. **Is it time for some *new color choices* in your life?**

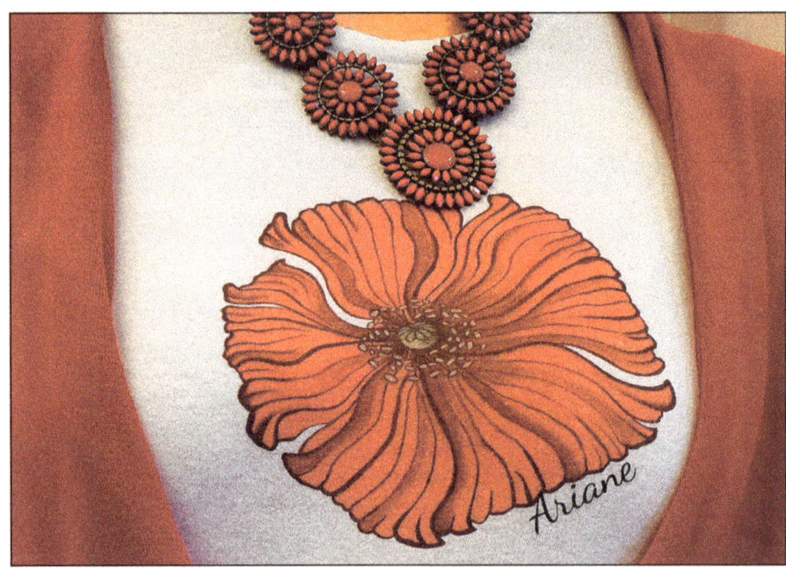

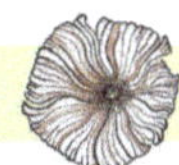

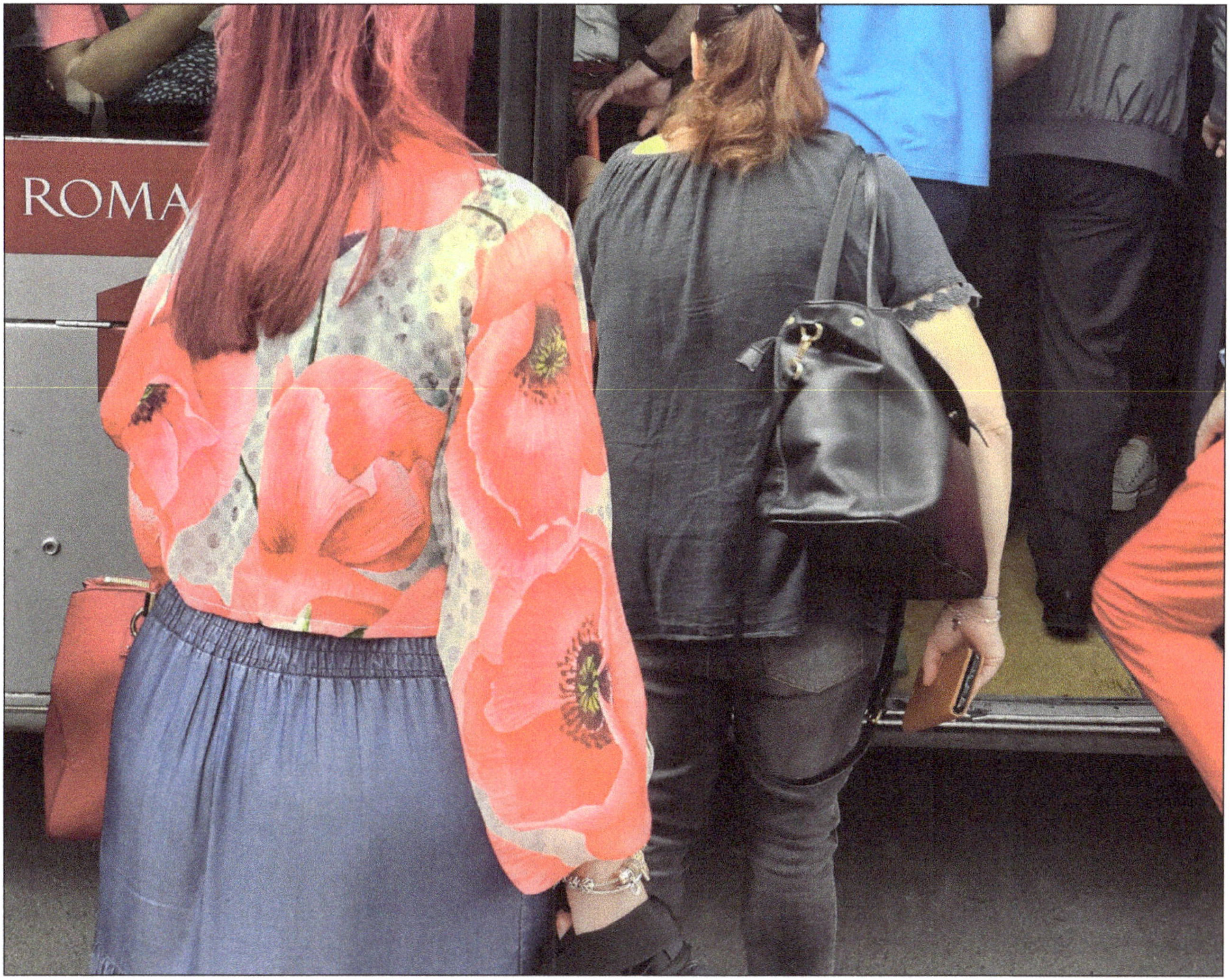

A little splash of red goes a long way!

On my recent trip to Italy, I took photographs of vibrant colors that caught my eye. Noticing what people wear is a solid way to start training your eyes to see and appreciate the vast array of colors that exist. **Fashion truly is art in motion. All we need to do is stop and look. Take some time to observe what people wear.** What colors delight you? What two color combinations draw you in? Are they variations of the same color or are they entirely different colors?

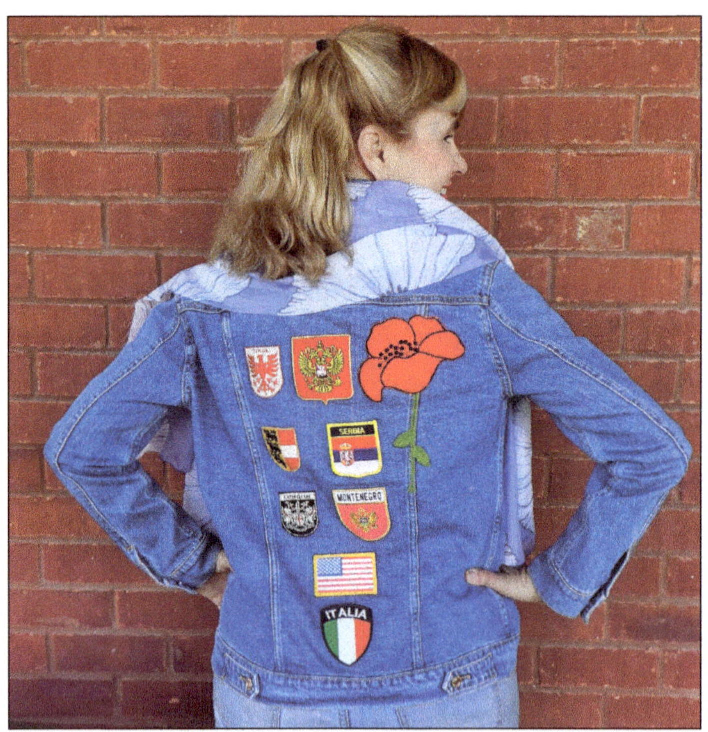

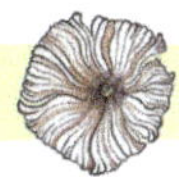

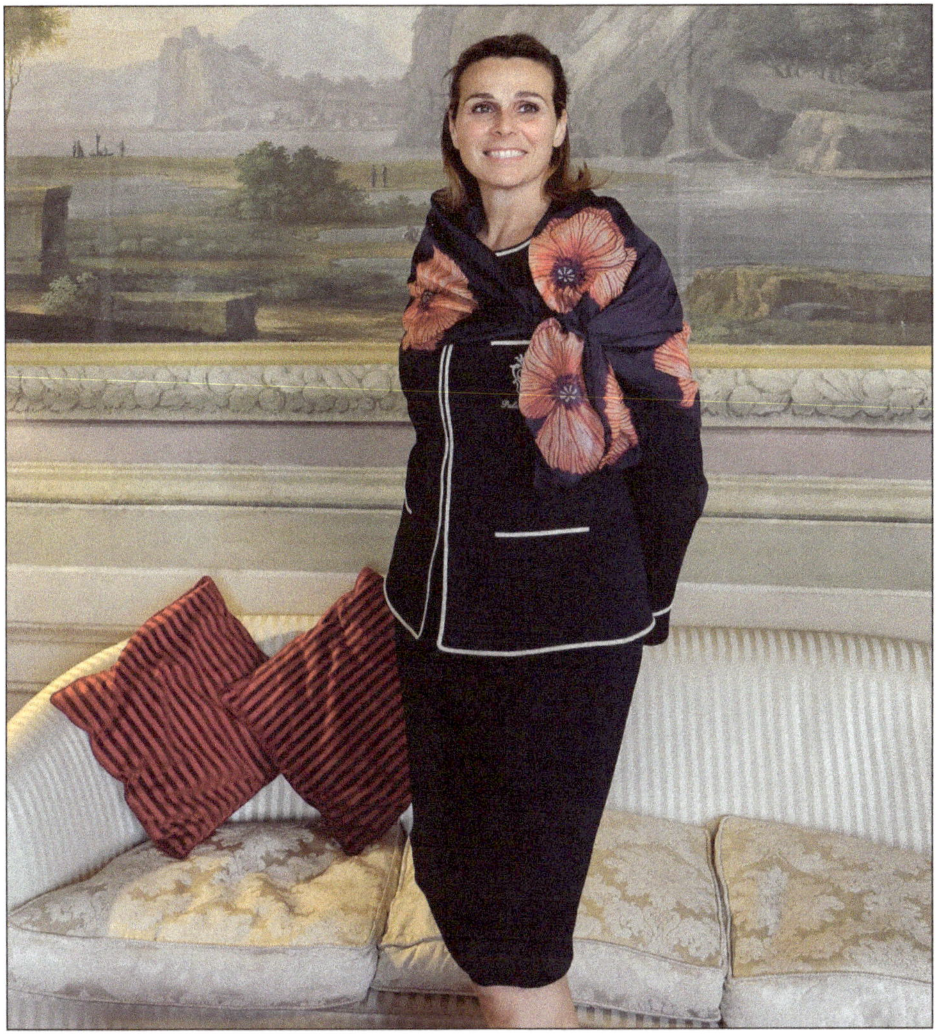

Elegant colors! The stylish owner of a vegan travel company in Tuscany, Italy (thepoppyland.com).

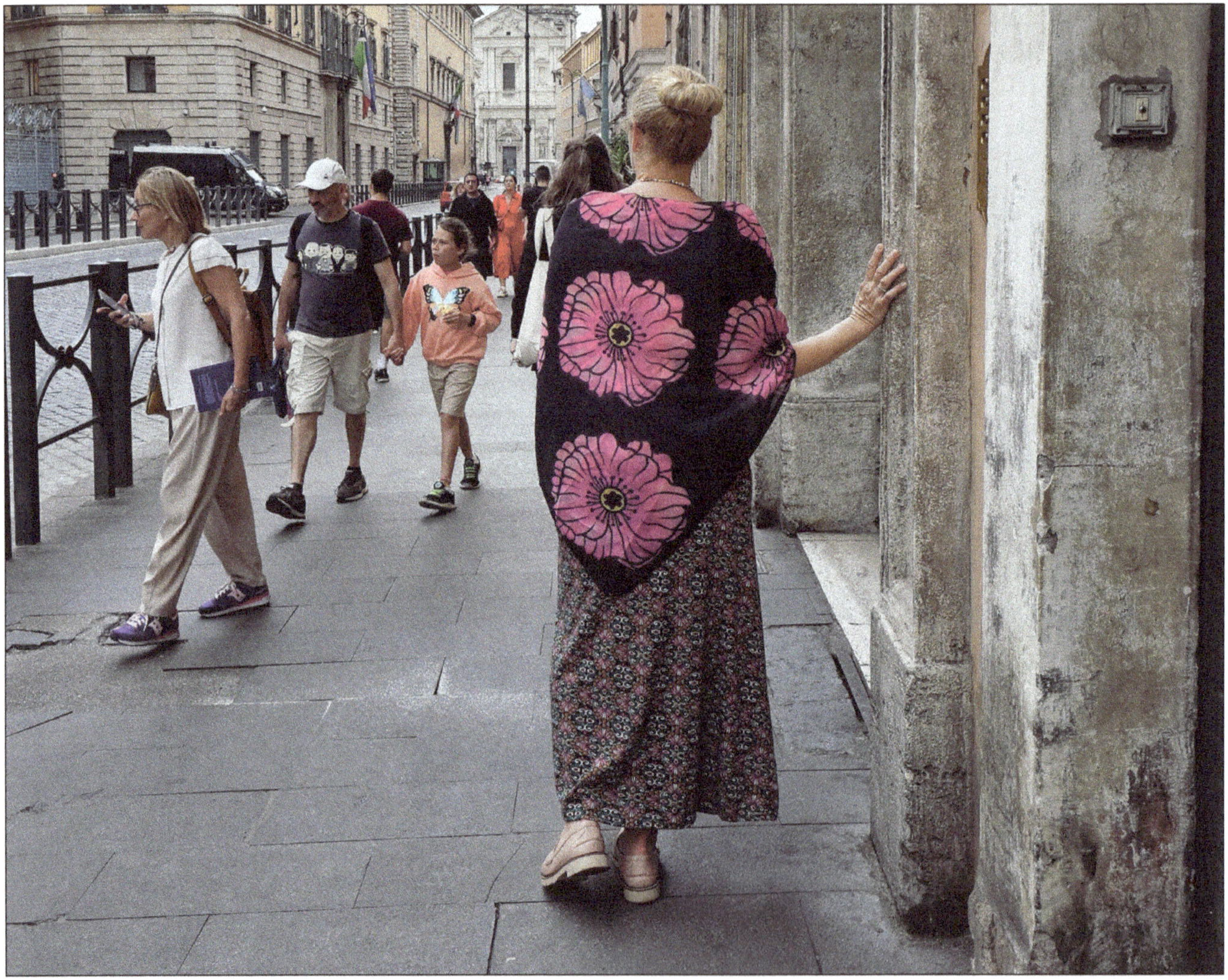

A little pop of pink brightens any day.

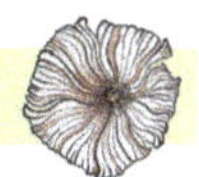

Go home and take a fresh look at your wardrobe. Do you see a variety of colors there or a select few? Are they intense colors, muted or somewhere in between? Do you like **cool colors** like blues or blue-greens, or perhaps blue-violets? Or, do you like **warm colors** like yellows, oranges, reds and red-violets?

Out of all the elements of art design, color is the one element that most everyone has a strong opinion on. Usually, our feelings about color stem from childhood. We get stuck with what our childhood eyes saw regarding color and stop seeing anew. We are remembering what we first felt about color. As a result, we often hang on to preconceived stereotypes.

When was the last time you really took the time to notice the variety of colors in front of you? Our color preferences change over time. Maybe it is time to revisit how you perceive color.

Stop for a moment and look outside. How many different green hues can you find? There are a multitude of variations of this color! Look at moss, grass, pine, basil, sage, mint, and fern green. Each of these color tints is a hue of green. *Some we like more than others.*

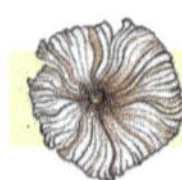

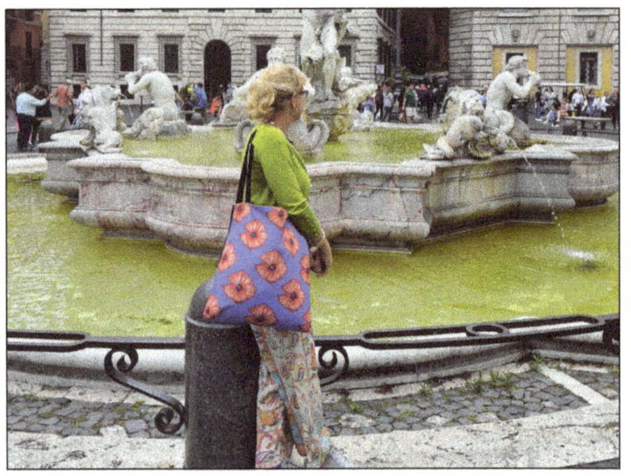

Fountain water green.

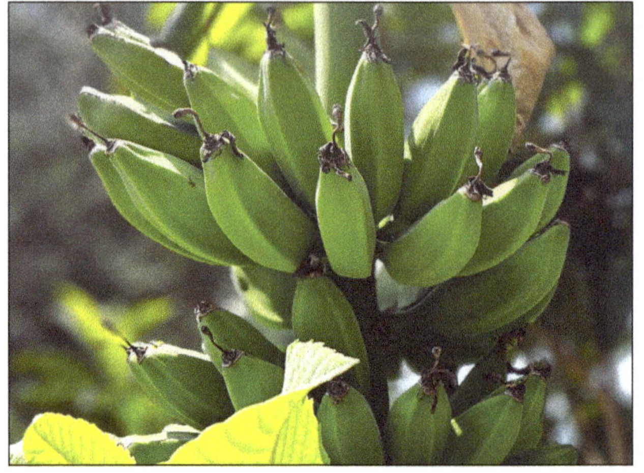

Unripened green bananas.

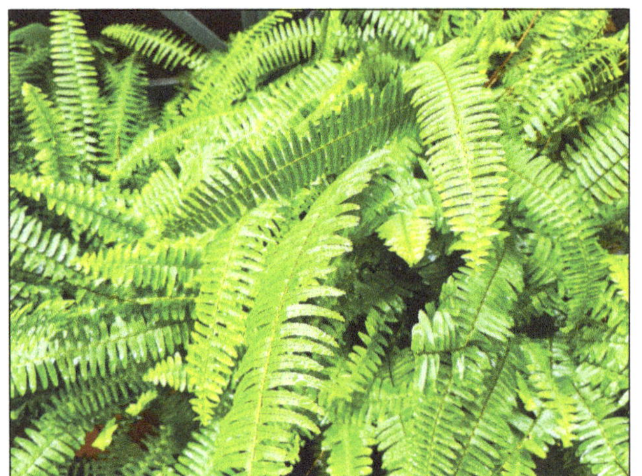

Fern green.

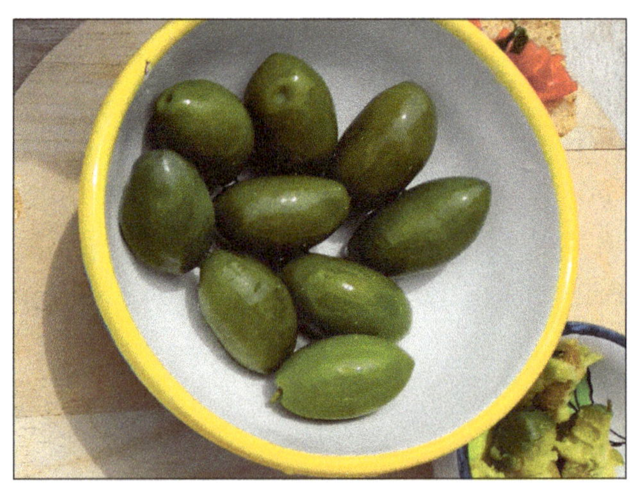

Olive green.

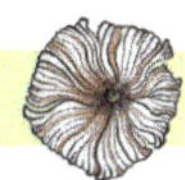

Color Preference Check-In:
Collect and paste or tape on a few examples of colors you love here.

I remember once being in a boat in the Florida Keys just in time for a magnificent sunset over water. It was a glorious vision of reflected color! I will never forget its beauty. Take note of the next sunset you see. **Count the colors.** One sunset is an explosion of color: Blues, purples, oranges and yellows, just to name a few. Some are intense and some are subtle. **Spend a few days going outside to watch the sunset, then complete the sunset exercises on the next two pages.**

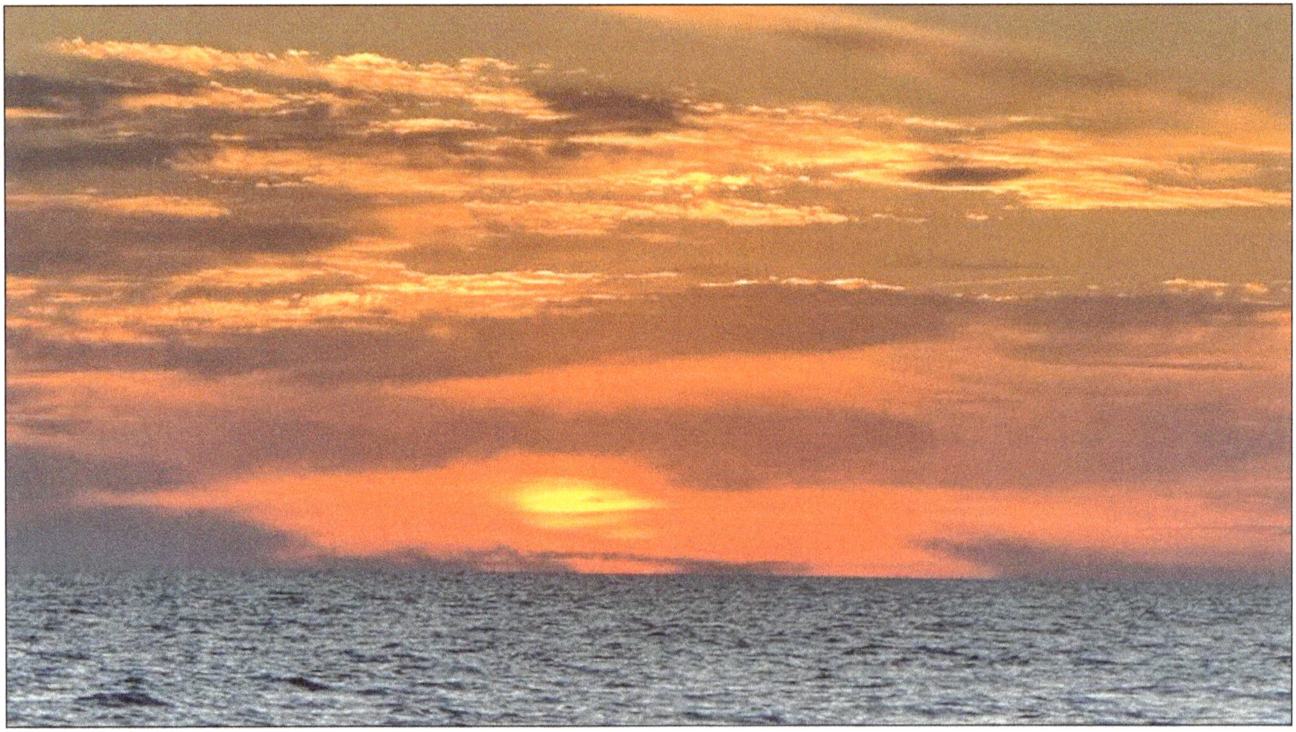

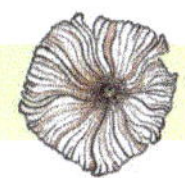

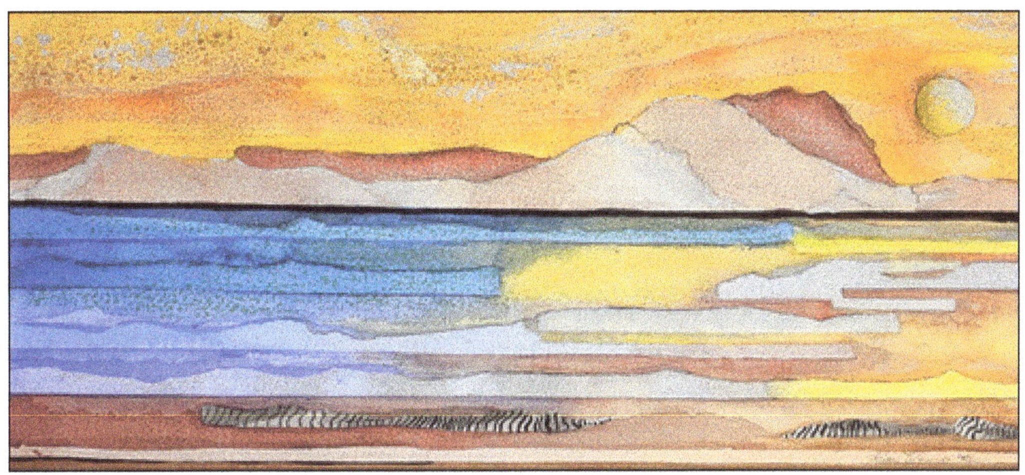

Lakeside Sunset watercolor by Ariane Trifunovic Montemuro, 1985.

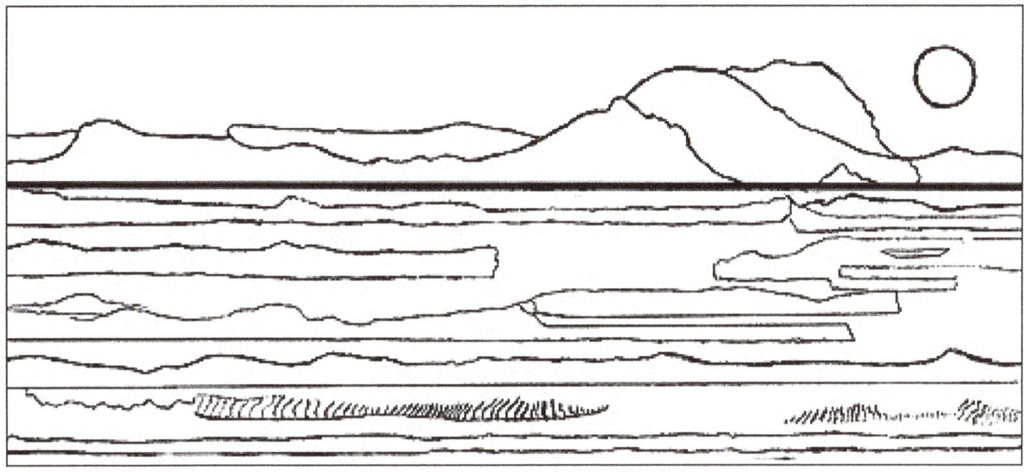

Use your colored pencils to recreate Lakeside Sunset here.

Draw your favorite sunset with colored pencils.

 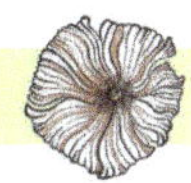

As you begin to see like an artist, you will become fluent in a new visual language. So, keep searching out and copying art that speaks to you. ***Studying and copying other artists' work is a great way to develop your artist's eyes.*** Plus, it's fun to see how others use color! This is one of the best ways to practice seeing like an artist. Focusing on one particular artist and studying their use of color refines your visual language skills.

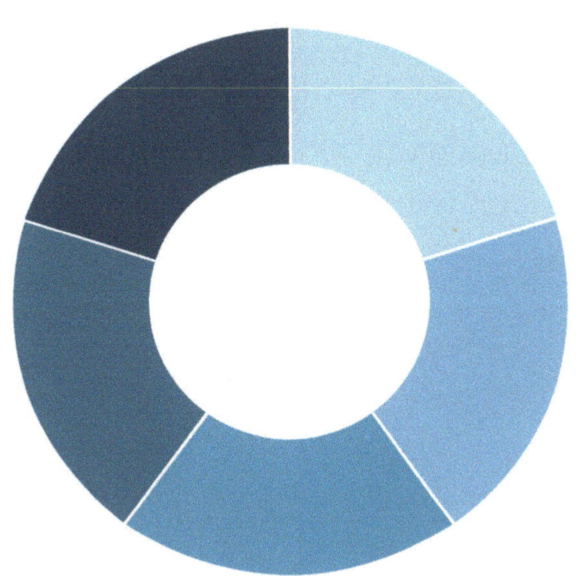

One of America's best known artists was the magnificent colorist, **Georgia O'Keeffe (1887-1986).** Look up and study her energetic and vibrant painting of *Lake George* (1922).

In that painting, O'Keeffe creatively manipulates blue to express an entire composition. She plays around with the color like a musical scale; from dark to light.

This amazing artist once said that she was able to say things through her paintings that she wasn't able to describe with words. **Colors and shapes became her language of expression. As you practice, they will become your language, too.**

O'Keeffe's words truly inspire me. *She's right.* **There is a real language to everything we see.** As you get to know certain artists, it's important to collect their sayings and even memorize your favorites. This way they'll stick with you when you see something that really moves you to create.

It's a good idea to take time to do a sustained investigation of artists of your choice and their works. See what you do and don't like about their art. Hang reproductions of their work around your home. Switch up these images from time to time. Pick new artists to study. It's important to see new images by new artists in order to learn and grow. Train your eyes to see a variety of images. **The more you draw, color, and copy artists' work, the better you will see.**

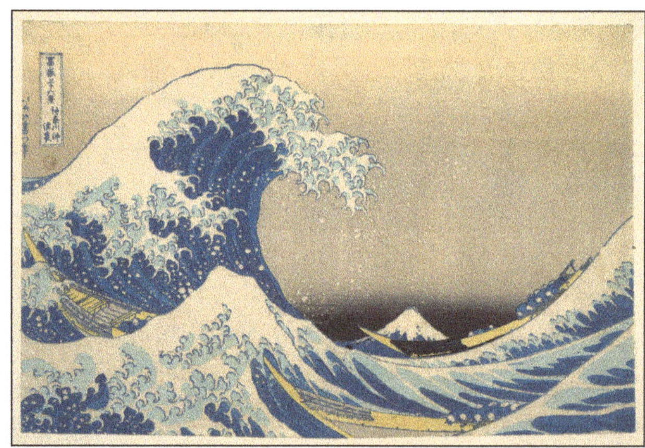

Impressionist painters to present-day artists continue to copy The Great Wave Off Kanagawa, *by Japanese artist, Katsushika Hokusai, (1760–1849). This is a great work of art to practice copying.*

 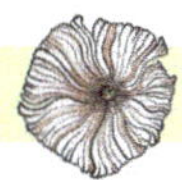

Continue studying a variety of artists and how they use color. By doing so, you'll refine and develop your artist's eyes. Practice makes perfect as you cultivate seeing the visual language of line, shape, and color. *As you start to understand what speaks to you visually, you'll eventually be able to articulate why.*

Colors can be warm like the sun or cool like water. Some colors you see and some you feel. Colors tell us so much about our world and ourselves. Authors color a story with colorful words. Colorful birds make us smile. We go to salons to color our hair. A mid-life crisis brings on a colorful little car. Change the color in your place, and it feels like a whole new space! So, if it's been a while, and you're bored with your style, it's time to rewind... *pick a new color and unwind!*

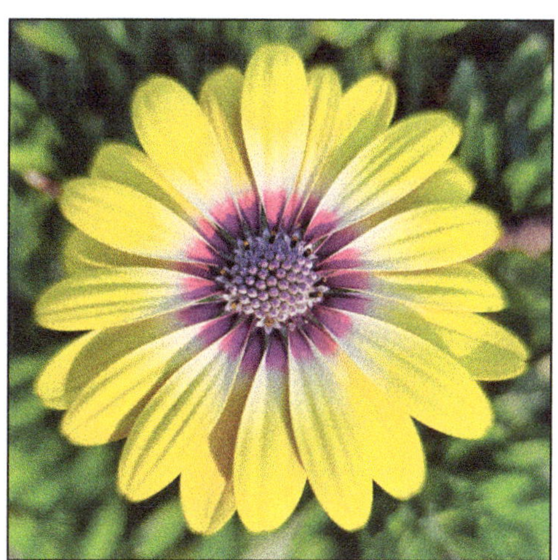

When I was a little girl, my grandfather came to me in a dream right after he died. He said, "You of all people would absolutely love the colors in Heaven! They are so incredibly beautiful. They are so vivid, like nothing you can see on earth." Of course, this childhood dream fueled my already colorful imagination with joy and curiosity. I tried to imagine the colors he spoke of. It was hard because there were already so many beautiful colors here on earth!

First things first, though, let's strive to relish the everyday beauty we see. After that is achieved, then maybe we can perceive even greater beauty. **Our artist's eyes must be able to see and appreciate the beauty surrounding us at this very moment.**

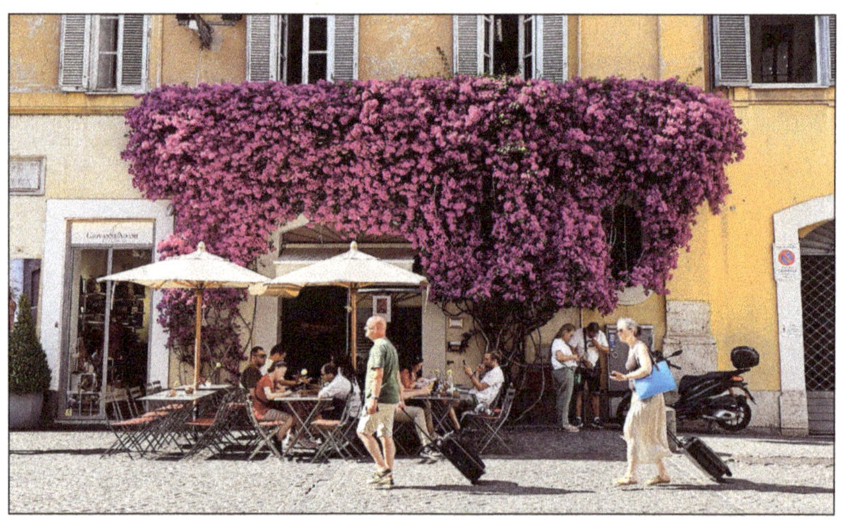

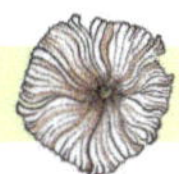

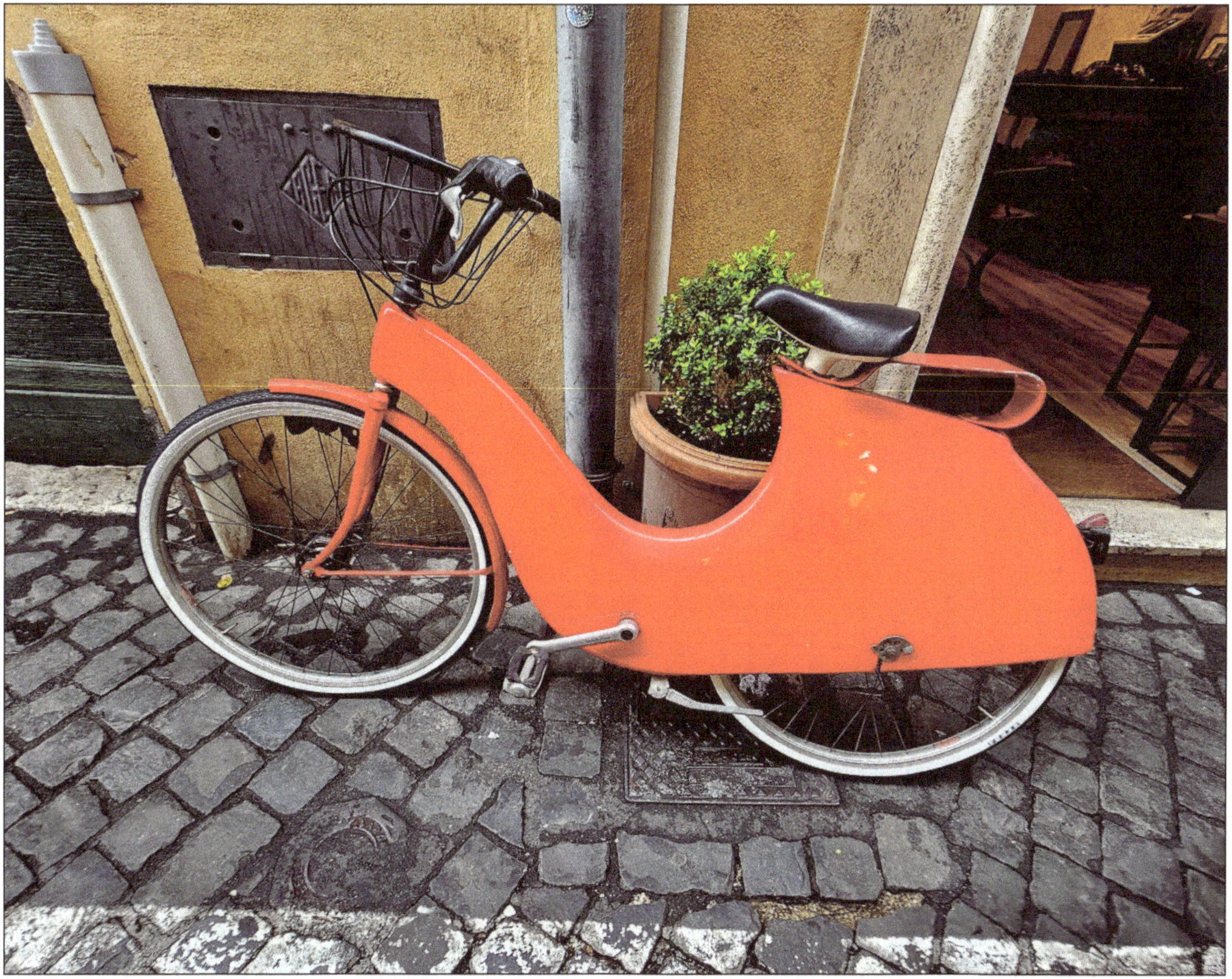

Who wouldn't love this colorful, shapely bike?

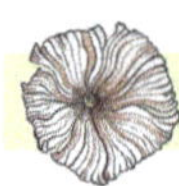

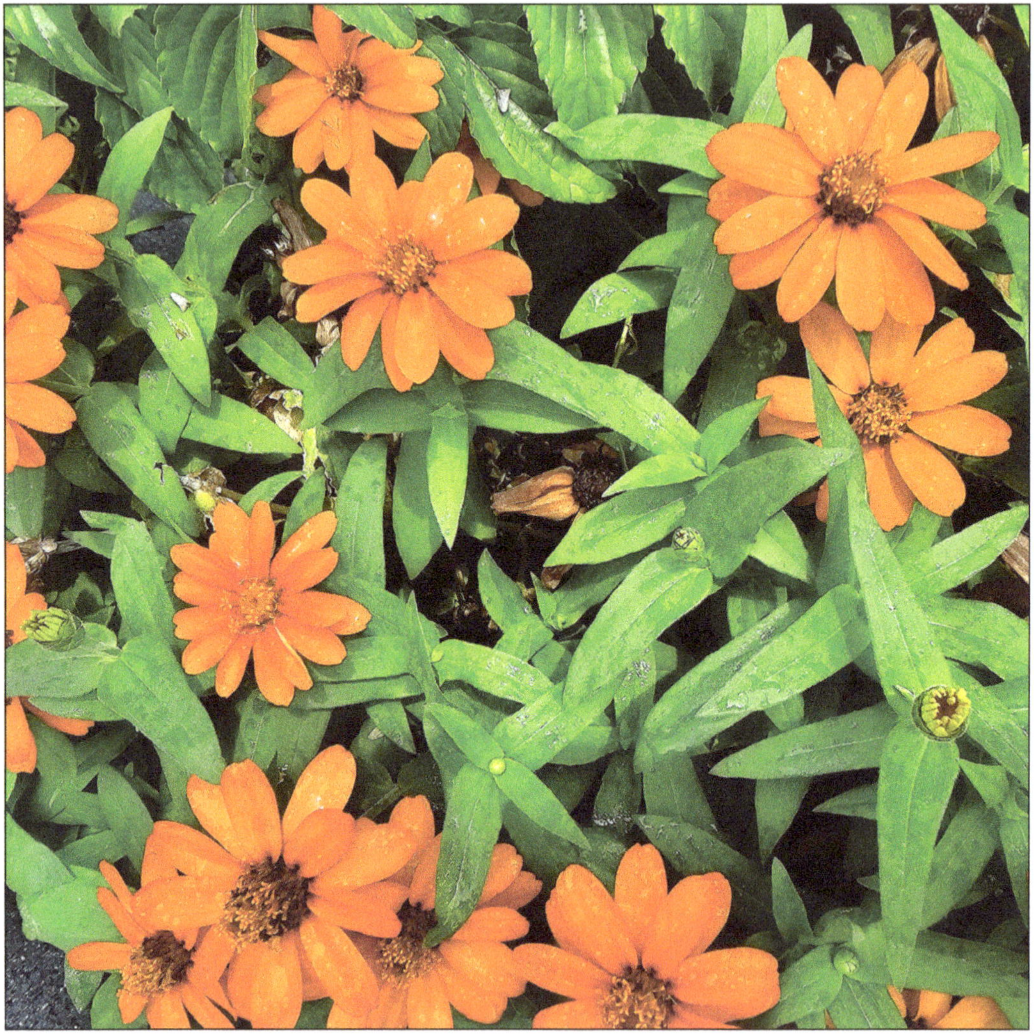

Color, color, everywhere!

 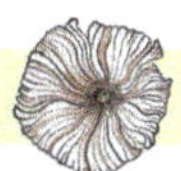

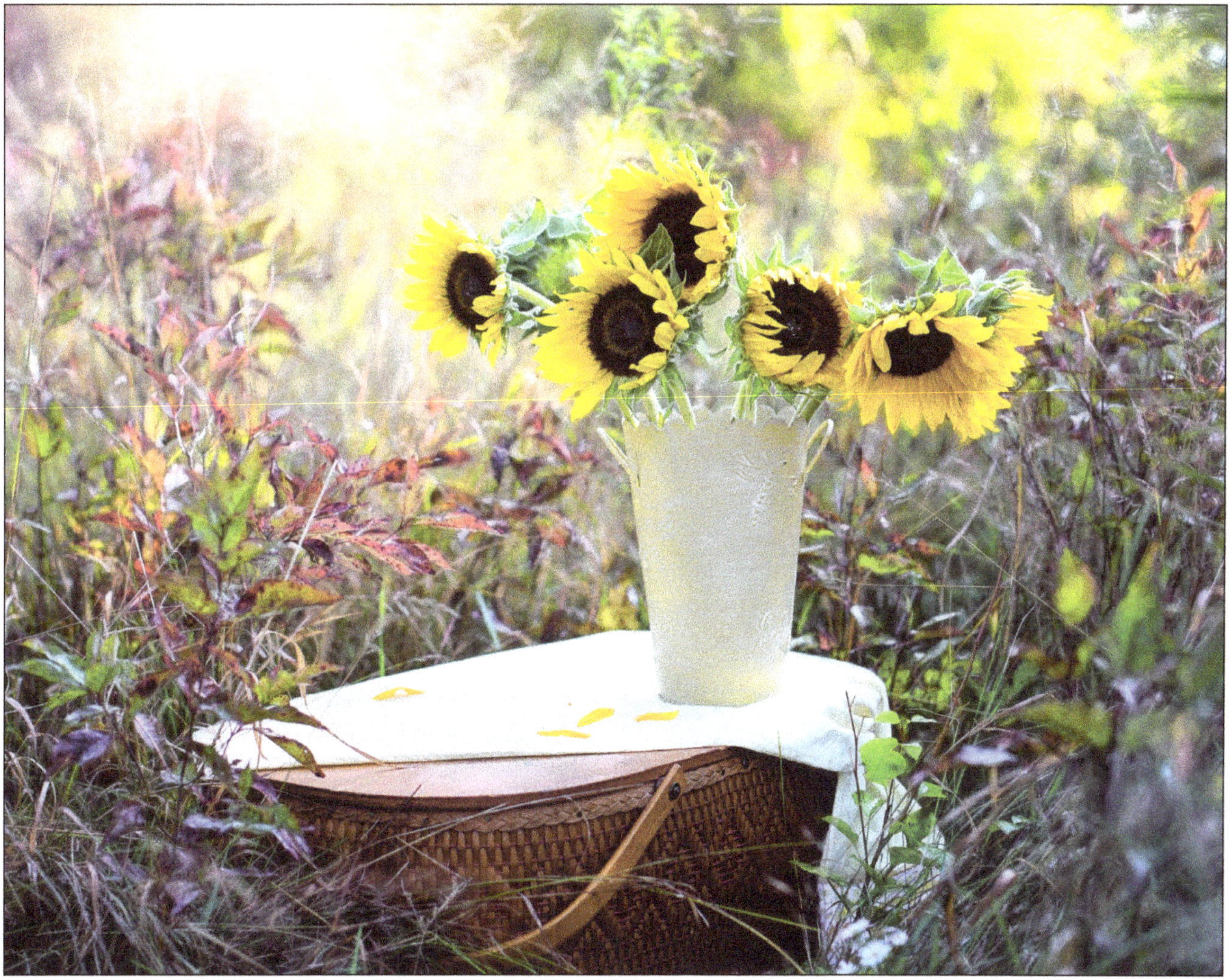

Yellow sunflowers delight and inspire!

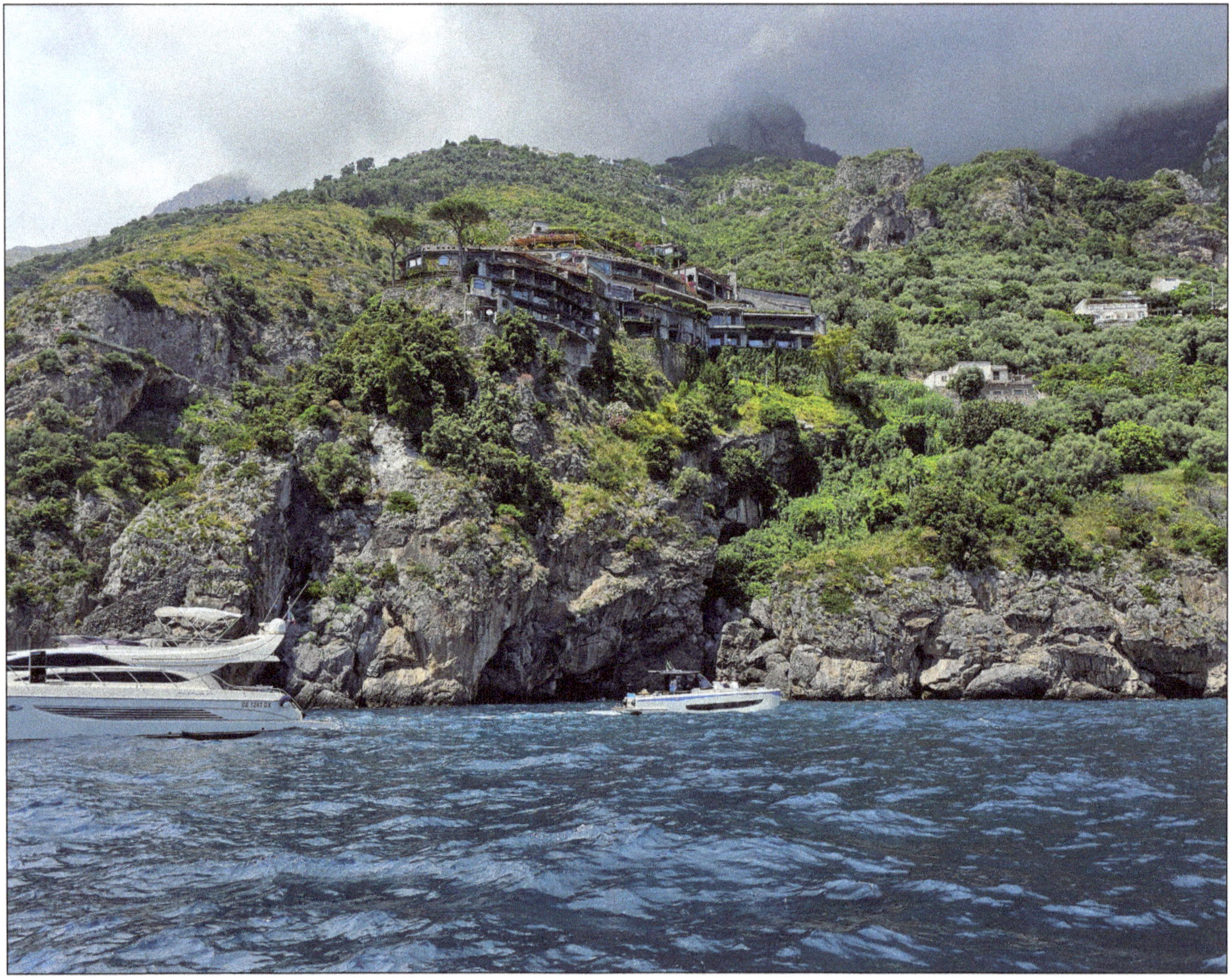

The majesty of a cool, crisp color palette.

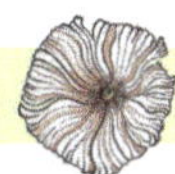

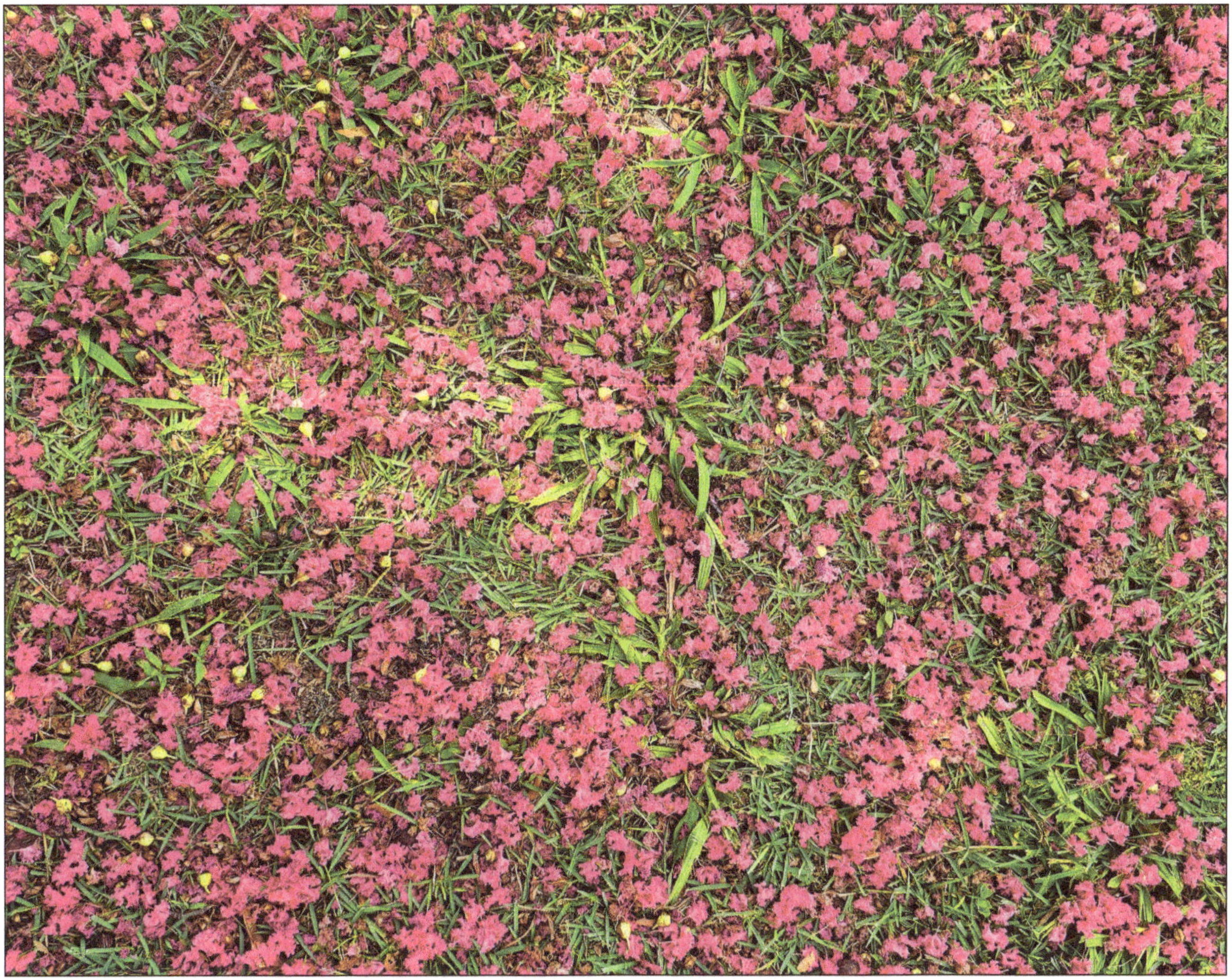

Nature's confetti: Colorful Bougainvillea petals on the ground.

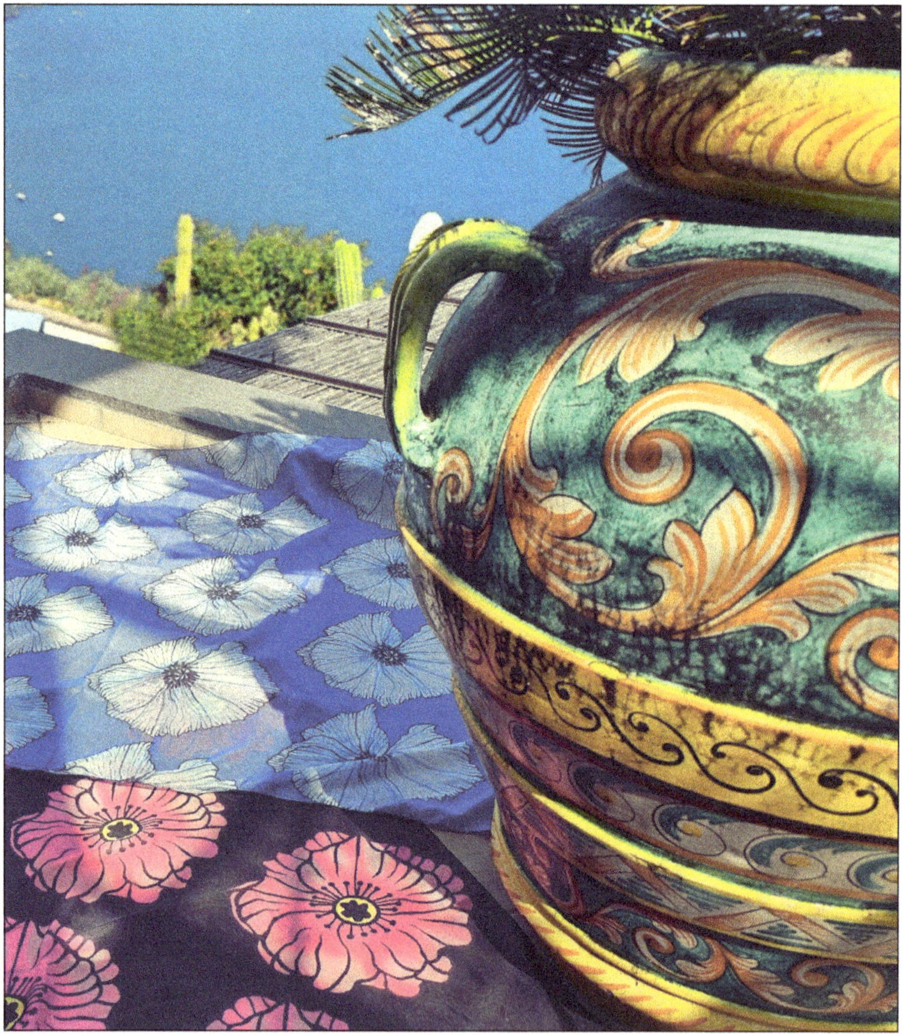

Seaside Amalfi Coast colors.

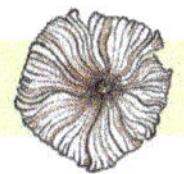

As you get to know and appreciate the design element of color, it is also important to understand the following vocabulary words an artist uses to describe color. These words are vital in understanding the nuances of different colors. Each of these terms explains certain color qualities.

Color Vocabulary Terms

Hues: Hues describe pure color. This is color in its purest form. A hue has nothing added to it to change its properties.

Tints: Tints are created anytime white is added to any hue. When this happens, the hue is lightened and the color's saturation is reduced.

Shades: Shades are created when black is added to any hue.

Tones: Tones are created when grey is added to a color. The amount of black and white added determines the final tone. Tones can be darker or lighter than the original hue.

Values: Value describes the lightness or darkness of a color relative to white, black, and grey. If you take a hue (like green) and add white or black to it, you manipulate the value.

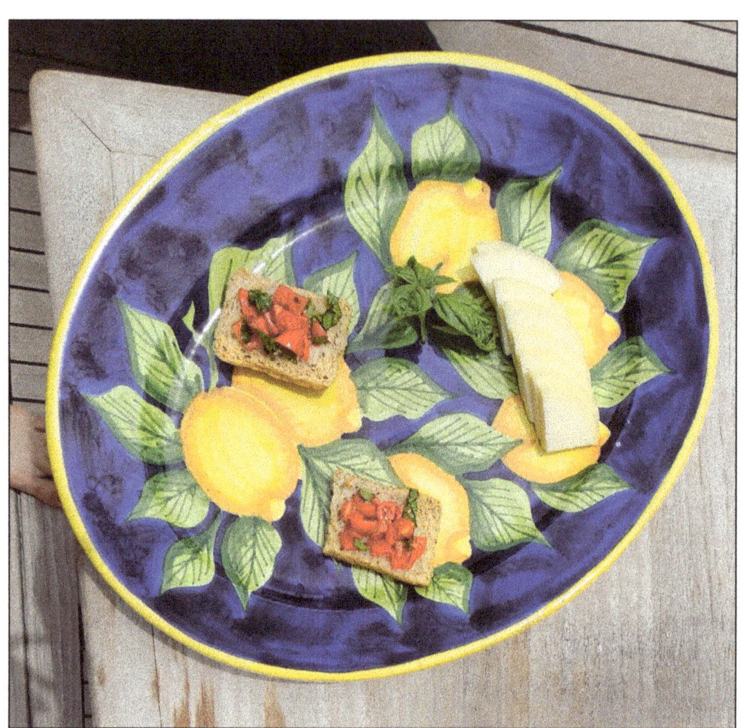

When you see like an artist, you see beauty everywhere, even in the presentation of the simplest of life's everyday activities, like the delicious pop of red on an already colorful plate. A splash of red can bring *a lot of happiness*! Notice how colors have a powerful way of inspiring and igniting our senses. They convey a mood and tell a story about who we are at this very moment. That's why it's important to revisit our color choices on a regular basis.

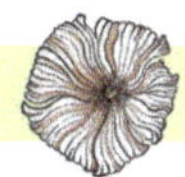

Revisit your current color choices. Take a moment to think about how you can refresh your personal color palette in your home and in your closet. *Little color changes can inspire new beginnings!*

Collect paint swatches. Draw colorful and muted color landscapes. Get to know which colors speak to you at this very moment. How many favorite colors do you have? One, two, or more? It's a great idea to focus on one color and get to know all its possibilities.

Ditch all those childhood opinions. It's time for a change. Declutter decades of old shades of color. Add nuances of color to refresh your wardrobe and your home.

Surround yourself with color choices that make you smile. Allow yourself some updated style. *You deserve it.* One small change can potentially result in a big inspiration in any area of your life!

Use color to tell your story in a new stylish way! You will be surprised and delighted when you look at your spaces transformed with new color picks. A fresh palette of new possibilities opens unexpected doors in life!

Newly awakened artists' eyes begin to see inspiration at every turn! Get ready for more beauty because your next step is to spice up your lives with texture!

Chapter Four Fun Fact

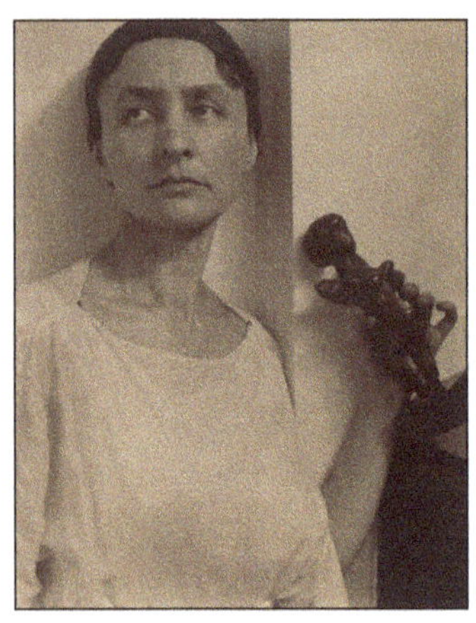

Georgia O'Keeffe holding a Henri Matisse sculpture. Photo by Alfred Stieglitz (1864-1946), 1921.

Georgia O'Keeffe (1887-1986) was an American modernist artist. She was influenced by realism early in her career. However, one summer course taught by **Alon Bement (1876-1954)** in 1912 changed her towards a more distinctly modernist style. Her greatest influence, **Arthur Wesley Dow (1857-1922)**, encouraged her to pursue a style of art that emphasized personal expression through composition and design. She took his teachings to heart and used her art to express ideas and feelings. As a result, O'Keeffe's art became more modernist and abstract. Her colorful, powerful, abstract images are now regarded as timeless and memorable. She is regarded as one of America's best-known female artists.

Look up and study her colorful flower paintings. The luminous colors and shapes of her flowers draw the viewer in. O'Keeffe's attention to detail and smooth color gradations introduces the viewer to the beautiful visual world inside each flower. The artist inspires us to not only stop and smell the roses, but also to carefully stop and observe the beauty of each and every detail within the flowers themselves.

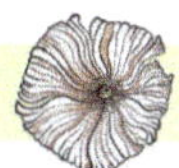

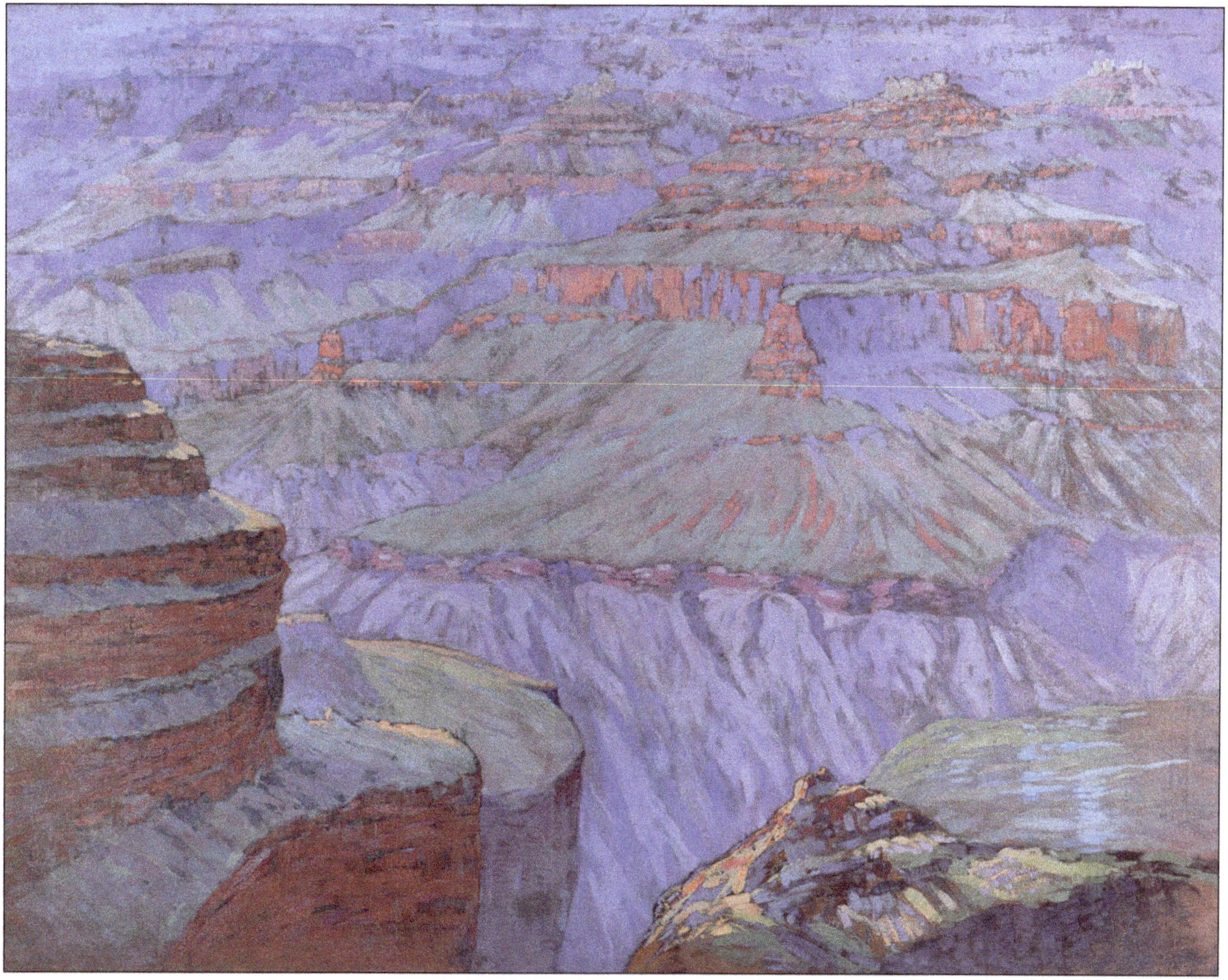

The Grand Canyon, *by Arthur Wesley Dow, Georgia O'Keeffe's greatest artistic influence.*

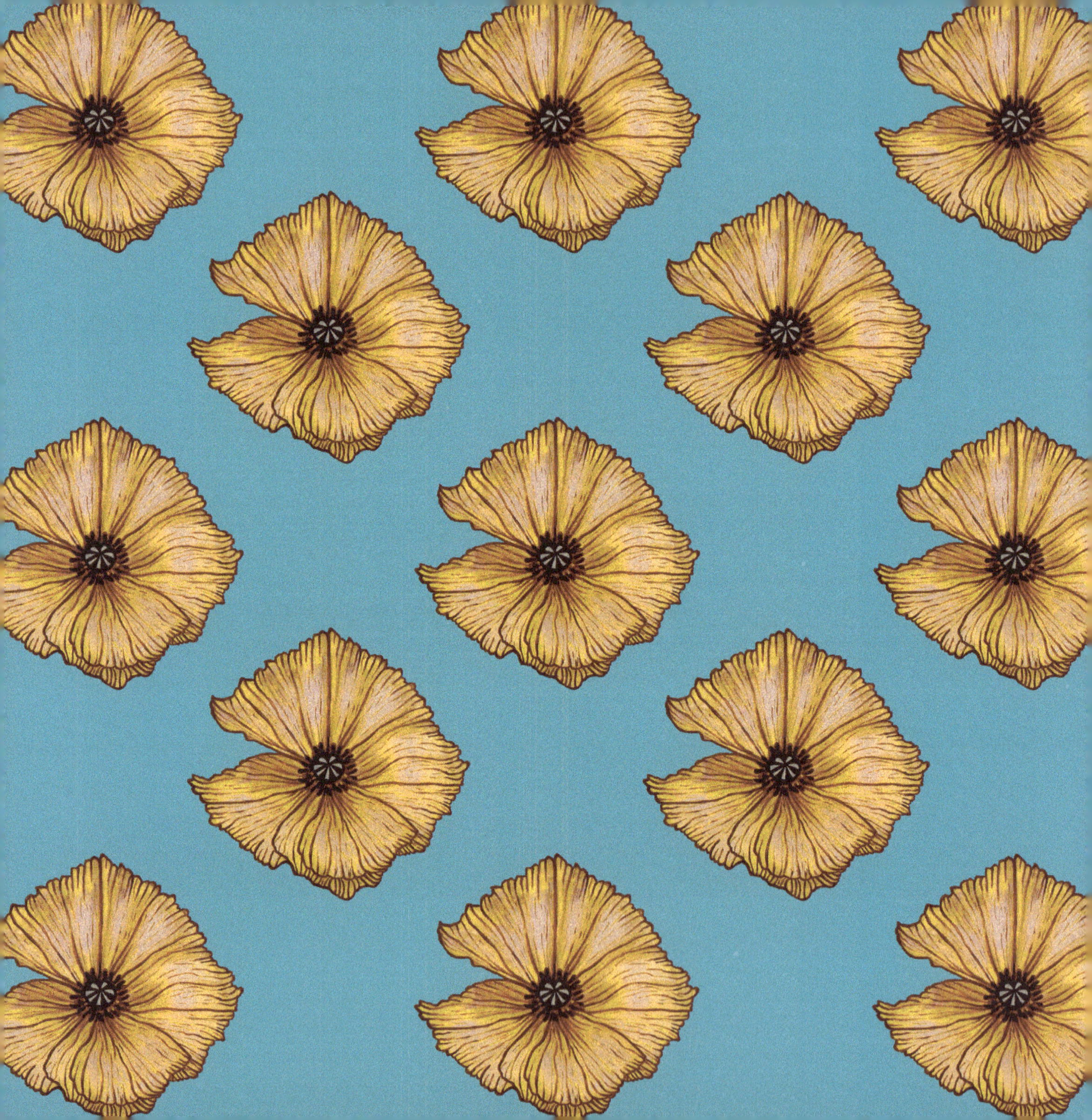

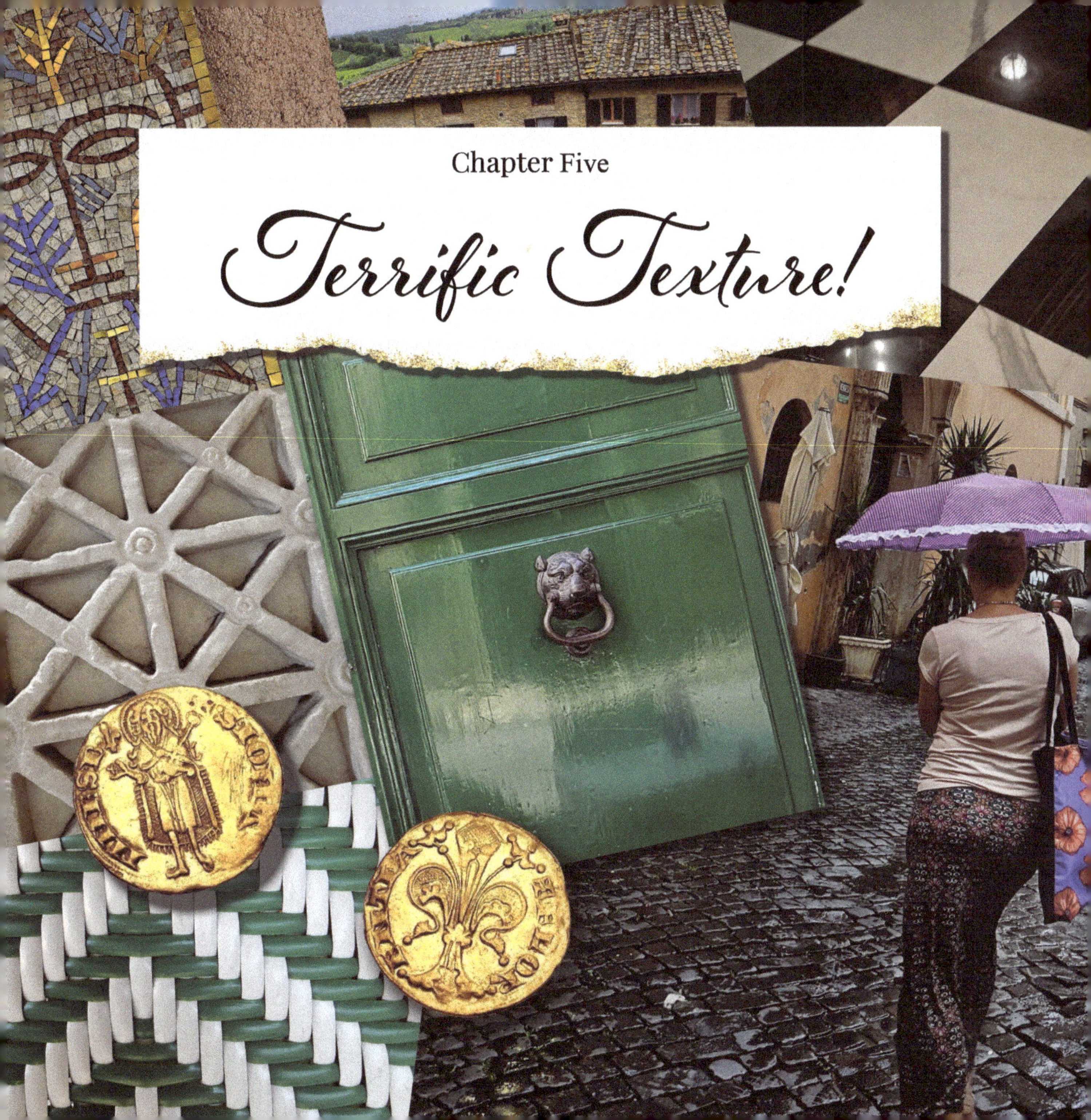
Chapter Five
Terrific Texture!

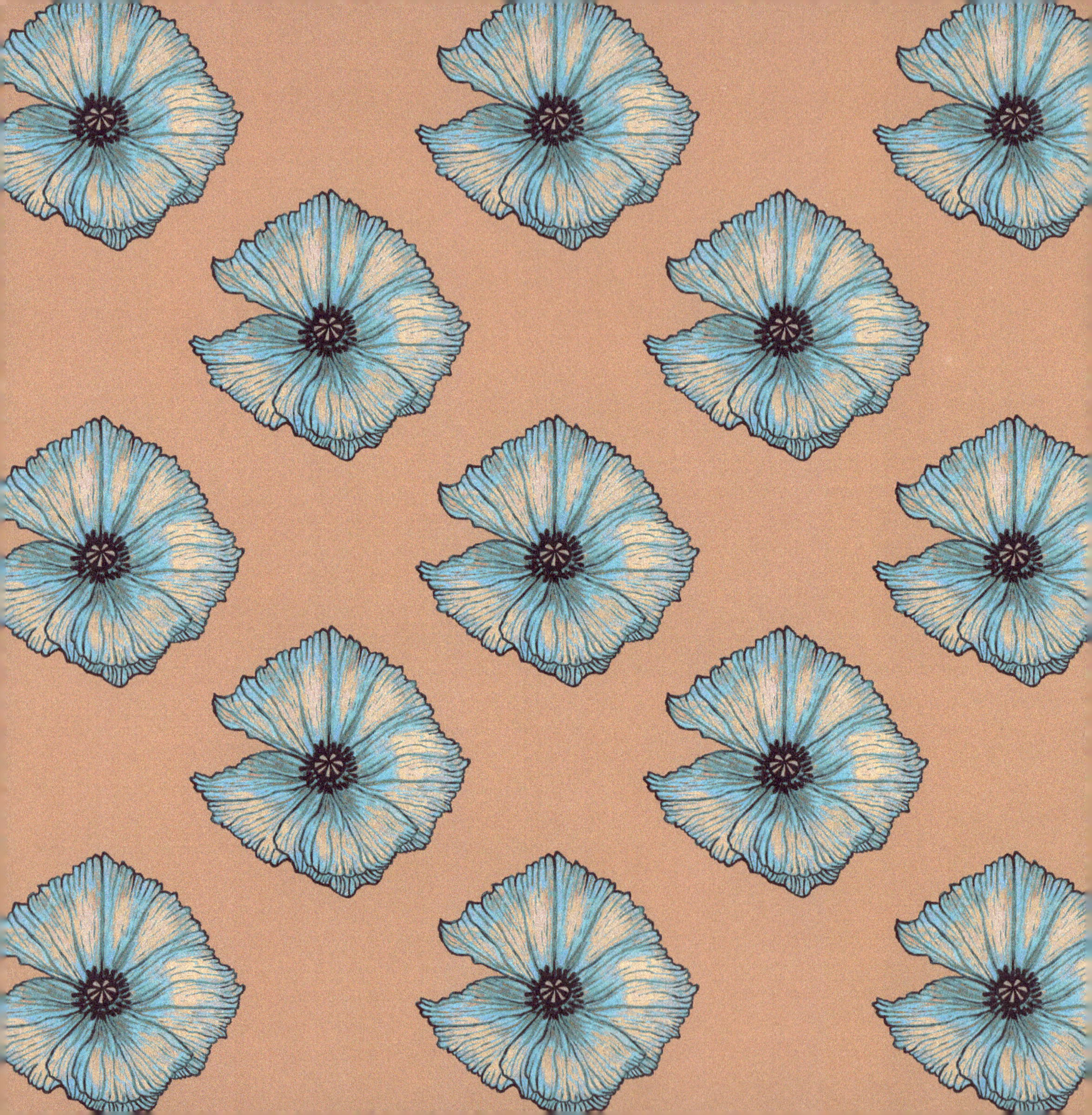

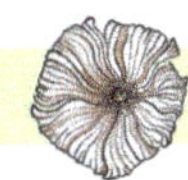

Chapter Five

Terrific Texture!

We've studied **lines**, **shapes**, **form**, and **color** — but there is a surprising and delightful detail missing in our conversation thus far. It is an art element that is essential in helping us perceive and understand the subjects and objects we depict.

Have you ever noticed a painting with an incredibly realistic surface quality, created with refined brushstrokes? It's hard to believe you are seeing a two-dimensional painting and not the reality of what is being depicted. This surface quality is known as *texture*.

Note the realistic texture on the jugs in the painting on the next page, *The Waterseller of Seville*, by Spanish artist Diego Velázquez (1599-1660).

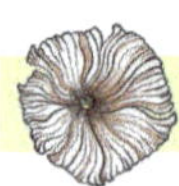

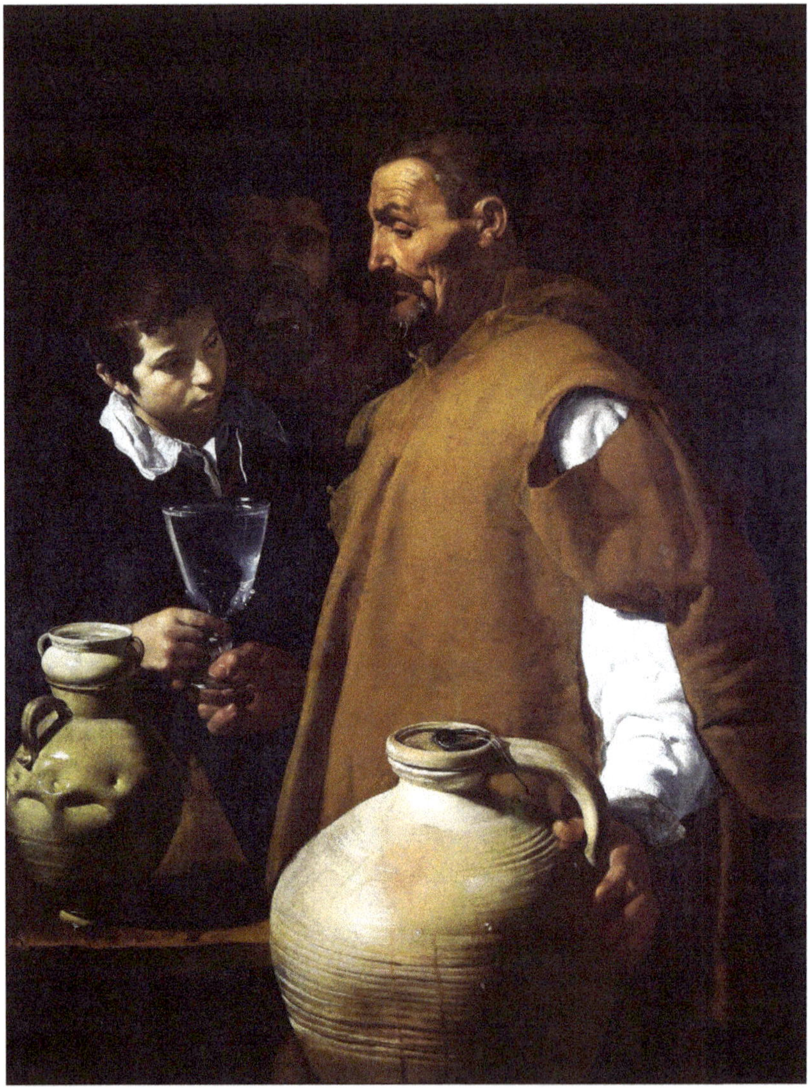

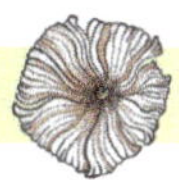

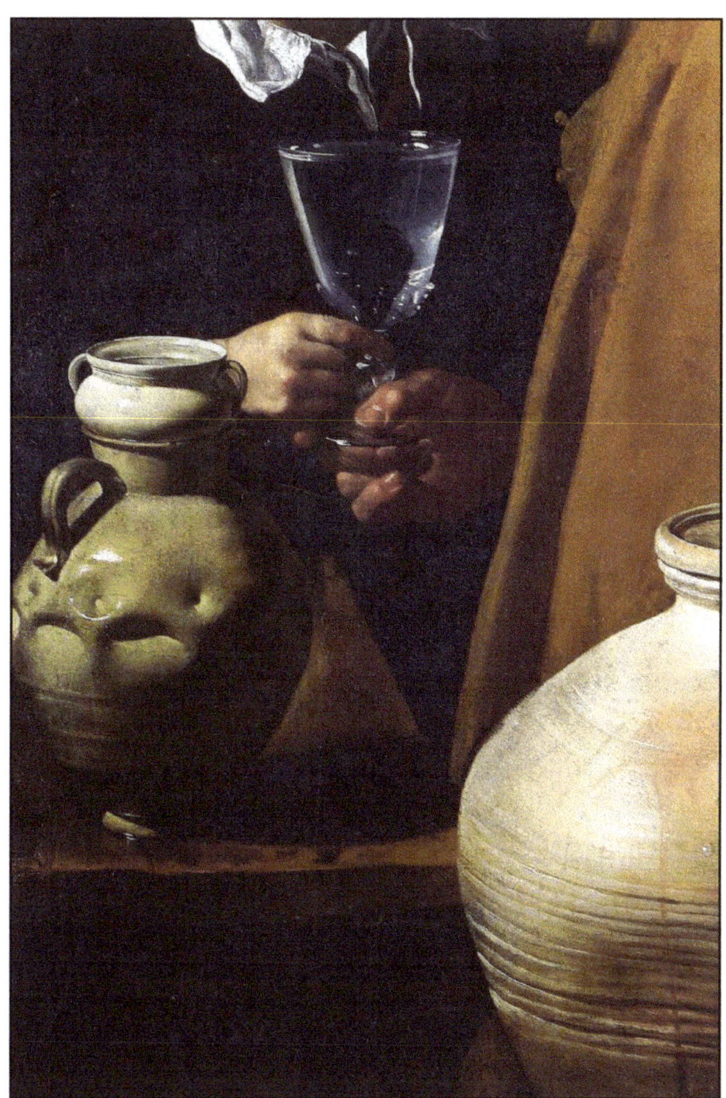

Carefully study the jugs and glass. It's hard to believe you are seeing a two-dimensional painting and not the actual object depicted.

Texture in art is the visual and tactile surface characteristics added to a work of art. It also refers to the illusion of physicality you see. Texture adds depth and movement to art.

There are two main types of textures in art. The first is ***implied texture*** which can be seen but not felt. Implied texture can be achieved through lines, patterns, colors, and brushstrokes. The second is ***physical texture*** which we can actually feel. Sometimes artists use a painting technique called impasto to depict physical texture. Impasto refers to the use of thickly textured, undiluted paint that appears almost three-dimensional on canvas.

Vincent van Gogh (1853–1890) was a pioneer in his use of this technique. If you view some of his paintings from the side you see the paint sticking out in lumps and ridges. He used impasto to add emotion and movement to his art. This is clearly seen in his most famous painting, ***The Starry Night***.

Van Gogh once said in a September 2, 1882 letter to his brother Theo, "Sometimes the subject calls for less paint, sometimes the material, the nature of the subjects themselves demands impasto." He experimented with texture in groundbreaking ways by depicting the movement, energy and heartfelt feeling that he experienced sitting before his subjects. Even today Van Gogh's art still pulses with his energy!

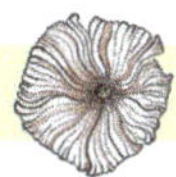

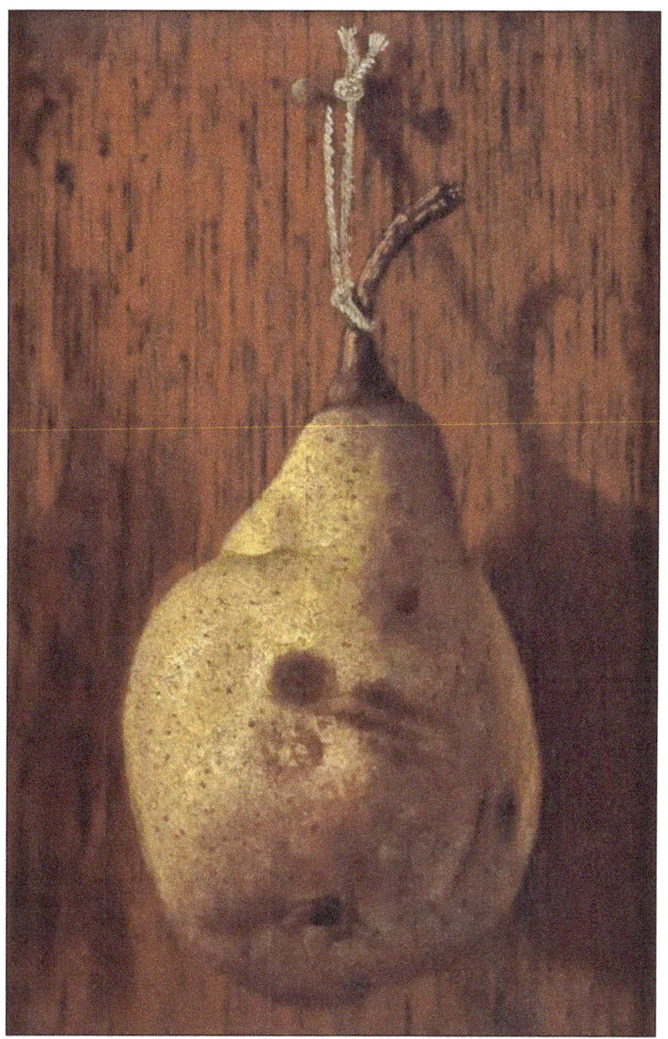

This painting is an example of implied texture. *unknown artist, American School of Realism, 1880.*

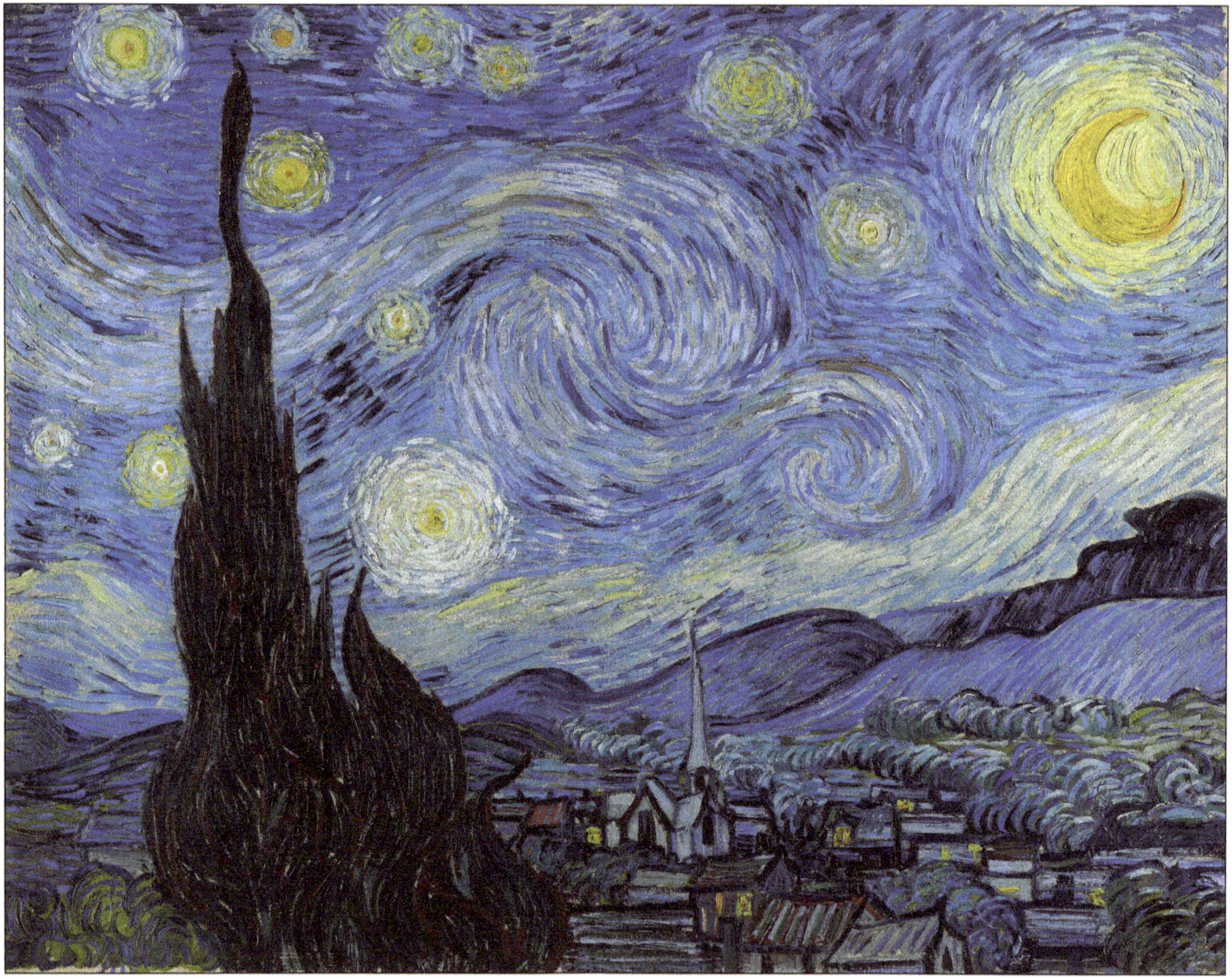

This painting is an example of physical texture. The Starry Night, *1889, by Vincent van Gogh.*

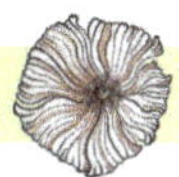

Texture is what makes the viewer want to reach out and feel the artwork. It may not seem as important as the other design elements we've reviewed — *but it is*. There is an old saying to that effect: **art is in the details**.

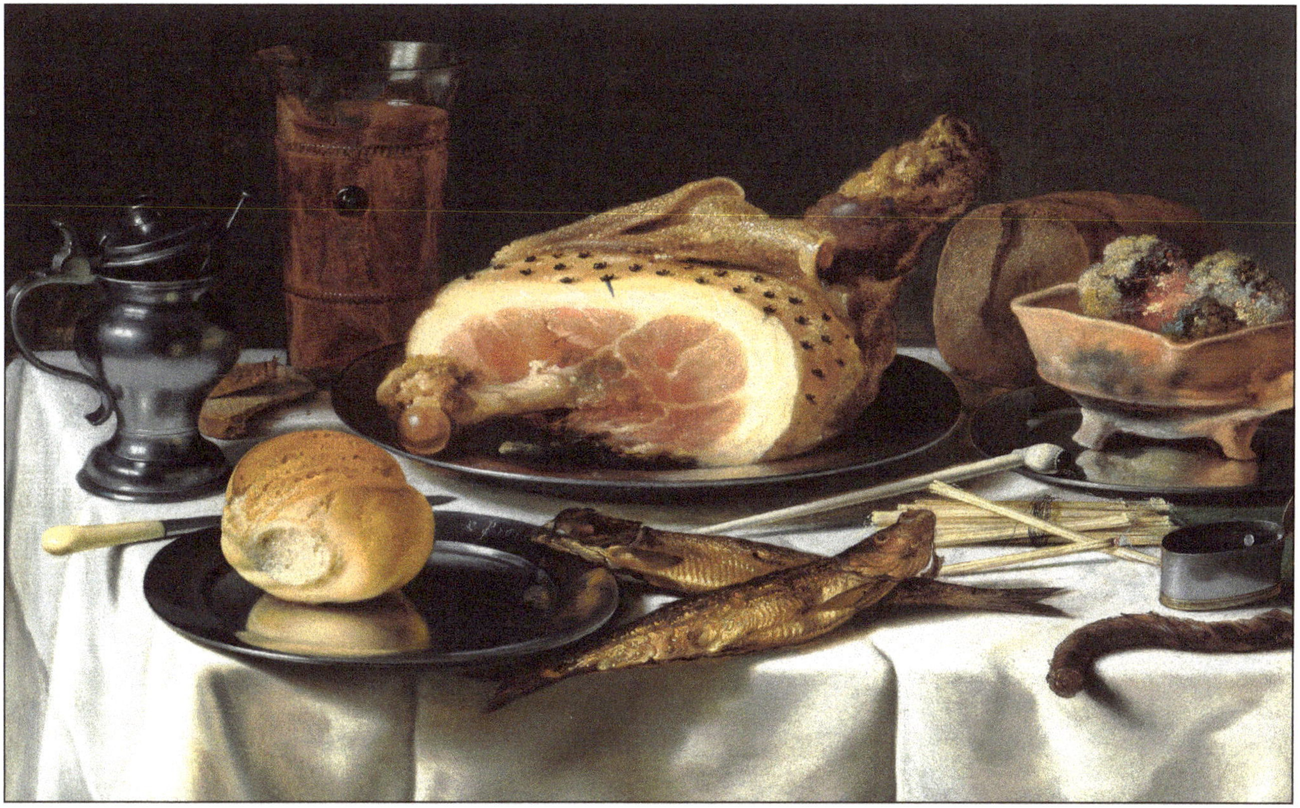

When I see art like this still life by Dutch artist Pieter Claesz (1597-1661), the texture looks so realistic I always want to reach out and touch what I see.

I remember seeing a sculpture once where the artist made large balloon dogs out of stainless steel. They looked exactly like helium balloons. It was hard to imagine they were made out of metal… but they were!

Texture is an important detail that works in conjunction with the other art elements of line, shape, space, and color. These elements combine together to make impactful art.

Simply put, texture is the element in art that relates to the *"surface quality"* of any artwork. This element sparks our imagination and brings everything in a composition to life. Whether it's a drawing, sculpture, or painting, texture can be created and found in almost any artwork.

Generally speaking, texture can be rough, smooth, matte, or glossy in terms of surface finish. There is a rich and endless vocabulary of descriptive words for texture for those of us who want to delve deeper into discussing texture in art. Some of these are: **shiny**, **reflective**, **lustrous**, **glossy**, **coarse**, **bumpy**, **patterned**, **solid**, **prickly**, **bristly**, **etched**, **incised**, and **cut**. And those are just the tip of the iceberg!

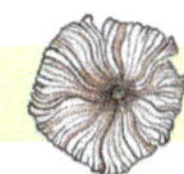

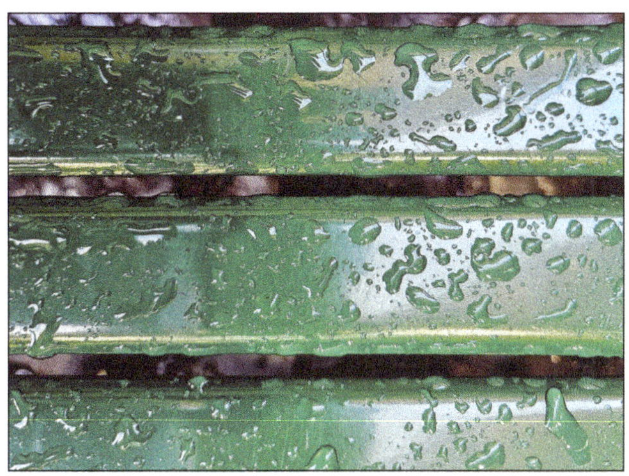

Shiny wet texture.

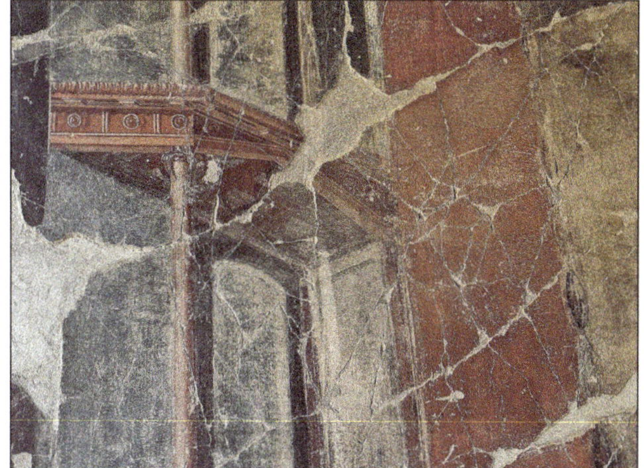

Herculaneum fresco texture.

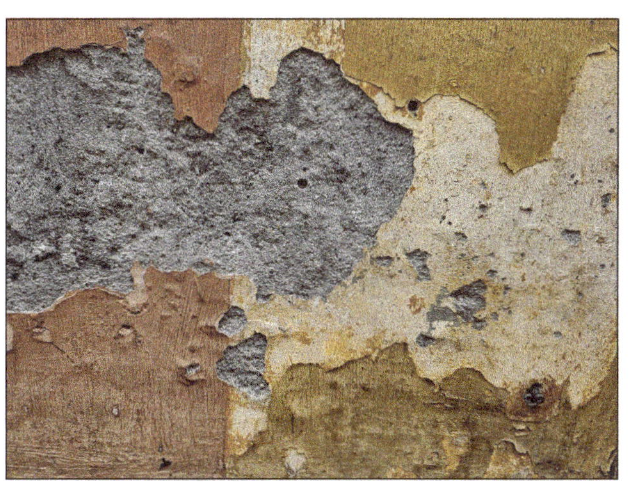

Ancient Roman wall texture.

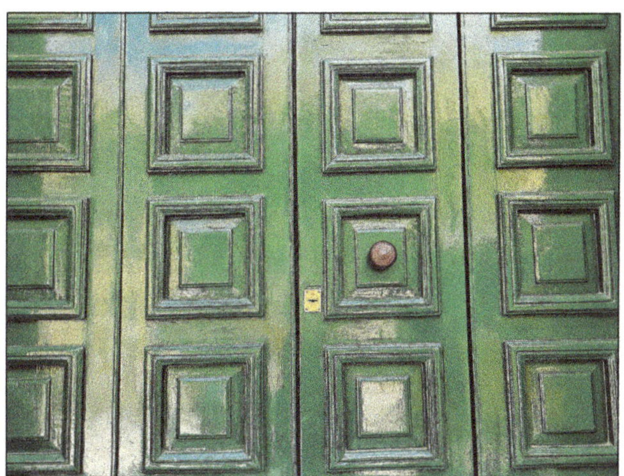

Glossy doors texture.

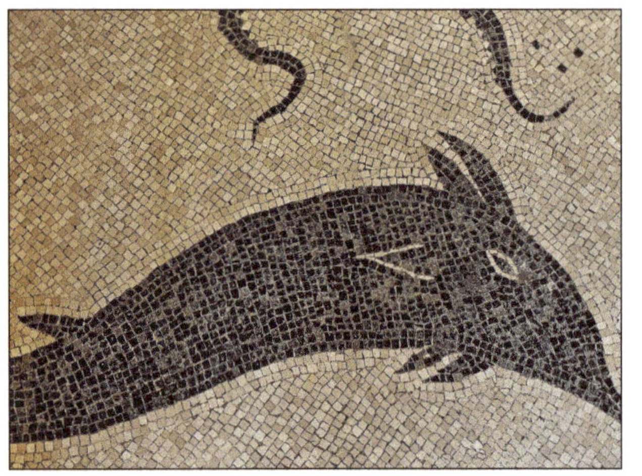

Mosaic texture.

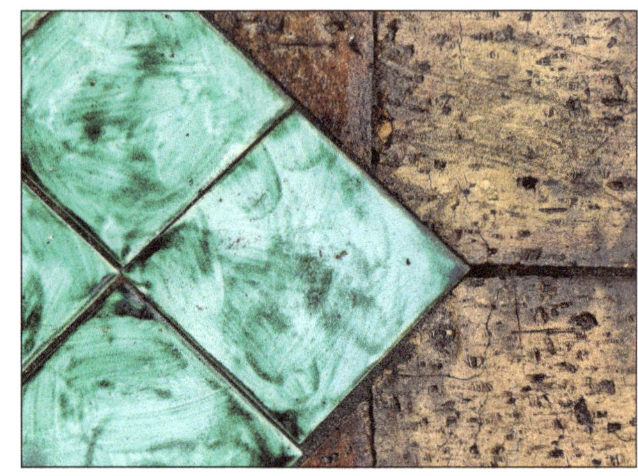

Amalfi tile texture.

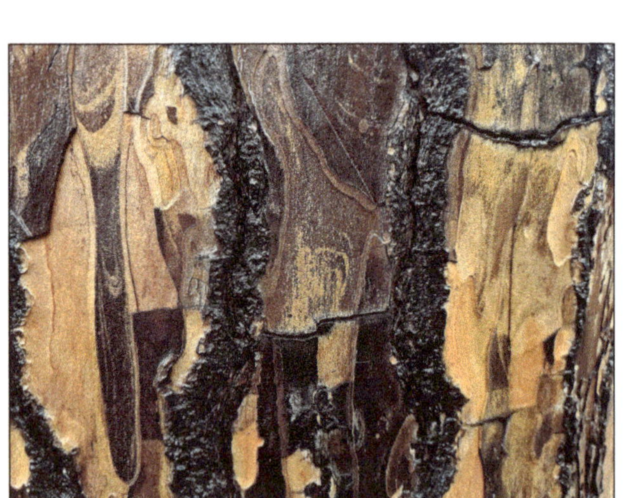

Crusty pine bark texture.

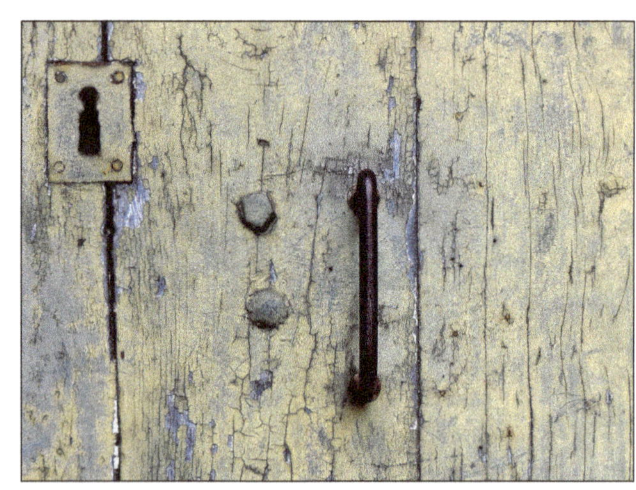

Dry, cracked paint texture.

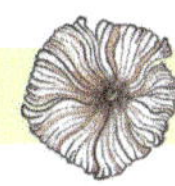

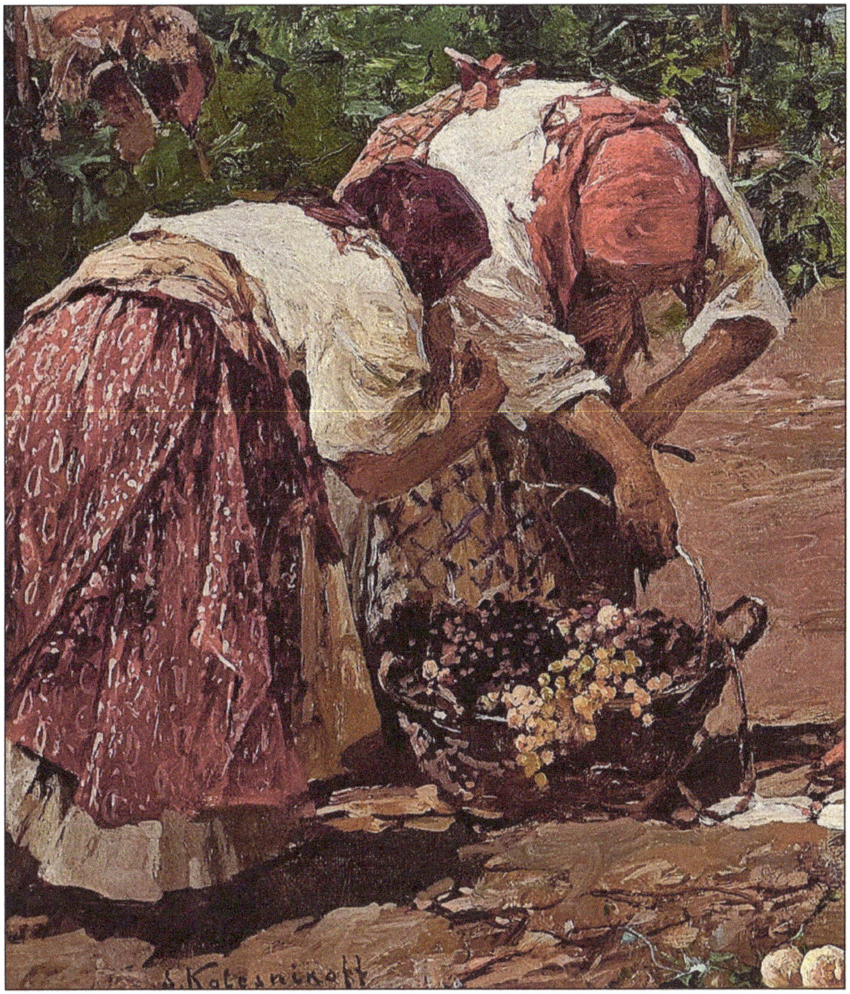

Notice how the distinguished realist painter Stepan Kolesnikoff (1879-1995) depicts the implied texture of fabric in this painting.

To see with the eyes of an artist, it's important to not just see, but also to be able to recognize and appreciate the variety of textures that we encounter in our everyday world. **Just look in your home, texture is all around.** You see wood and metal mixed in with a variety of textiles. Some textiles are cotton, leather, velvet, and silk. Your home might have a brick wall exposed or is covered with a patterned wallpaper. You might see shiny accessories like vases and trays. Or patterned textile pillows on a polished leather sofa. Take a good look around you. You are surrounded by texture! There are so many terrific textures out there to choose from like jagged rocks, wood, grain, feathers, and fur.

Now it's time for you to practice rendering texture. In the following still-life photos, observe the texture. Is it smooth, sharp, rough or bumpy in certain areas?

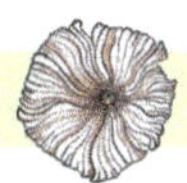

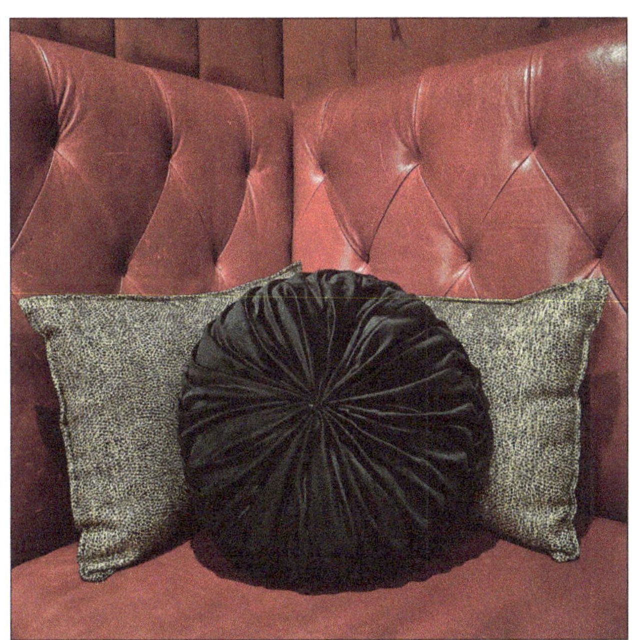

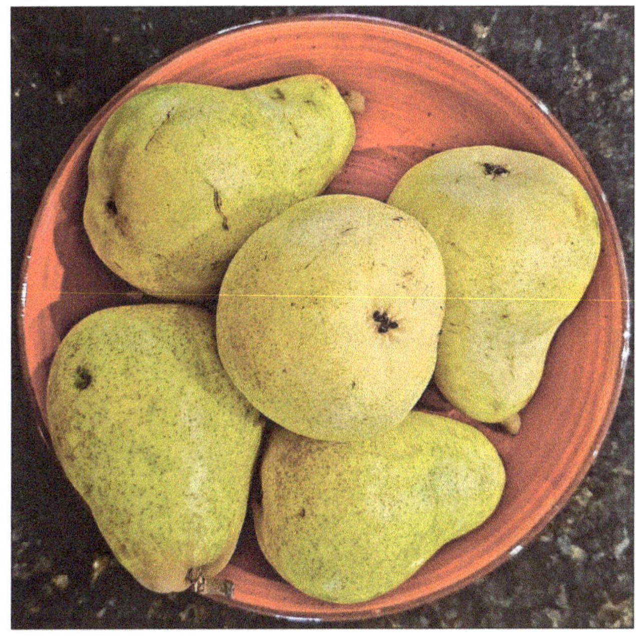

Reproduce the next two still-life photos on the following pages with your drawing pencil. Be sure to model each form using some of the shading techniques we reviewed in Chapter 3. Use **hatching**, **crosshatching**, **stippling**, and **blending** to depict a few of the textures you see.

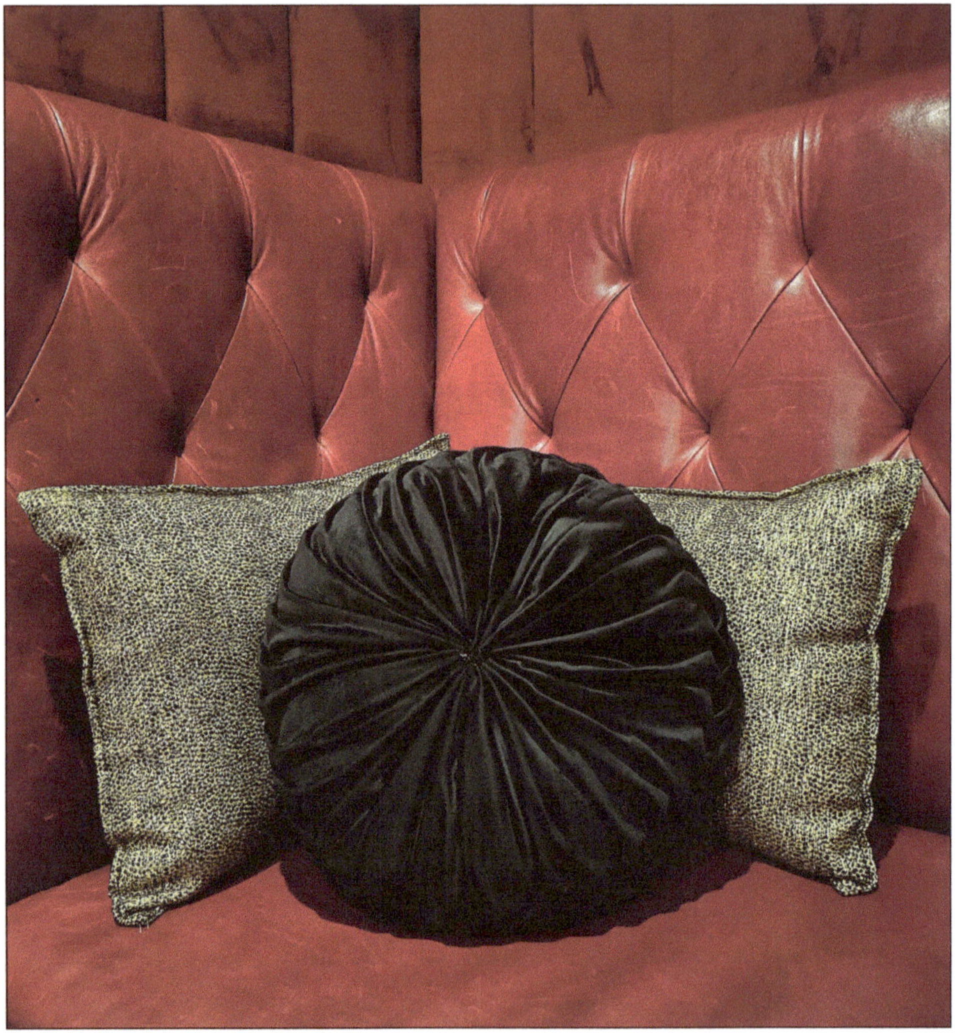

Texture exercise 1: Sofa fabric textures.

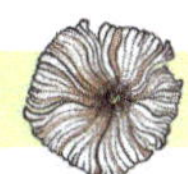

Texture exercise 1: With your drawing pencil, copy the sofa still life.

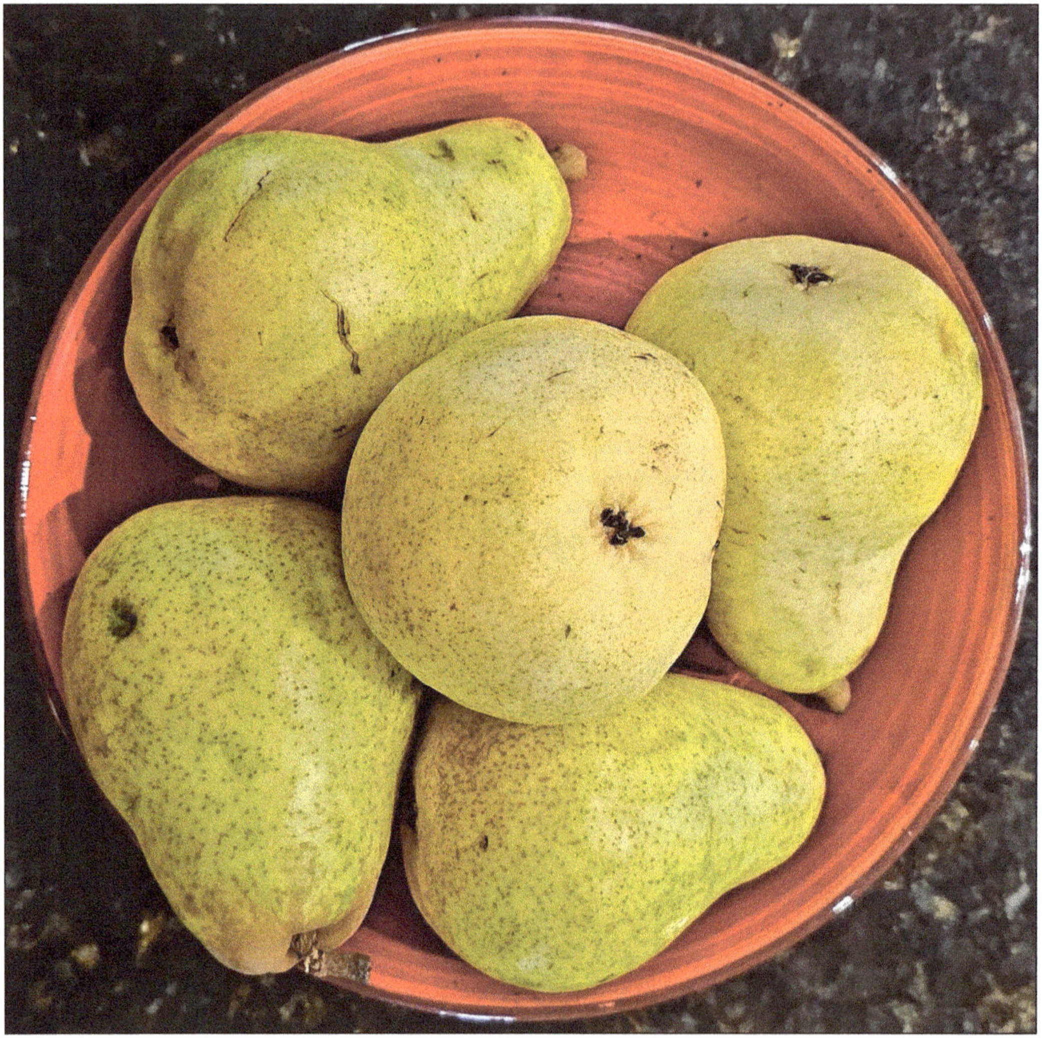

Texture exercise 2: Bowl of pears subtle textures.

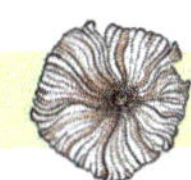

Texture exercise 2: With your drawing pencil, copy the bowl of pears.

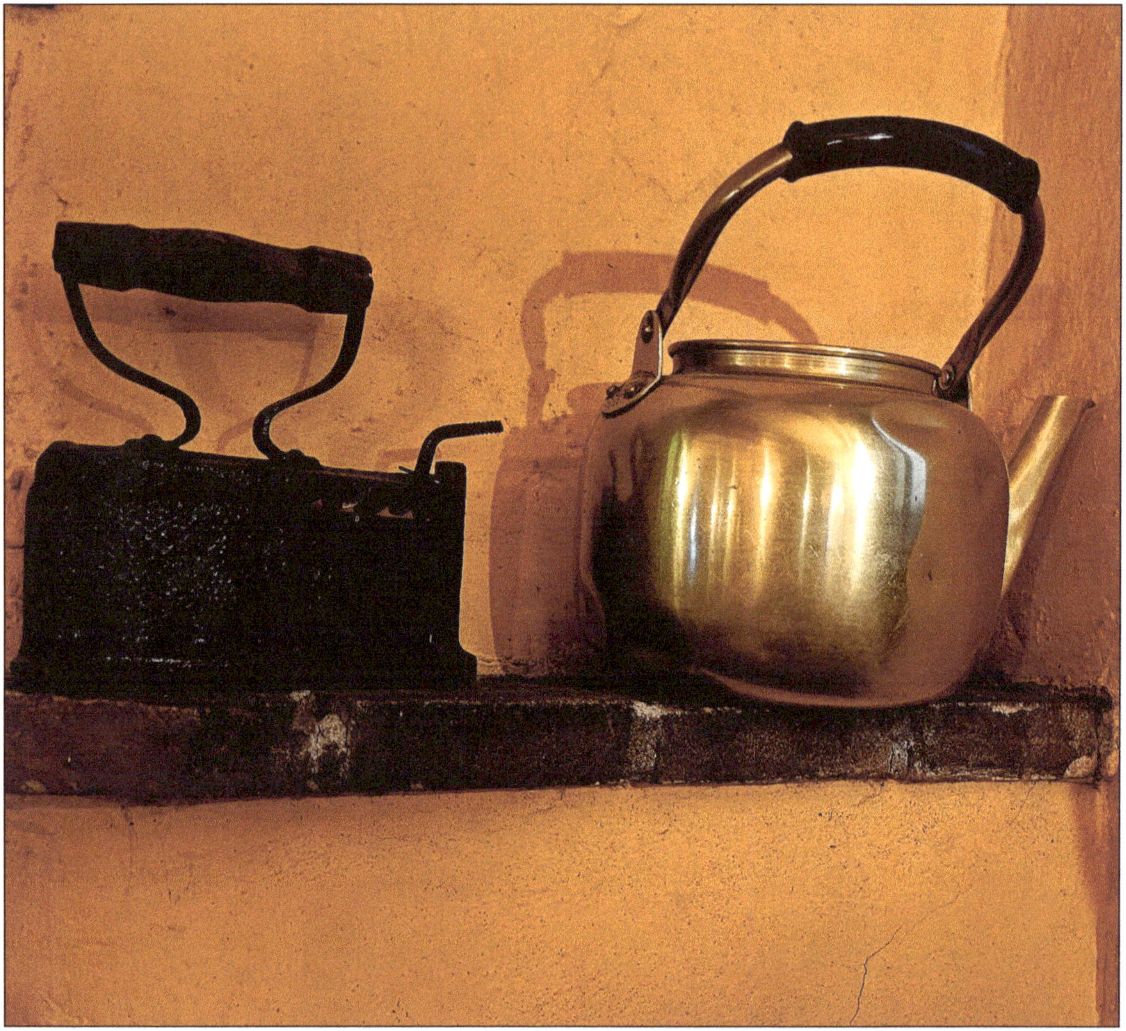

Contrasting textures add visual interest to a composition..

 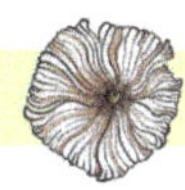

Chapter Five Fun Fact

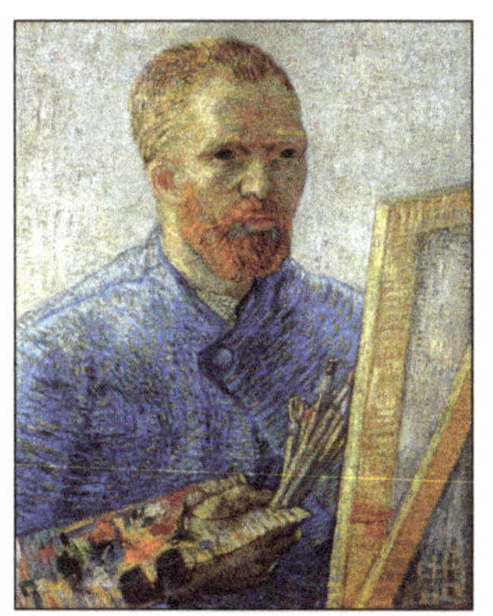

Vincent van Gogh (1853–1890) was an artist who embraced texture in his work.

He was a Dutch painter known for his expressive brushstrokes and bright complementary colors. After trying different careers, he decided to pursue art at age 27. Like **Georgia O'Keeffe (1887–1986)**, he also believed his paintings could tell you things that words could not express. He suffered from depression and often felt like a misfit in society. One could say he used his art as therapy. He loved painting and sometimes painted all day without stopping to eat. His paintings of sunflowers, landscapes, night skies, and self-portraits were filled with emotion, color, and richly textured brushstrokes. Even though he only sold one painting in his lifetime, he never stopped doing what he loved. He often said that if you thought you could not paint, then by all means you should try to paint because if you did your negative thoughts would be silenced. His endurance, passion, and devotion to his art is an inspiration to anyone and everyone. He teaches us to keep doing what we love no matter what!

Pick your favorite Vincent van Gogh painting, then recreate it on the next page with your colored pencils.

Investigate and choose your favorite Van Gogh painting and copy it here with colored pencils.

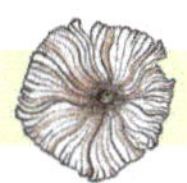

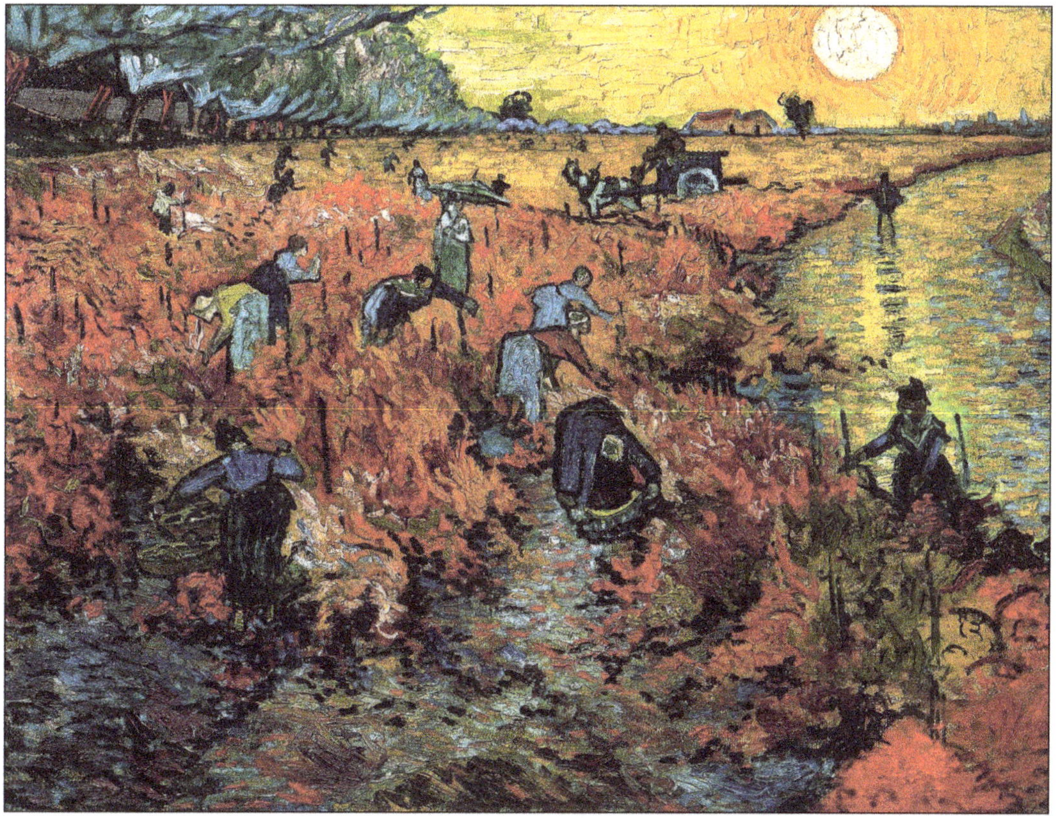

This painting of **Red Vineyard at Arles** *is believed to be the only painting Van Gogh sold during his lifetime. Fortunately, he left over 2,000 other paintings, drawings, and prints.*

*"Great things are not done by impulse,
but by a series of small things brought together."*

— Vincent van Gogh

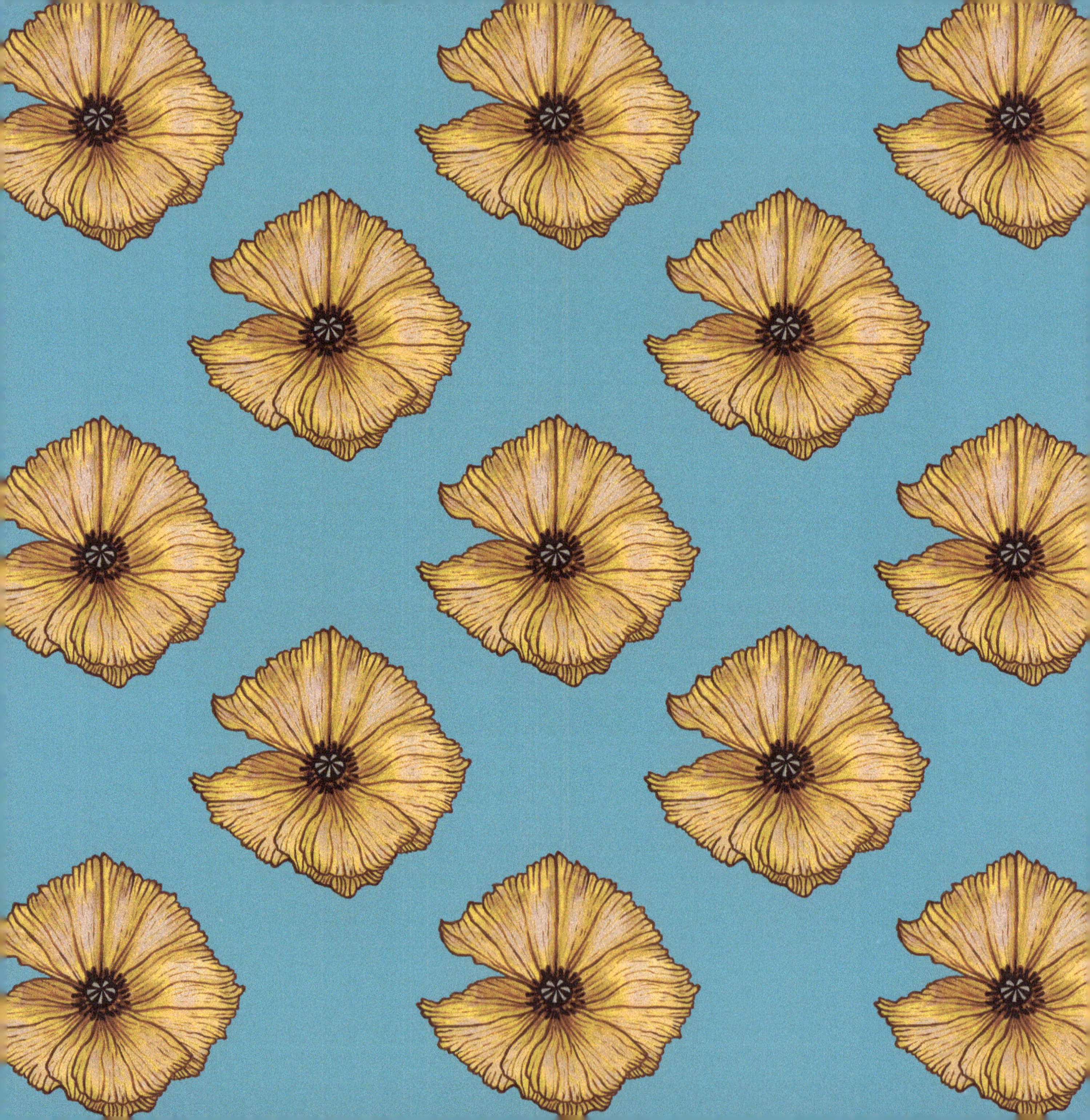

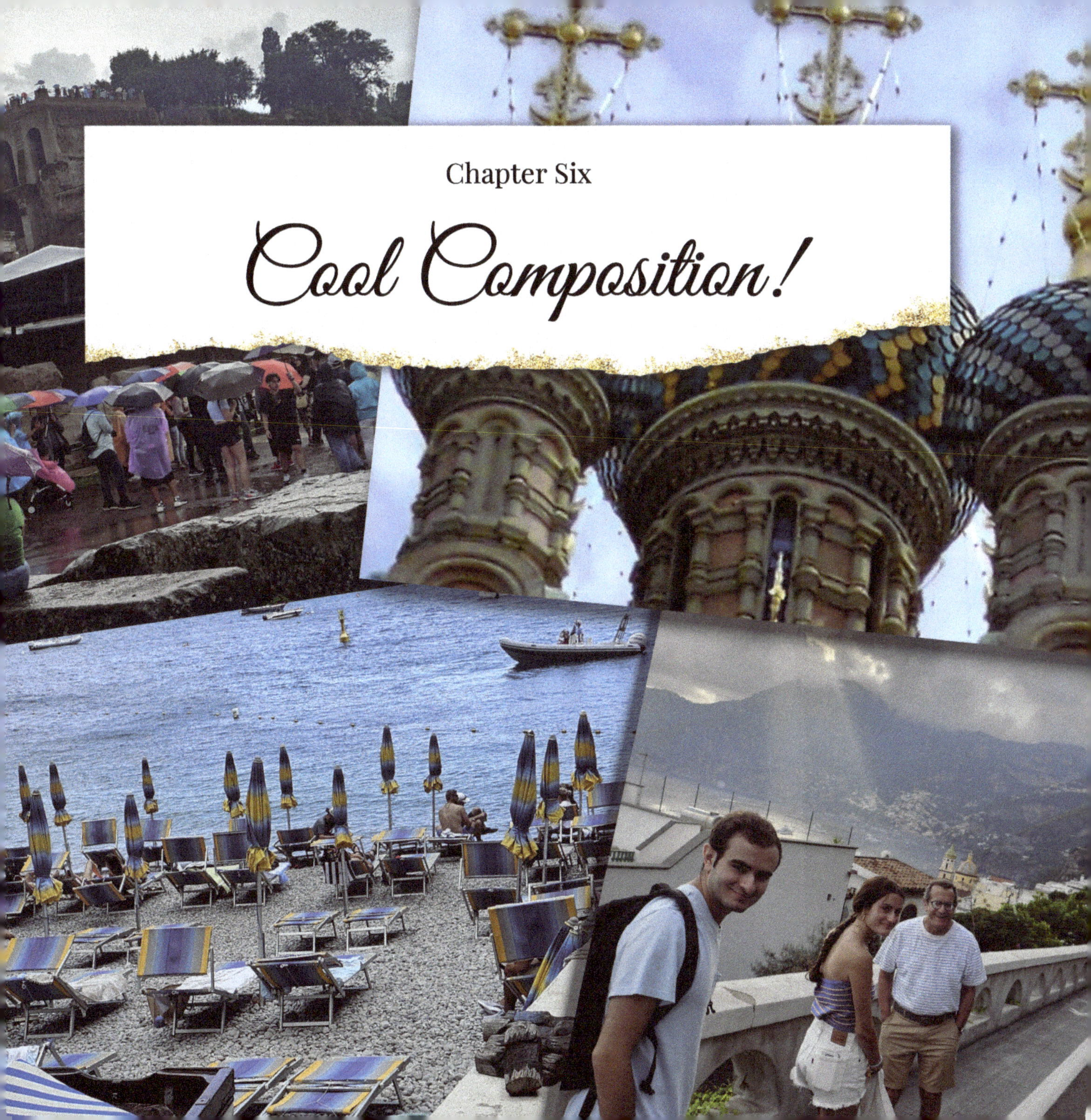

Cool Composition!

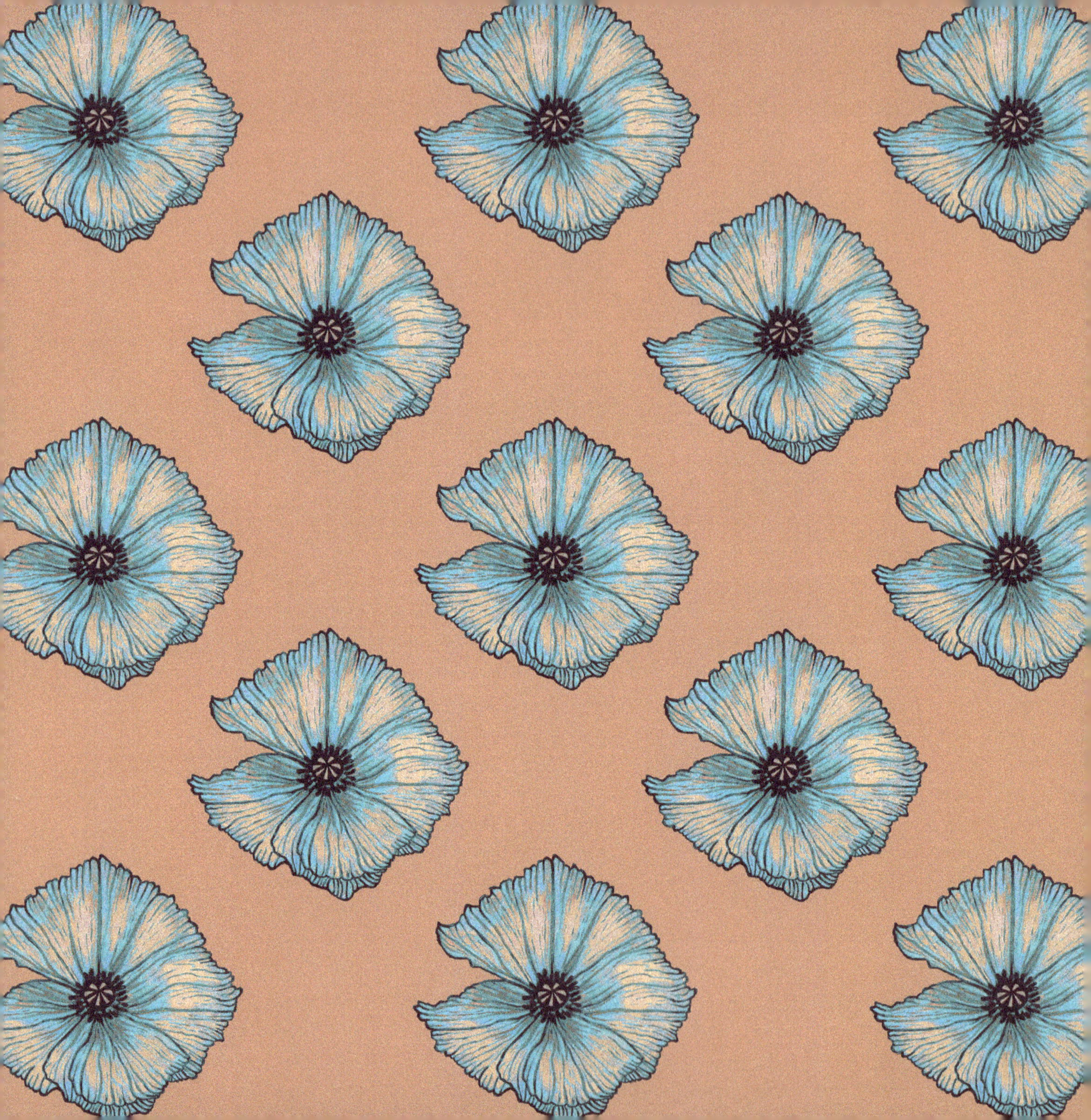

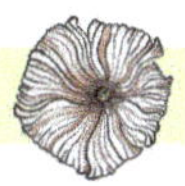

Chapter Six

Cool Composition!

The term composition means 'putting together.' Composition describes the visual ordering or formal arrangement in art. Artists determine what the center of interest of each artwork will be. Music is composed in the same way. You have something important to say and arrange things accordingly. We are always arranging things in our lives. From our hair to flowers in a vase, we adjust things until they are just right.

Size and position is how objects relate to each other in a composition. We carefully measure the placement of things. Or, sometimes we use our intuition. Heavy things on the bottom of a page. Tall ones in the back and short ones in front. It's a balancing act. We adjust things in our picture frame until they are in the right position.

Artist **Henri Matisse (1869–1954)** said it best, "Composition is the art of arranging in a decorative manner the diverse elements at the painter's command to express his feelings." After all, we compose whenever we look through a window. **Each of us possesses a special way of seeing and noticing things others might not.** Our field of view is uniquely our own. Wherever we look, what we see with our eyes and feel with our hearts is special and one of a kind. It is our vision.

Here are composition vocabulary words to reflect upon as you begin to express your vision.

- **Shape and proportion**
- **Positioning**
- **Cropping**
- **Negative space**
- **Color**
- **Contrast: the value, or degree of lightness and darkness, used within the picture**
- **Lines**
- **Lighting**
- **Repetition**
- **Perspective**
- **Harmony or disharmony between objects used to express a thought**
- **Blurred or busy background**
- **Emphasis**

It's important to incorporate these principles of organization in your art. They will help you depict what you are trying to say with your work. **Compare them to a recipe, and use these ingredients to help organize your composition.**

 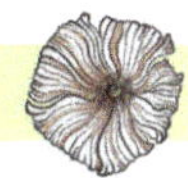

There is an exceptional artist who helps us see the value of a beautiful composition. **His name is Juan Gris (1887-1927).** He was a Spanish painter who lived and worked in Paris, France. His work is described as Cubism.

Cubism is an early twentieth-century art movement. It revolutionized the way artists see and depict the world. Instead of presenting realistic views of the world, Cubist artists strived to show every part of the whole subject in their compositions. Juan Gris and others abandoned traditional perspective and depicted objects and people as dynamic new forms.

Study the next few pages of Juan Gris still life paintings and look for each of the design elements we've already discussed. For instance, you might spot examples of **physical** and **implied** texture in his art. You also clearly see **line**, **shape**, **form**, **color**, and **texture**, all coming together in his very distinctive compositions.

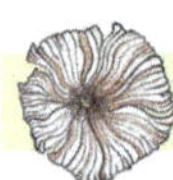

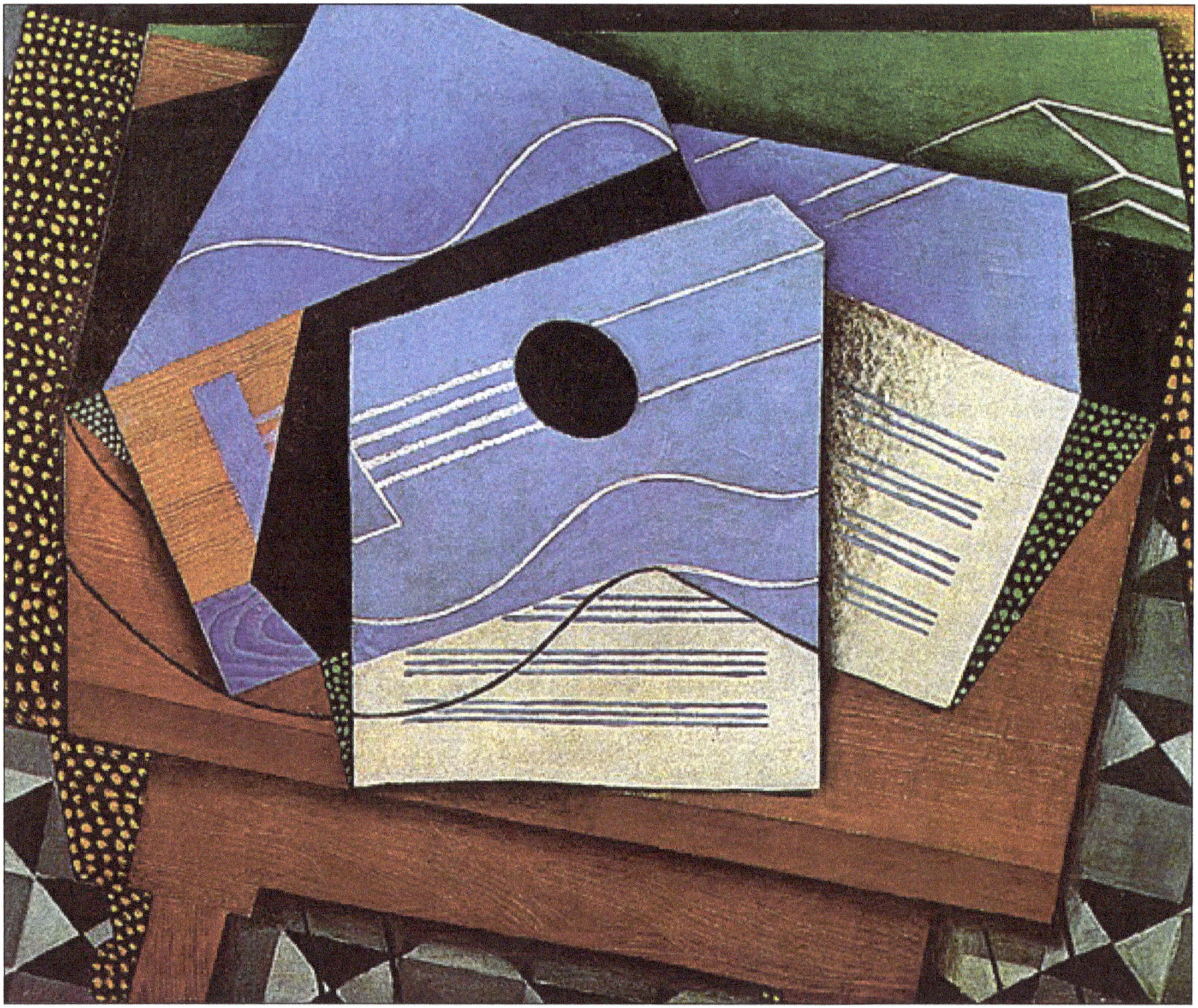

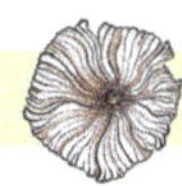

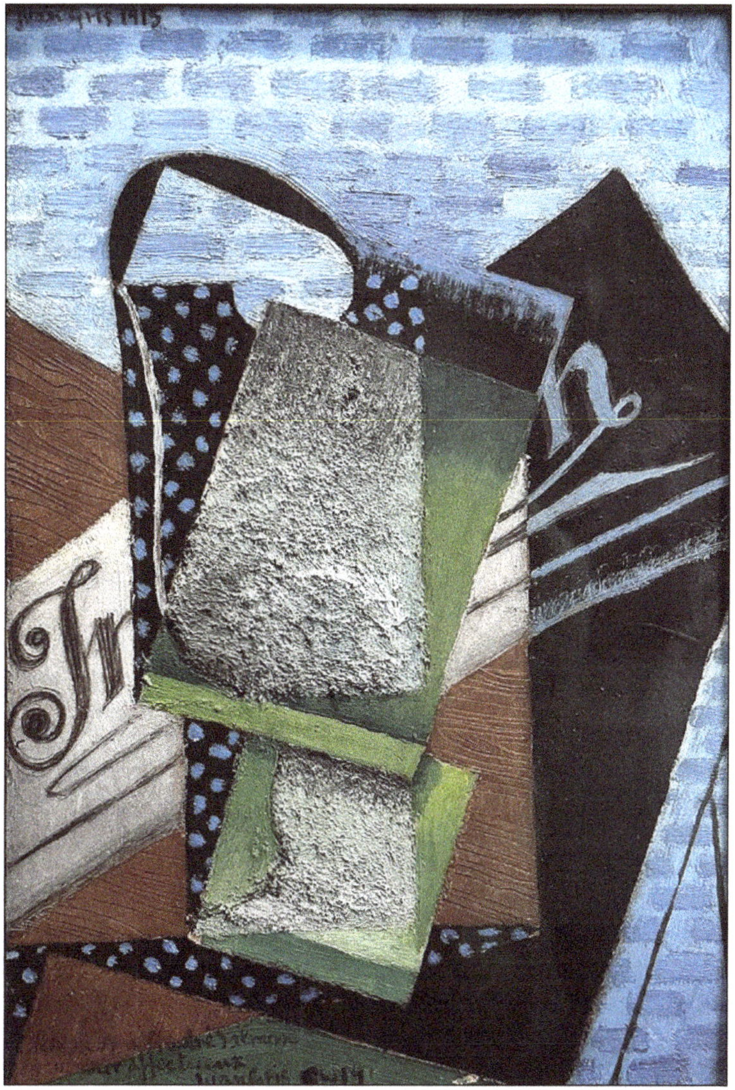

Juan Gris used many different mediums in his compositions to express his ideas. These included collage, gouache, chalk, and charcoal on canvas. He liked to mix things up and unexpected visual surprises would pop up in his art, like implied texture and calligraphy. He always pulled these diverse elements together, resulting in his unique compositions.

I love the fact that he liked to tell people "You are lost the moment you know what the result will be." Juan Gris always reminds me to relax a bit and be spontaneous when I create.

Drawing the same subject matter over and over helps you see something new each time. One of the things he inspires us to experiment with, is different color variations of the same composition.

Black Guitar *still life, Juan Gris, 1926.*

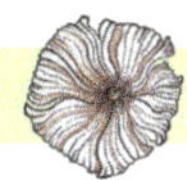

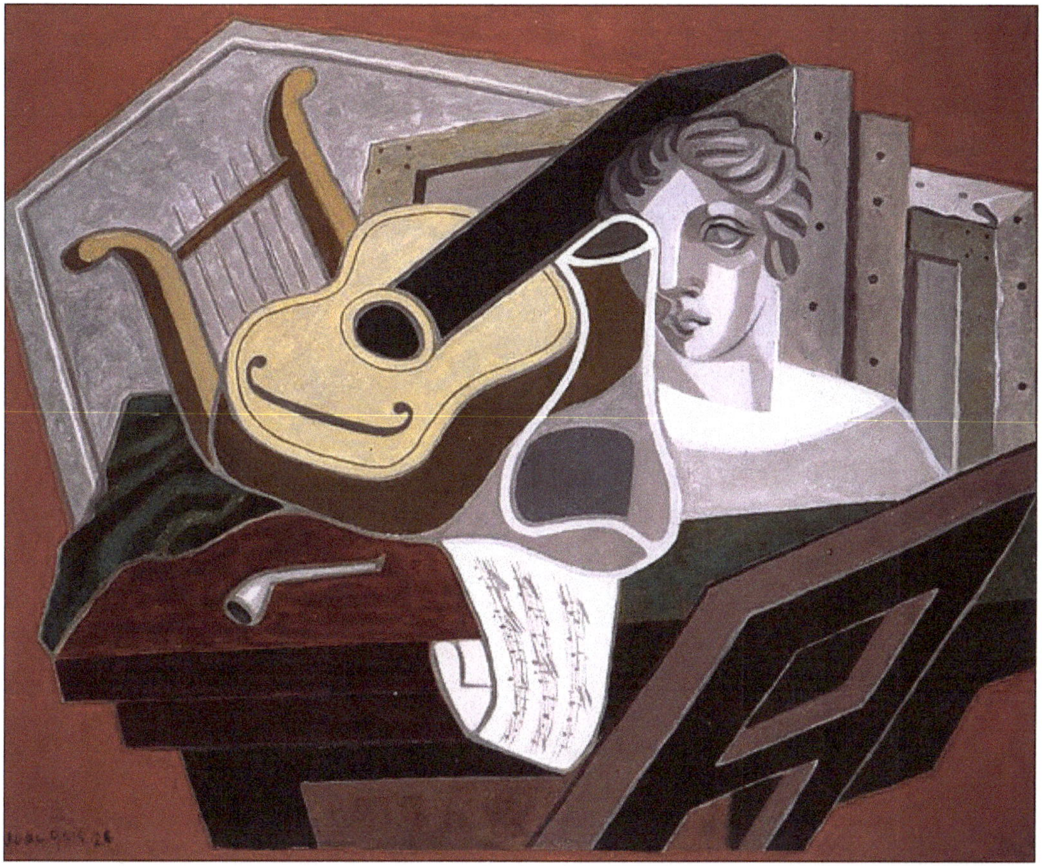

We often see elegant parts of bottles, vases, dishes, guitars, smoking pipes, tables, and decorative tablecloths in Juan Gris' works. *Repetition in art teaches us to see things in new ways.* He often painted the same objects over and over again. **We should follow his lead and do the same.**

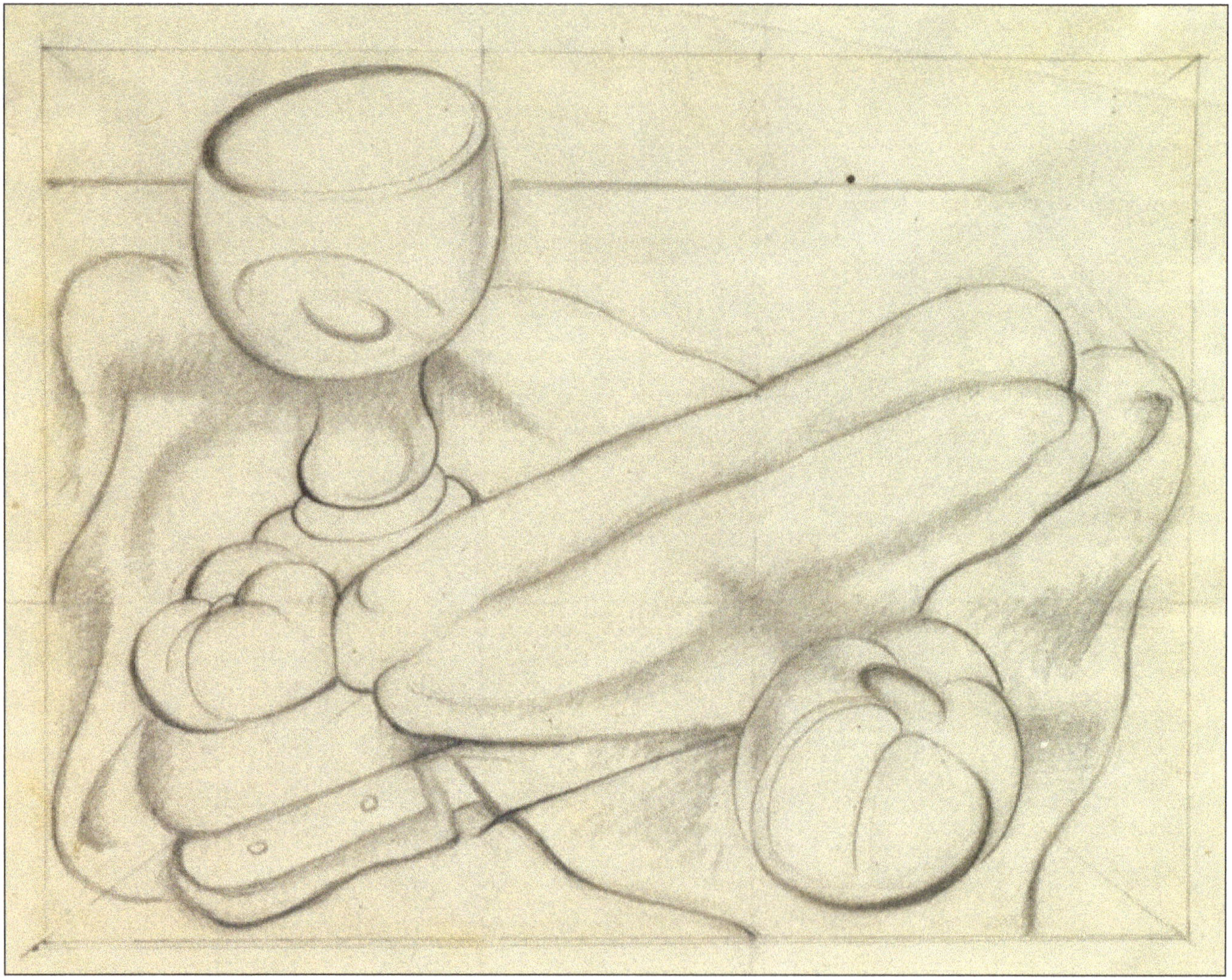

Composition exercise 1: Juan Gris still life.

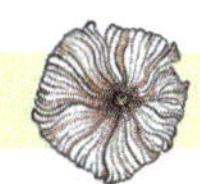

Compostion Exercise 1: Copy the Juan Gris still life with your drawing pencil.

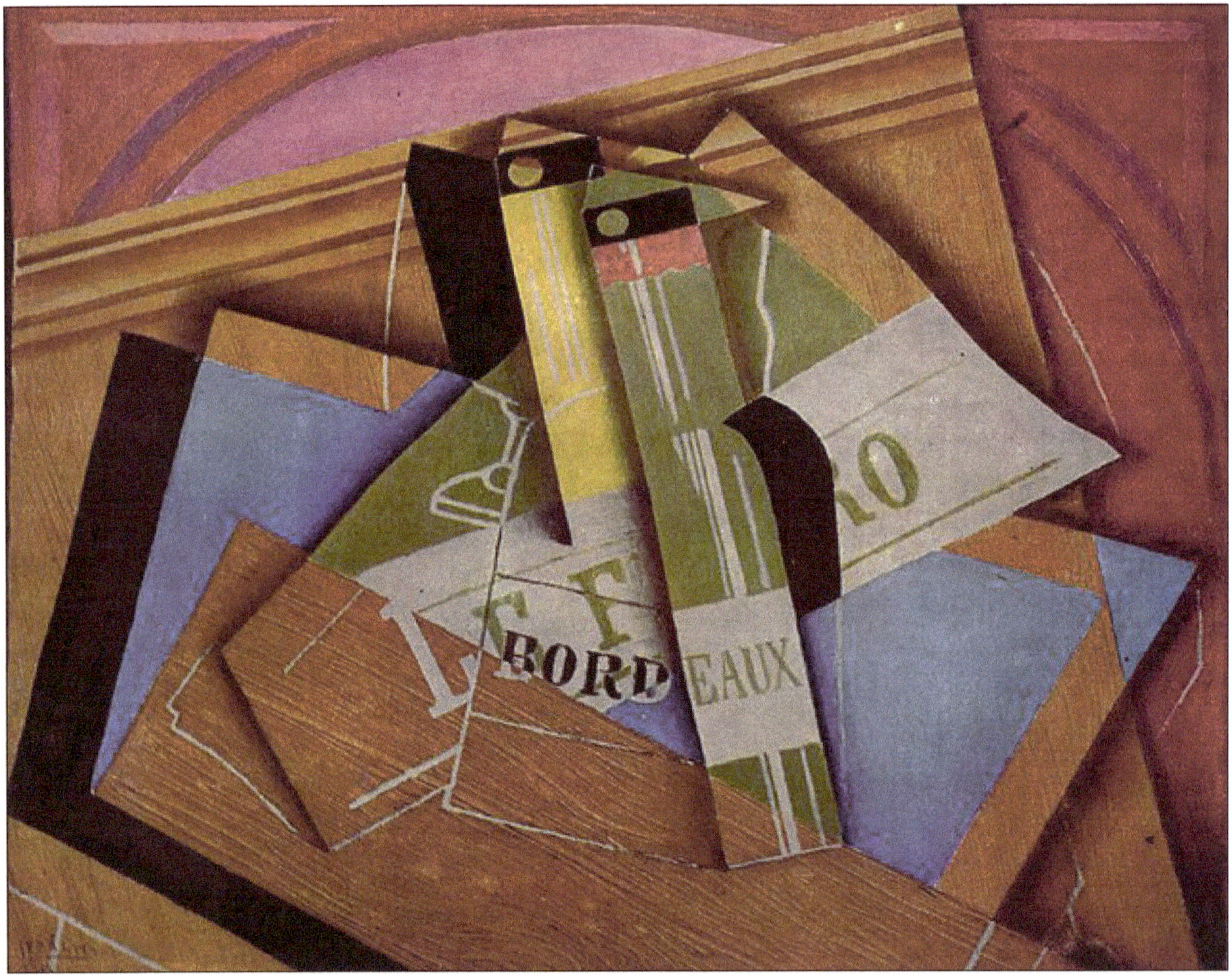

Composition exercise 2: Juan Gris still life with wine bottle.

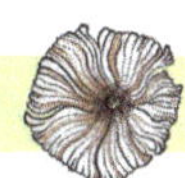

*Compostion exercise 2: Use your colored pencils to copy Juan Gris'
still life with wine bottle.*

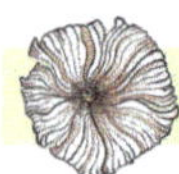

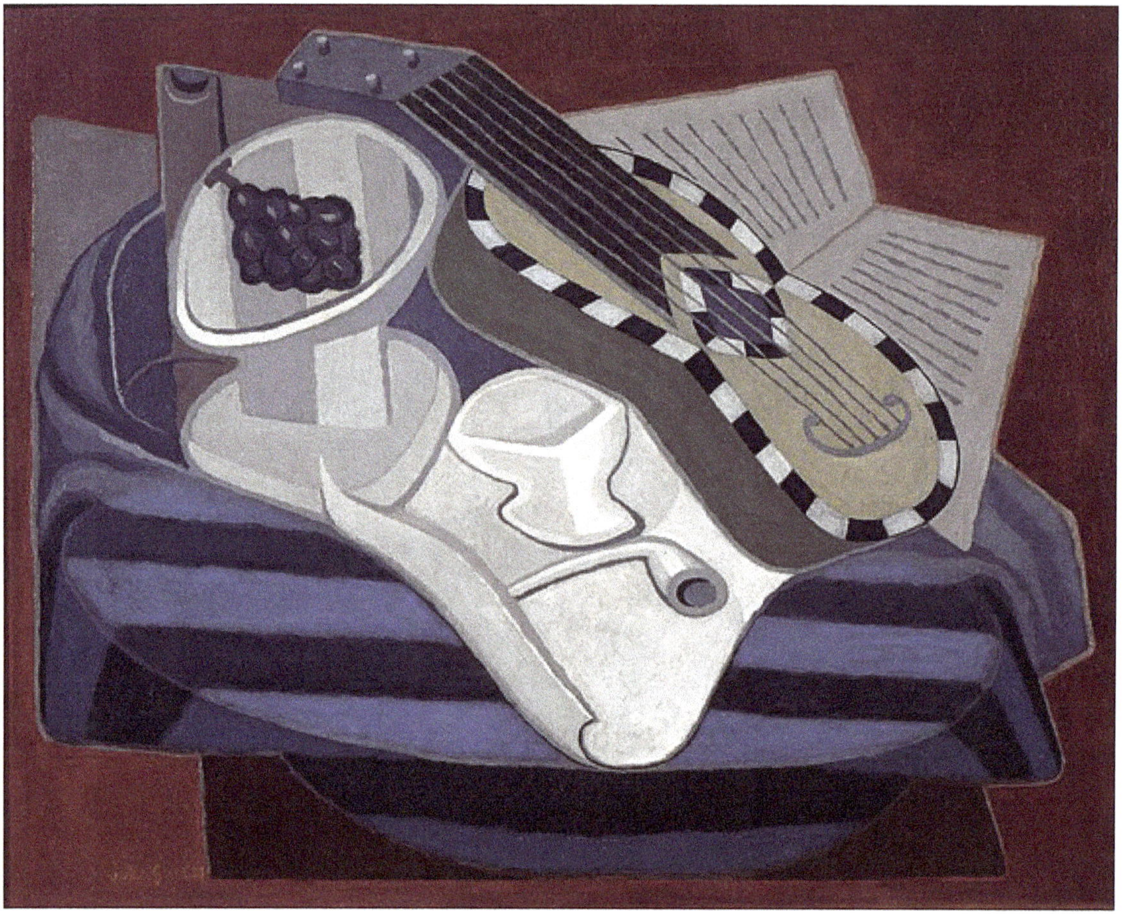

Juan Gris gave us the essence of the objects in the portions he chose to represent the whole. Like a virtuoso, he combines the parts so that they come together in a beautiful symphony that makes his compositions unique.

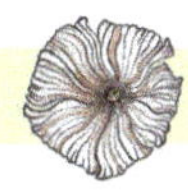

Chapter Six Fun Fact

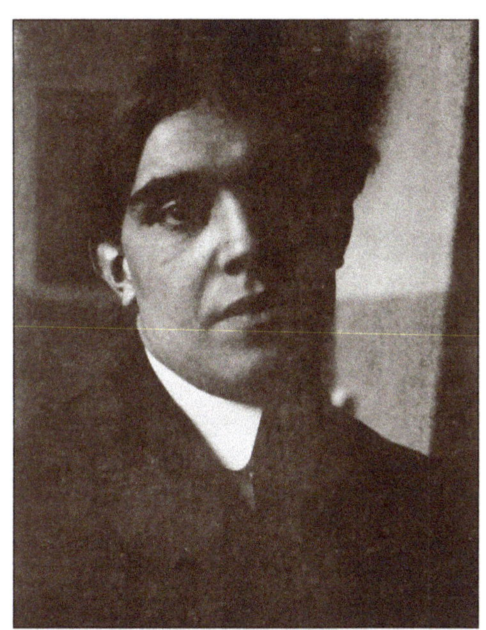

Juan Gris (1887-1927) was a famous 20th century Spanish painter. He sold all of his possessions and moved to Paris after his father died in 1906. While in Paris, he met **Pablo Picasso (1881-1973)**, for whom he had enormous respect. In fact, he viewed Picasso as a mentor. It is said that Picasso may have been threatened by Juan Gris' talents or perhaps was annoyed by his flattery. Either way, Juan Gris is considered one of the leading figures of the avant-garde Cubist art movement, along with Picasso, **George Braque (1882-1963)**, and **Ferdinand Léger (1881-1955)**.

Juan Gris' art shines with a certain childlike innocence and simplicity. It reminds us to study the world around us as if we've never seen it before.

"Every child is an artist. The problem is how to remain an artist once we grow up."

— Pablo Picasso

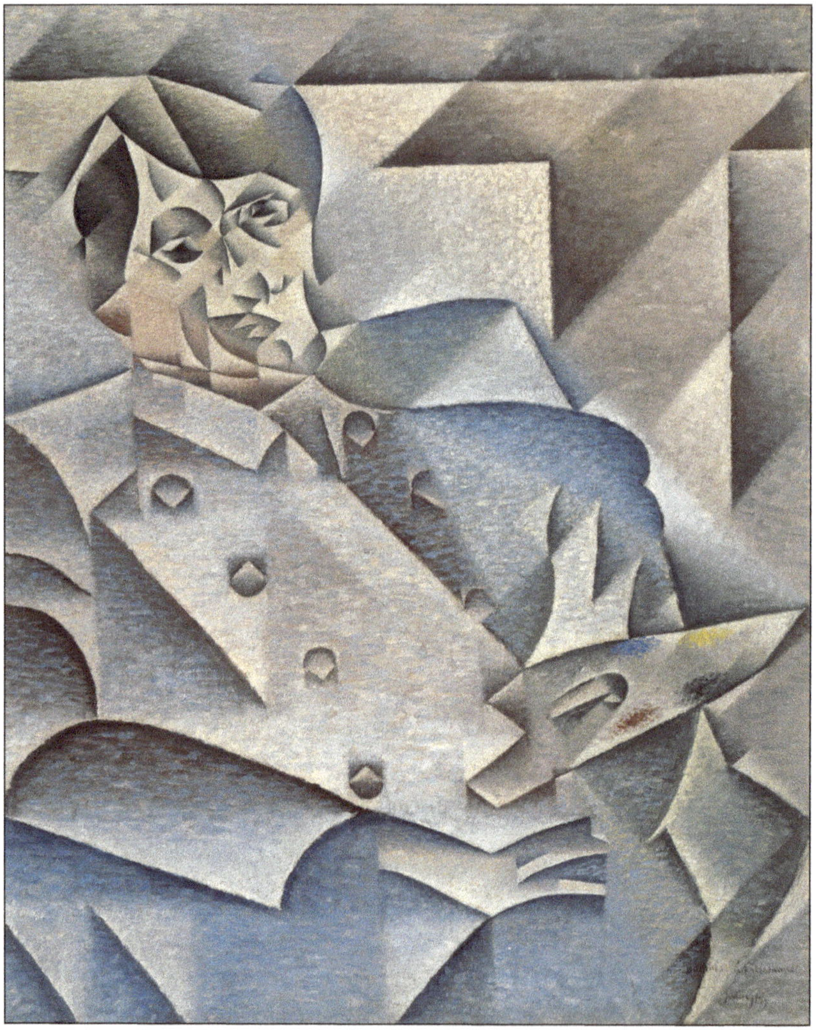

Juan Gris: Portrait of Picasso.

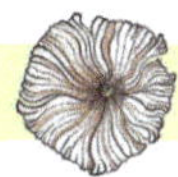

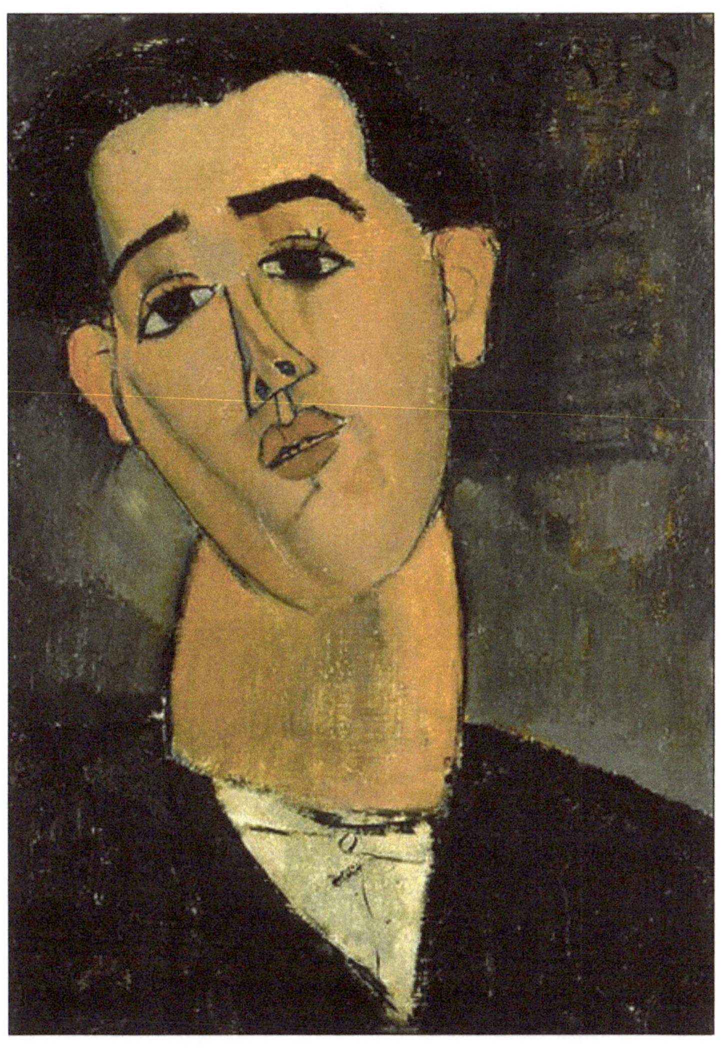

Portrait of Juan Gris by Amedeo Mondigliani

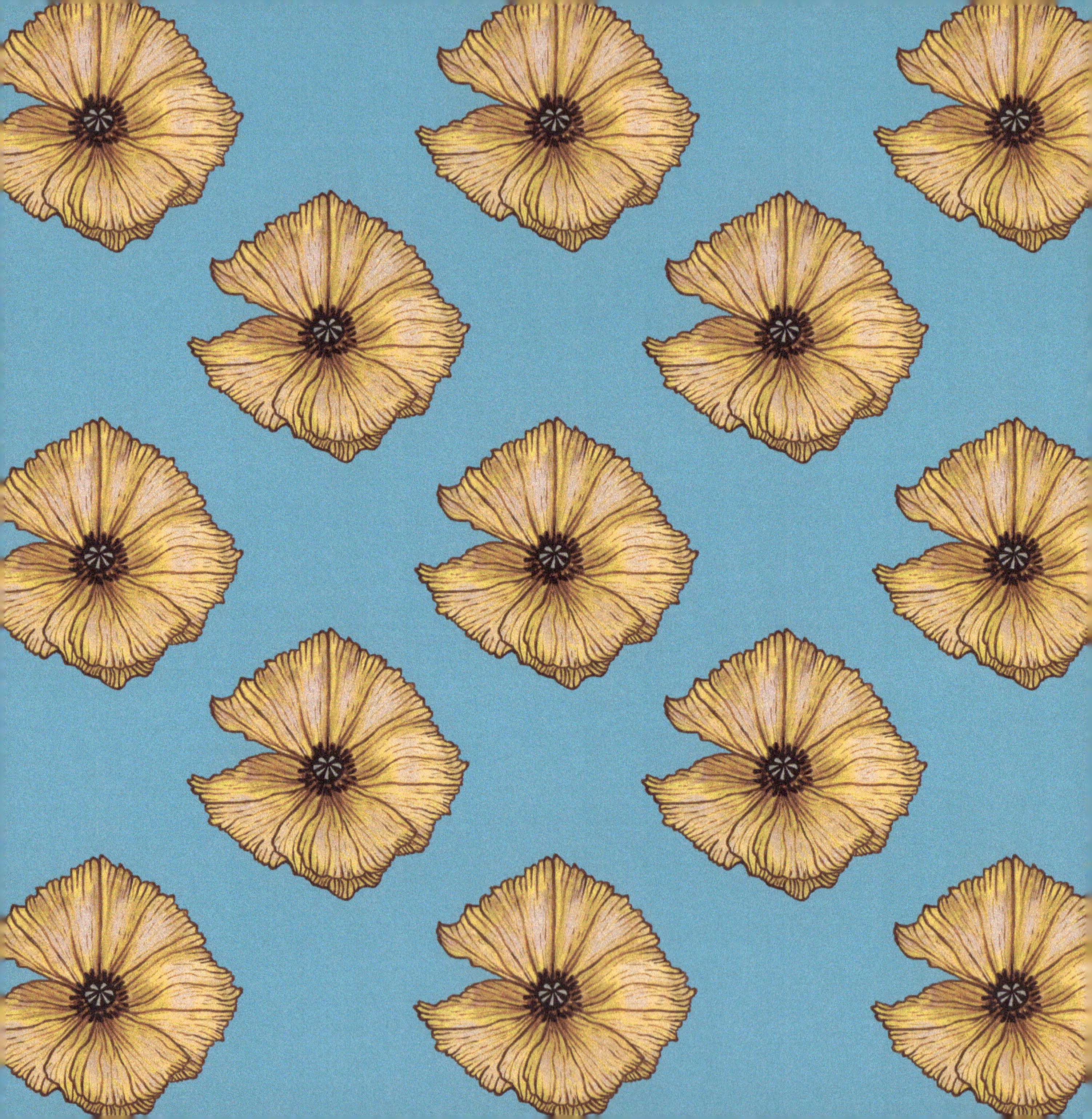

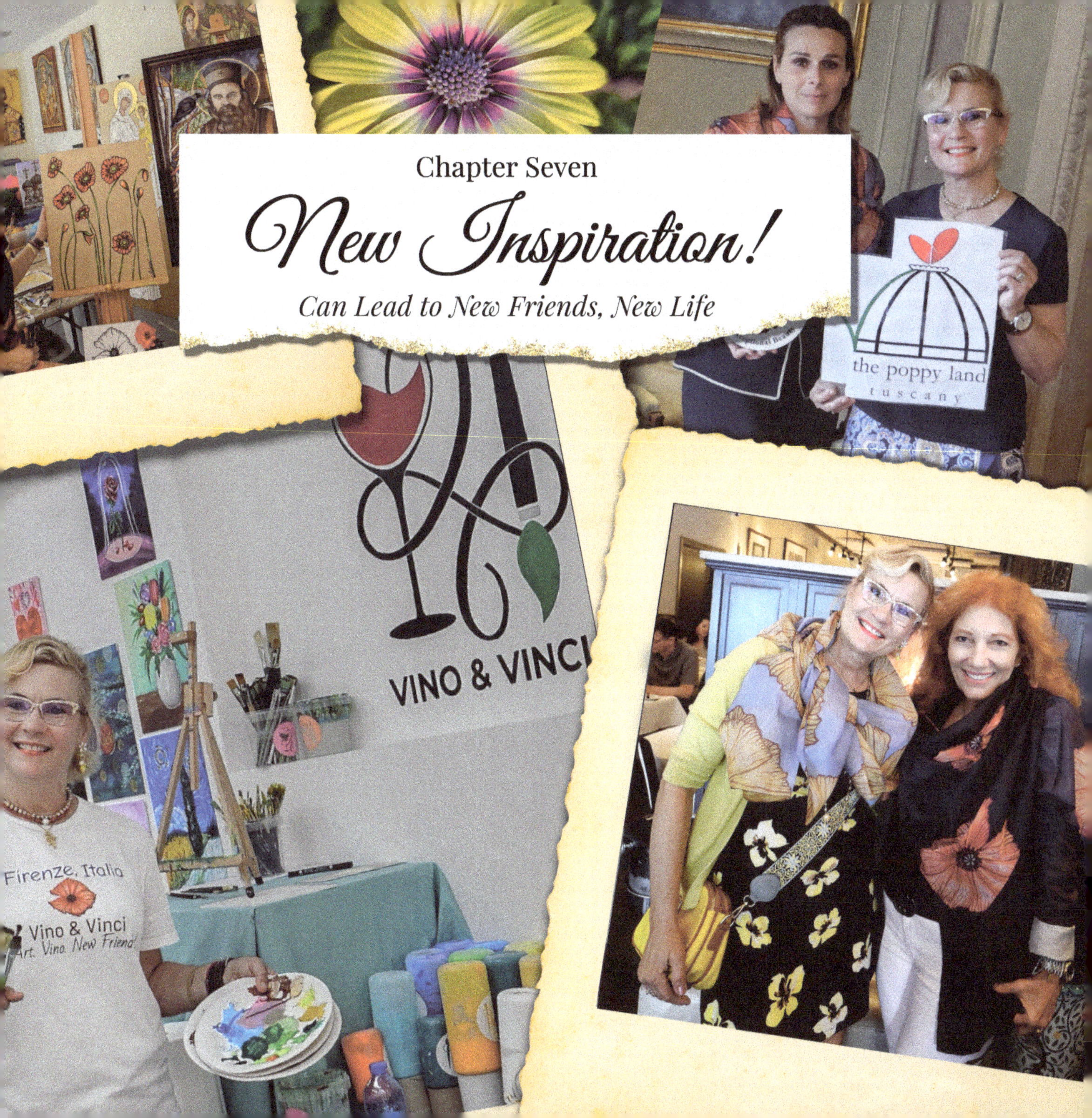

Chapter Seven

New Inspiration!

Can Lead to New Friends, New Life

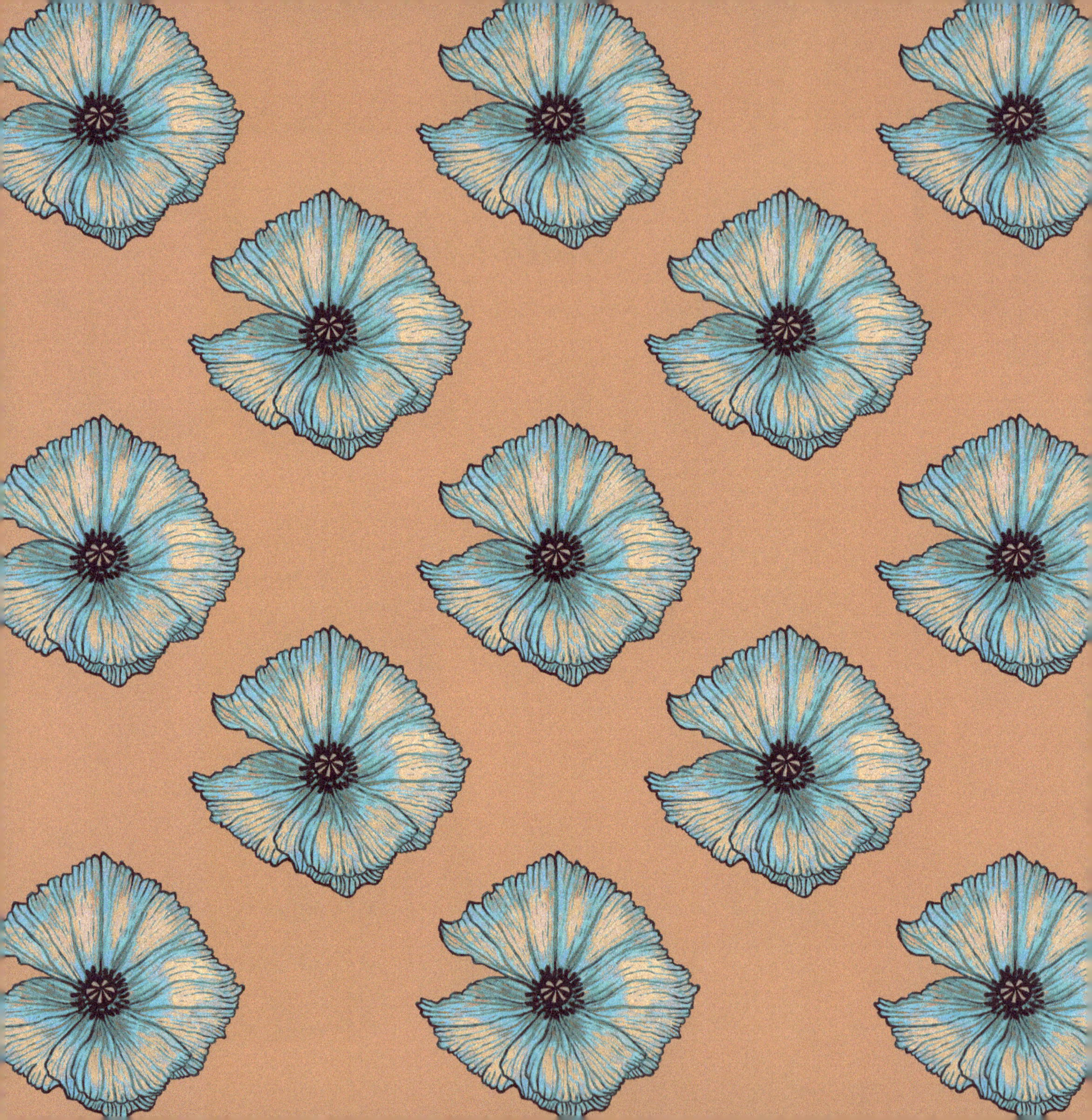

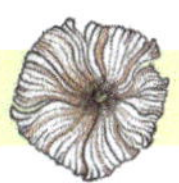

Chapter Seven

New Inspiration

Let Beauty ignite your senses.

The truth is **we are all artists**. In order to see beauty, we have to know how to recognize it. This little book is your primer and reminder on how to see beauty. Once you learn how, you cannot help but see it all around you.

Learning to see like an artist opens your eyes to seeing beauty that others often miss. This new way of perceiving the visual world will change you in many positive ways. **Beauty is good for the soul.**

Every part of your life will be touched by this new outlook. This perspective unleashes your own unique creativity and zest for life! Best of all, you will begin to allow yourself to embrace an ever-changing and refreshing new sense of style in your life.

Style is simply knowing what you like and savoring it. Just by opening this book, you have given yourself the chance to be creative. You are cultivating your creativity. **Keep trying and don't doubt your potential. *Self-doubt kills creativity.***

Seeing like an artist is all about changing your perspective and making life happen. Breathe in the inspiration of beauty! It is good for your health. Go outside and enjoy nature. Look around and enjoy the view. Grab inspiration from everything you see. **Your passion for life is ignited when you relish what you see.**

In order to experience beauty, we have to train our eyes to look for it. If we don't, then life happens to us. Instead, we need to be like little children and see what they see. When I was in Italy last summer, I saw these wonderful children playing in the rain with their colorful umbrellas. Everyone else was running for cover from the rain and waiting for it to end. Meanwhile, these kids played joyfully in the Piazza Navona (a public square in Rome). We all watched them as they twirled their colorful umbrellas and danced happily in the rain. They saw the rain as beautiful! I took pictures of them and even now thinking of them makes me smile. They knew how to behold the beauty in life because that's all they see!

These kids should inspire us all. We can all have this perspective in life if we keep practicing with what we discussed in this little book. **This way, we won't become blind to a world filled with unending inspiration and joy.**

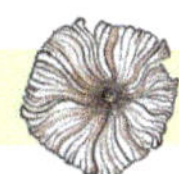

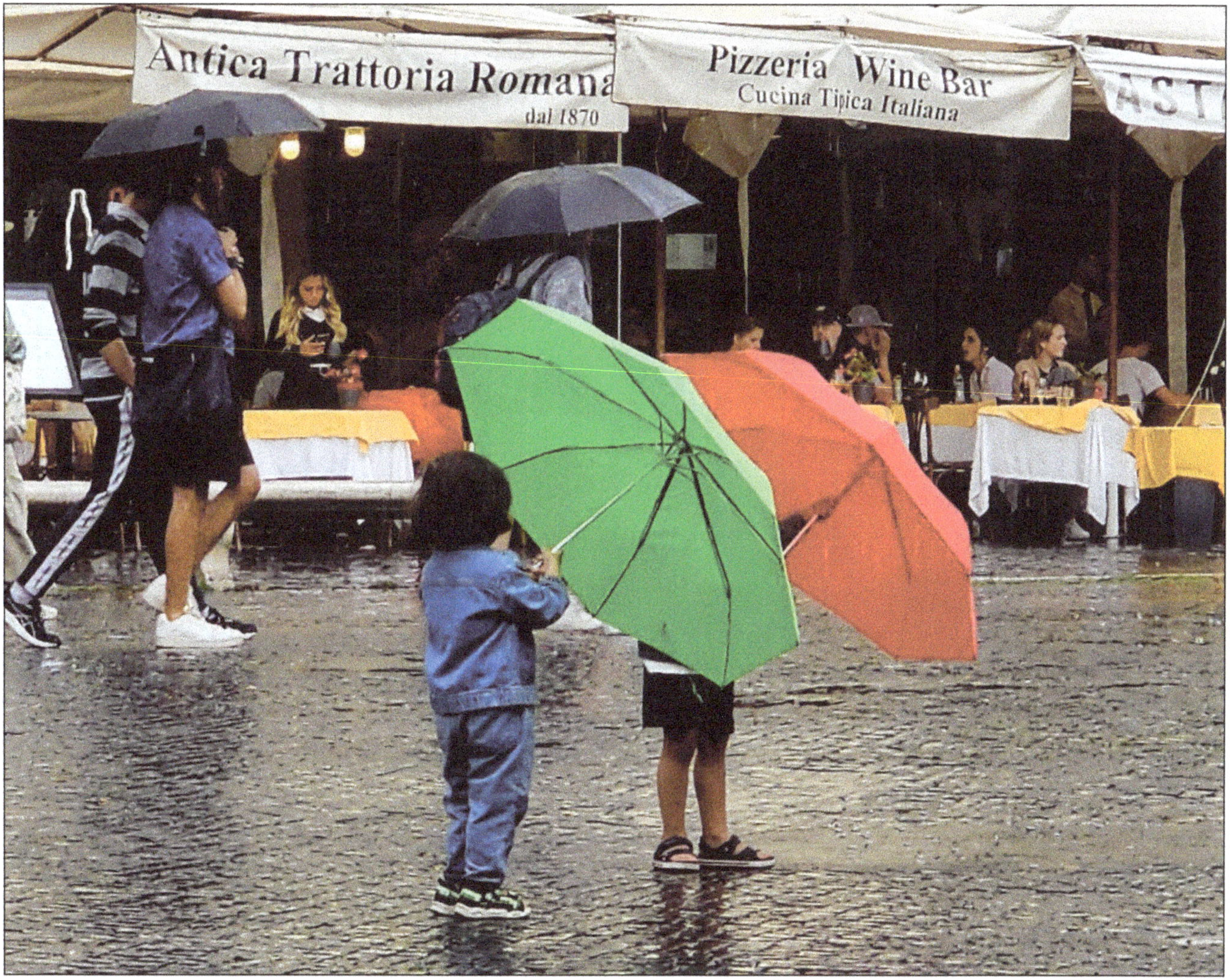

Children playing in the rain, Piazza Navona, Rome.

Little by little we will find the beauty that inspires our hearts and lives! All we need to do is keep a sketchbook handy and continue drawing and painting. Artists use their sketchbook as a wellspring of inspiration. Collect photos, postcards, ribbons, pressed flowers, color, and wallpaper swatches and more in your sketchbook. Write notes in your sketchbook about what you see and how it makes you feel. ***Collect quotes that inspire you!***

One of my favorites is the lighthearted title of a book about creativity by American painter and art instructor, **Bob Ross (1942–1995)**. I love how he reminds me to relax and be joyful when I create. As the title of his book reminds us, our mistakes are simply *Happy Little Accidents*. This lovely thought always reminds me not to take myself too seriously when I paint.

I also love what American poet and author **Sylvia Plath (1932–1963)** said about creativity. She reminds us ***that the worst enemy to creativity is self-doubt***. And that's the truth with a capital T! It's important to have a little faith in yourself. Give yourself a chance to let your originality shine!

Finally, there are some quotes that I find introspective and deeply inspiring. They remind me how our personal quest for beauty ultimately leads us to our Creator.

"Art is a shadow of Divine perfection."

— Michelangelo

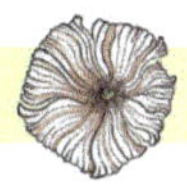

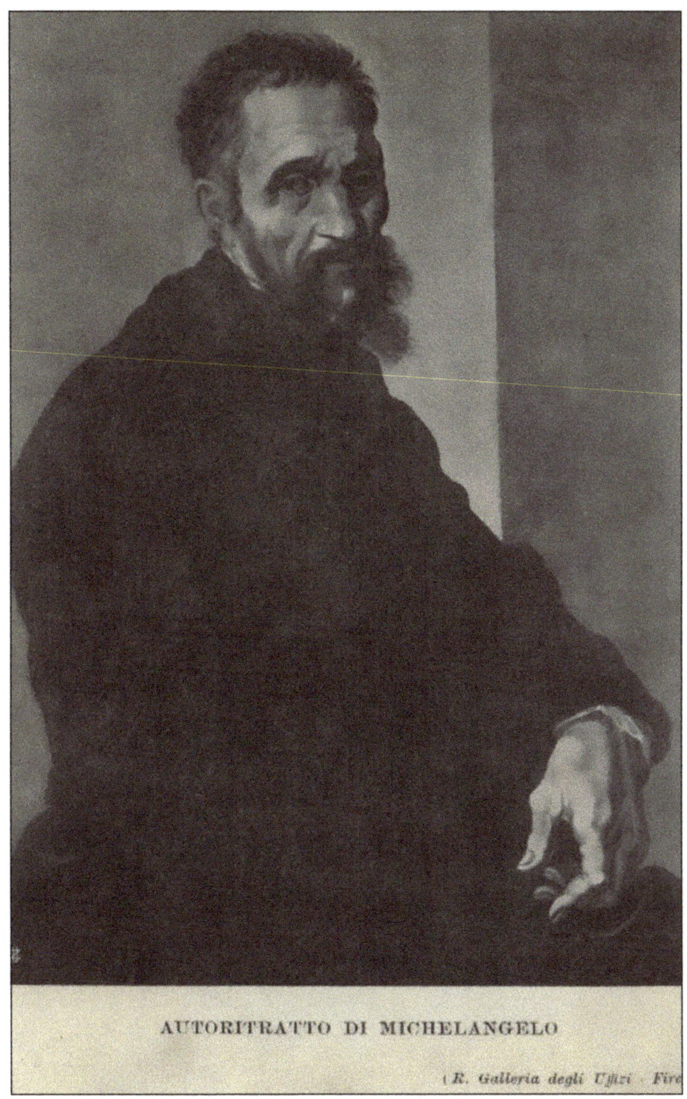

For example, time and again, I read and often ponder **Michelangelo's (1475-1564)** writings to art historian, **Giorgio Vasari (1511-1574)**. His words were written at the very end of his eighty-nine-year-old life. They speak of not only Michaelangelo's lifelong dedication to his art but also his heartfelt final lifelong realization which was that his faith in God was all that really mattered in the end. I find his words beautiful and deeply inspiring.

Which artist's words touch *your* soul?

On the Brink of Death
To Giorgio Vasari
Sonnet LXV

The course of my life has brought me now
Through a stormy sea, in a frail ship,
To the common port where, landing
We account for every deed, wretched or holy.

So that finally I see
How wrong the fond illusion was
That made art my idol and my King,
Leading me to want what harmed me.

My amorous fancies, once foolish and happy
What sense have they now that I approach two deaths
The first of which I know is sure, the second threatening.

Let neither painting nor carving any longer calm
My soul turned to that divine Love
Who to embrace us opened His arms upon the cross.

 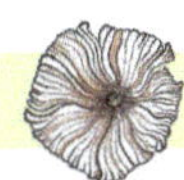

We all have our favorite quotes by various artists that continually inspire us. It's important to keep them around for inspiration.

Every time I read the simple words of a Greek Orthodox Saint named Porphyrios, I feel very inspired to be creative. Saint Porphyrios said that we ***must see the glory of God in the smallest flower***. His holy words make me slow down and study the tiniest flowers and objects that I encounter. His quote even inspired me to plant a poppy garden in my backyard. This special little garden made me realize that more than any other flower, poppies delight and inspire me in a unique way.

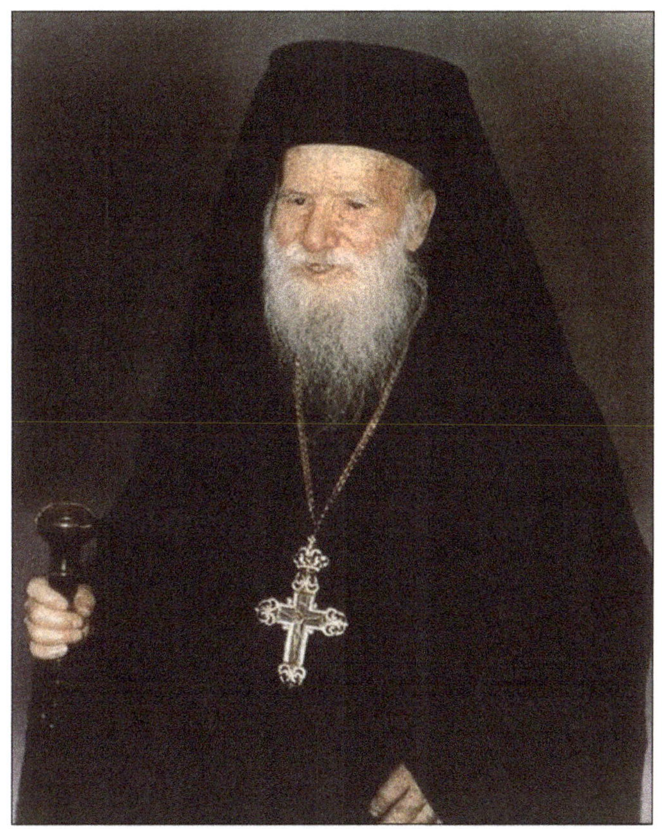

Saint Porphyrios of Kafsokalyvia (1906-1991) His beautiful quote inspired Ariane to start her poppy business.

Can you think of something beautiful you see around you that inspires you and brings you unending joy?

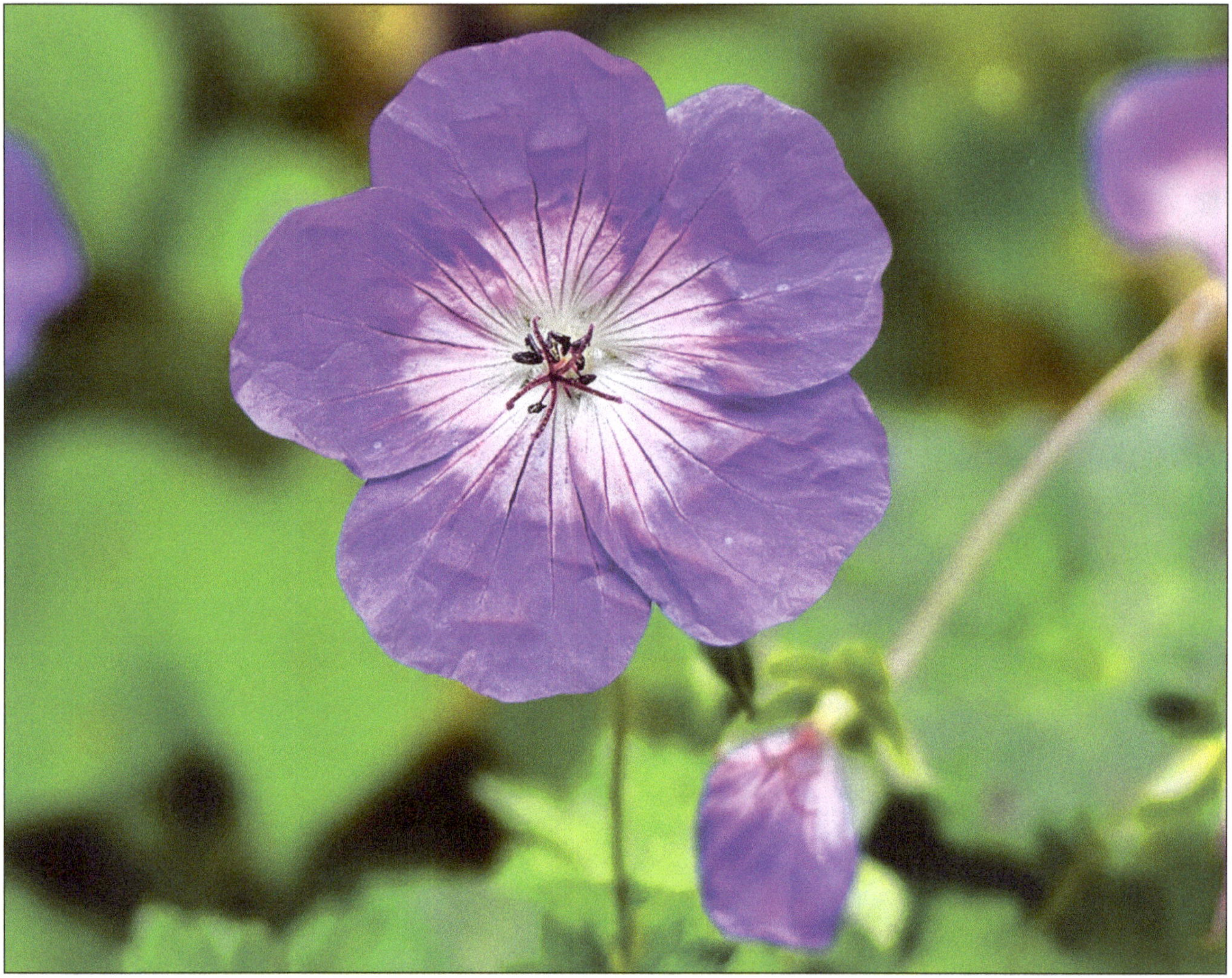

A tiny purple poppy from the author's garden.

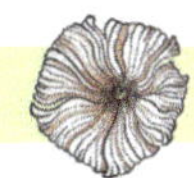

Whenever I sit down to study and draw little flowers, I see so many details and colors that bring me joy! I found myself doing this with poppies and drawing them over and over until I ended up creating a business called **Poppies with a Purpose**! You never know where the pursuit of beauty will lead you! It will be a positive journey — I can attest to that!

Now go out there and see like an artist. Find your joy. It's never too late! If you continue to work at seeing beauty, your original ideas will eventually begin to blossom. **Grab a sketchbook.** Collect quotes, color swatches, and keep drawing and painting! Don't give up! You were created to see beauty in your own special way. Lastly, remember practice makes perfect and always pays you back. **It's time for you to *Behold the Beauty* in your life!**

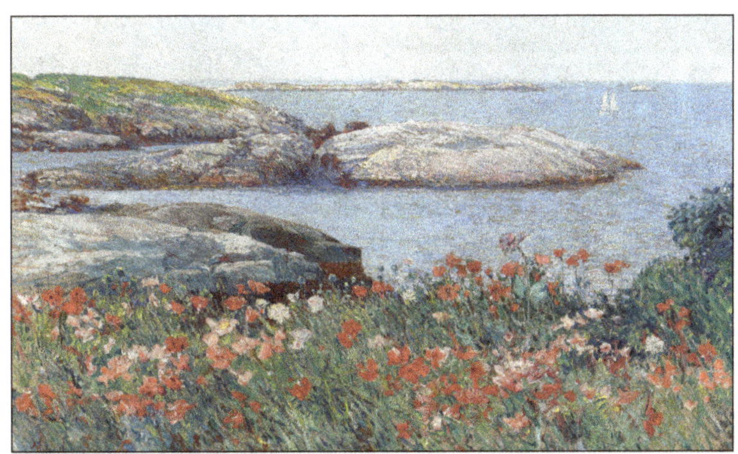

Unique shapes and soft colors delight the eye. **Poppies, Isles of Shoals,** *1891, by Childe Hassam.*

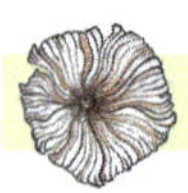

Make a list or collage of images and artists' quotes that inspire and bring you joy (favorite art and artists, colors, special travel destinations, seashells, flowers, trees, and more!).

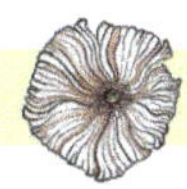

Chapter Seven Fun Fact

Seeing like an artist improves your overall well-being.

Now that you have read this book, keep it close as a reference and "travel" guide as you continue exploring the world around you. Remember, it's important to further practice the exercises we've discussed. As you sharpen your vision, new doors will open in life.

Seeing like an artist can reduce stress and help you perceive your world in wonderfully new and different ways. Creativity produces a refreshing change in perspective. It makes us happy to see something that inspires us.

It's also good for our mental health. Countless studies in the medical field have shown that engaging in creative pursuits has a positive effect on our mental and physical well-being. **Pablo Picasso (1881-1973)** once said, "Art washes away from the soul the dust of everyday life."

Since prehistoric times, our ancestors have left an artistic legacy of animal drawings and beautiful human hand-print outlines on the walls of various caves. **Now its your turn to express yourself!**

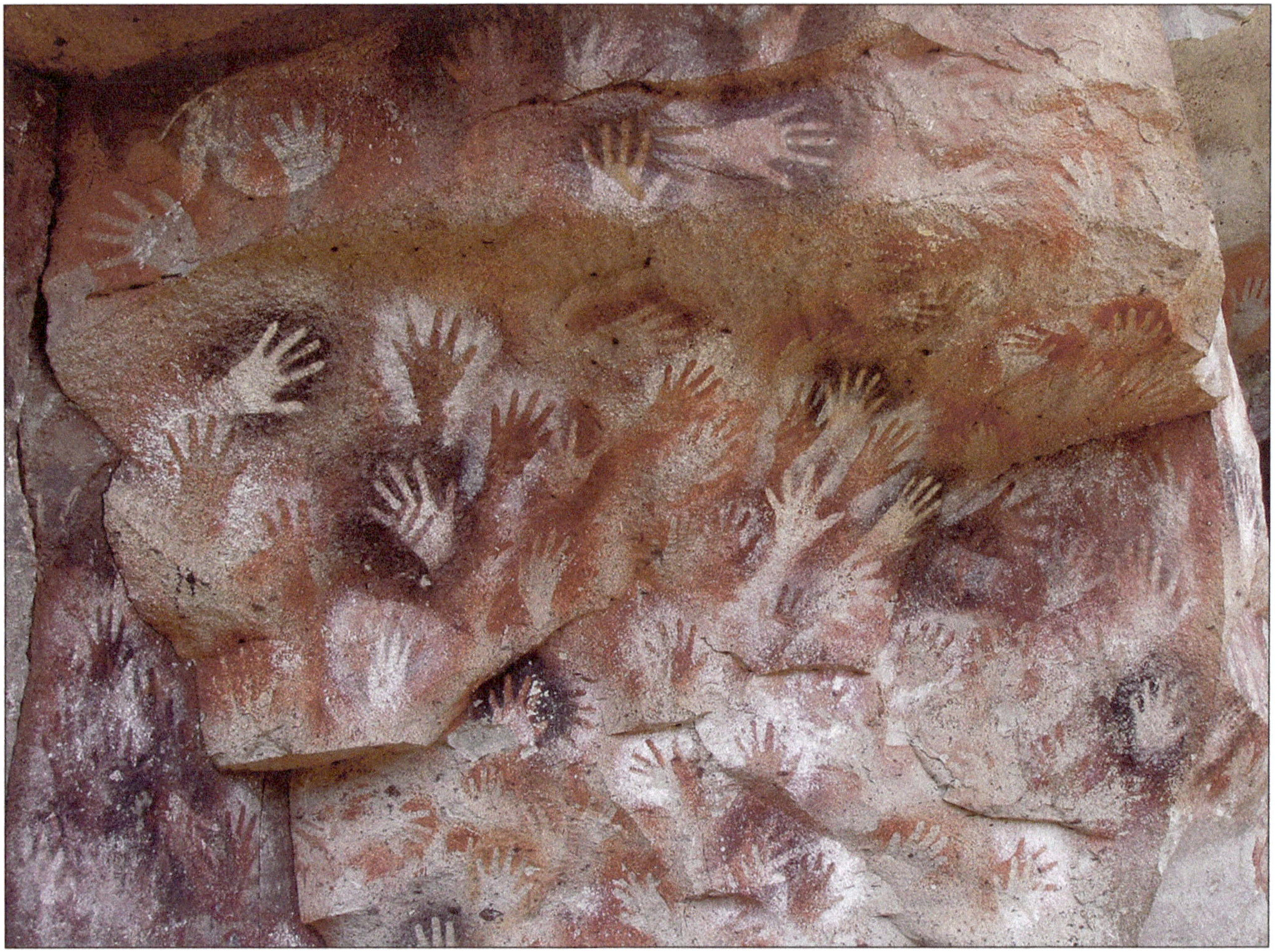

Art in caves is some of the oldest in the world. With around 10,000 years of history,
the Cave of Hands in Argentina offers us a connection to these ancient people.
These stenciled outlines of human hands remind us that being creative is an important part of who we are.

After all, you could say it's in our bones. **The desire *and need to create beauty* was and is absolutely part of who we are!**

Let's live a richer and fuller life, one filled with positive transformation. The end result of seeing like an artist is never-ending inspiration. Inspiration always brings us joy, happiness and style.

There is so much beauty to behold in the world. ***What inspires you?*** Maybe its time to change your color palette, personal style, or other areas in your life. When you see like an artist, you discover what lifts your spirits at any stage in life!

"One little poppy flower always brightens my day and inspires me to no end!"

Ariane Trifunovic Montemuro

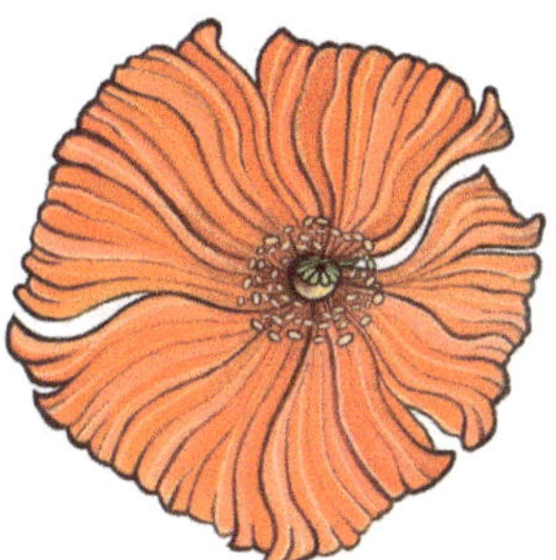

Final Assignment:

Keep practicing with this book

&

Behold the Beauty!

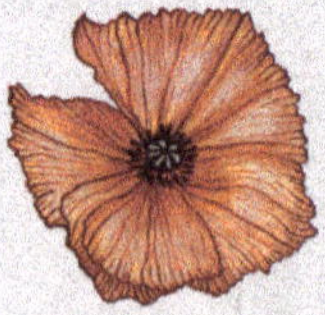

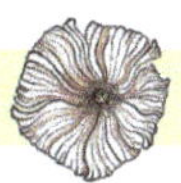

Ready. Set. Go! Begin your lifelong pursuit of beauty.

You are creative. Now it's time to practice. You won't realize your potential unless you try. So, give it a go! See what inspires you. Have fun and follow your heart. Observe and keep drawing everyday things, every day. You know the saying, use it or lose it!

Start by drawing a chair in your home. Study its lines, shape, color, and texture. The more you look the more you'll see. If you cannot find a chair you like, try drawing the elegant chair to the right on one of the following *Notes and Ideas* sketchbook pages (starting on page 200).

This chair wraps it up for our time together! Remember to open your eyes and study your surroundings wherever life takes you.

Now go out there, find your joy, and keep practicing!

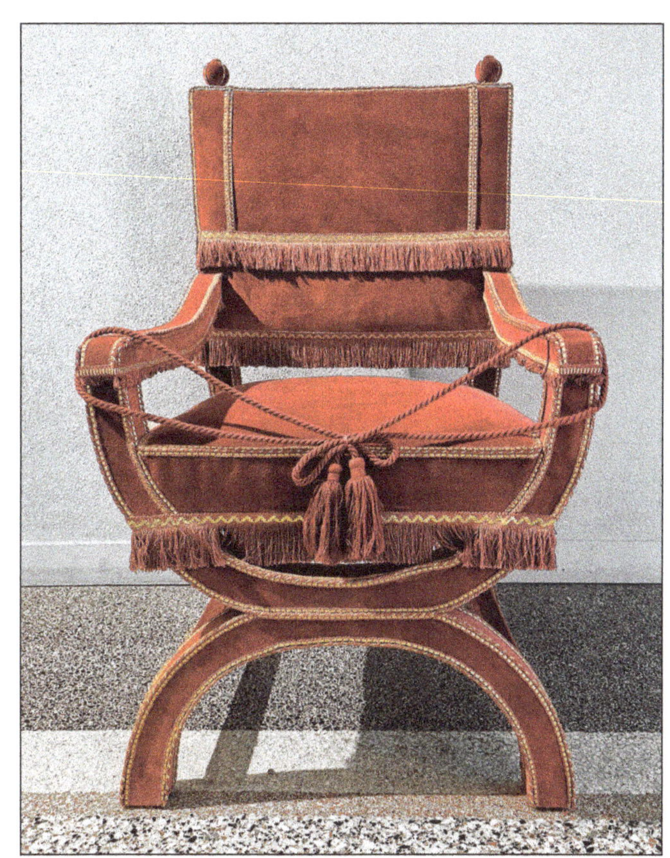

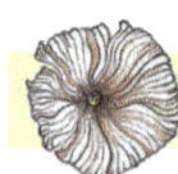

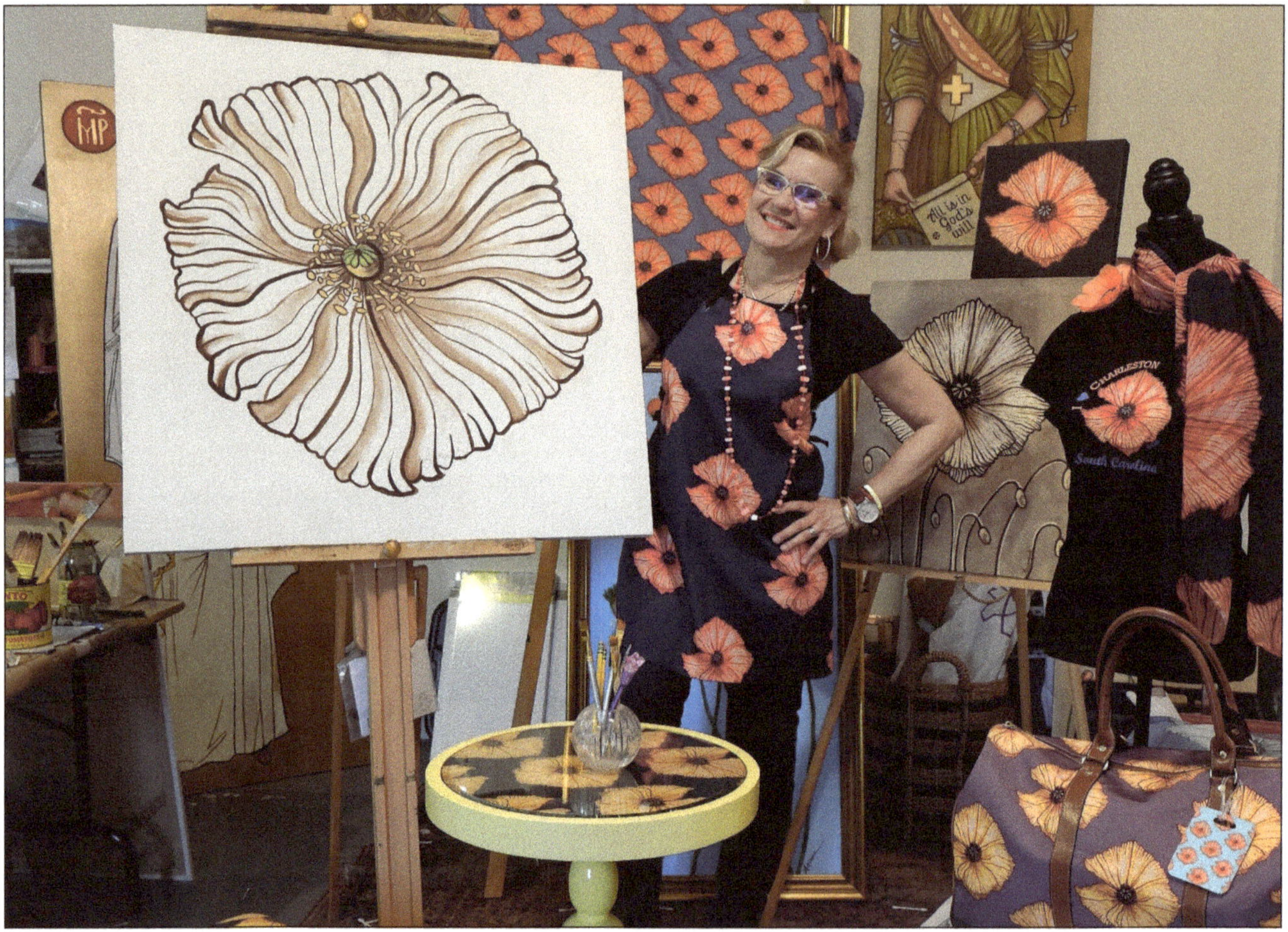

Ariane's favorite quote:
"We must see the glory of God in the smallest flower."
Saint Porphyrios.
Ariane in her studio with her original poppy product designs. Work in progress of painting.

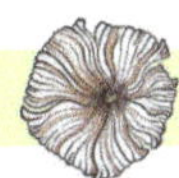

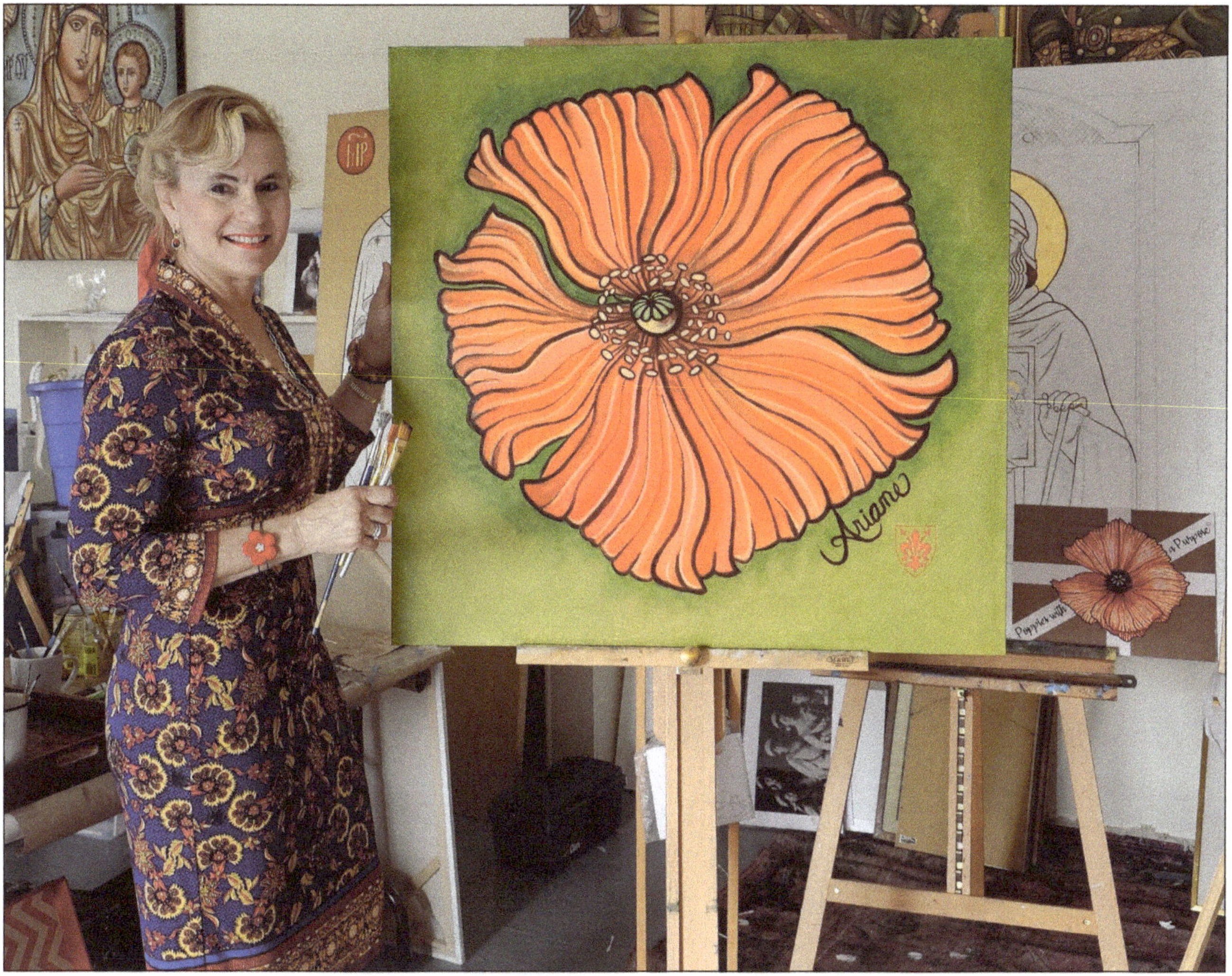

Ariane with her completed poppy oil painting: Pazzo for Poppies (pazzo means crazy in Italian).

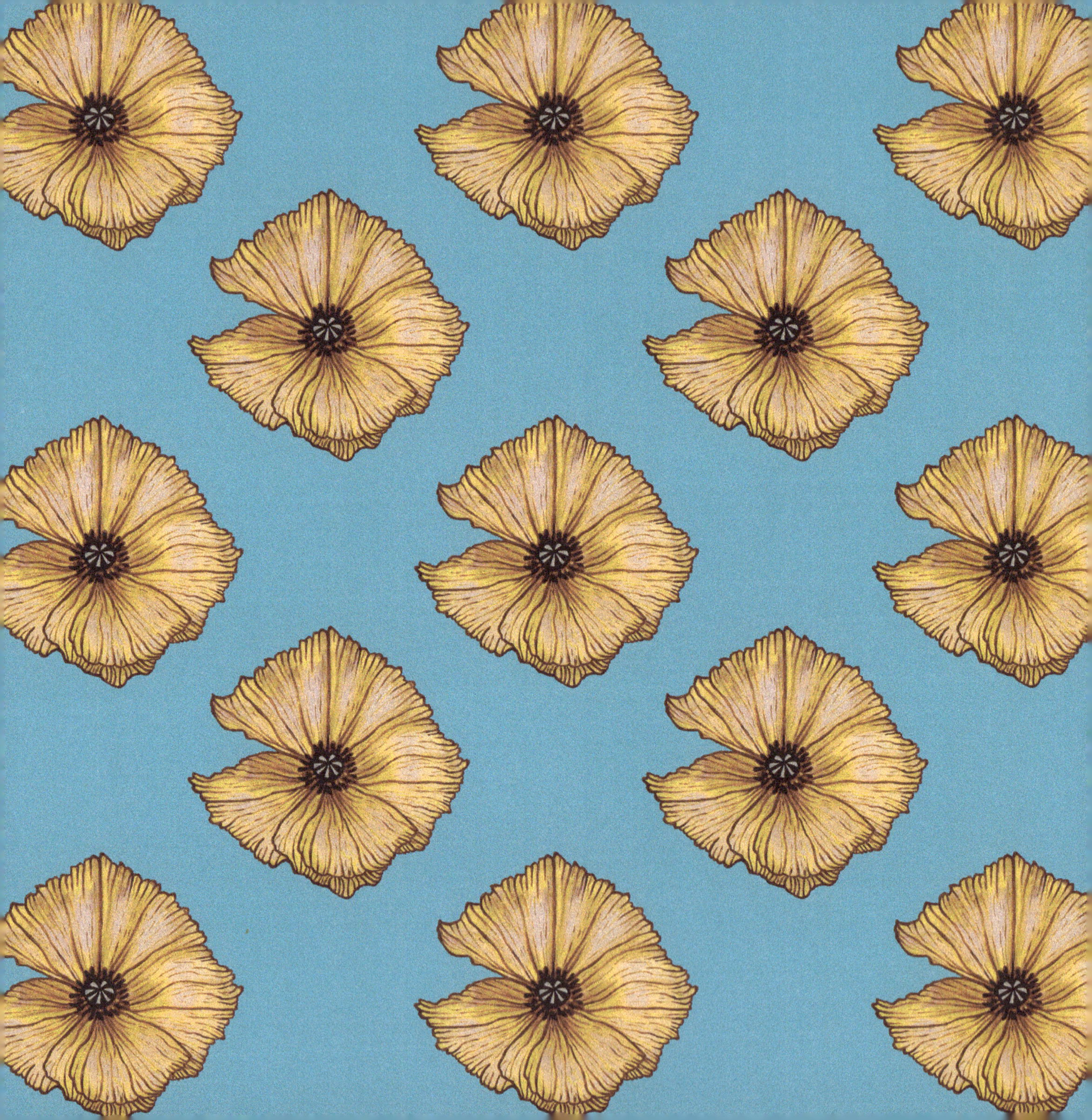

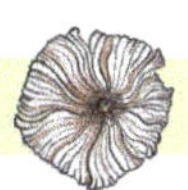

Notes & Ideas

Everyday inspiration and joy are waiting for you!

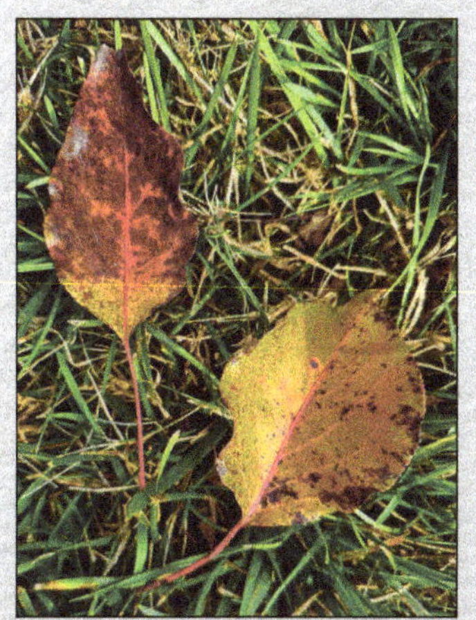

While writing this book, I found these two leaves in my front yard. I was delighted by their beauty, so I photographed them. The single red line running through each leaf made me happy, so I put the photo near my writing desk. This way I could see it every day. As a result, I was inspired to add a flourish of color at the top of every page of this book. One simple green line to run throughout my book — just like the red line in the leaves. A small book design detail that makes me smile. *We must always remember that beauty, inspiration, and joy can be found right in front of us.*

Take the opportunity to use the following blank pages at the end of this book to record, collect, and save the unique beauty that strikes you and makes you happy wherever you go!

Grab inspiration from everything you see. After all, that's what artists do!

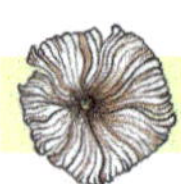

Notes & Ideas

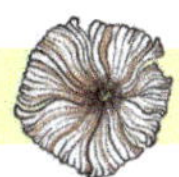

Notes & Ideas

Notes & Ideas

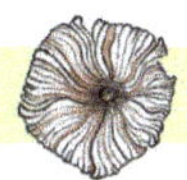

Notes & Ideas

Notes & Ideas

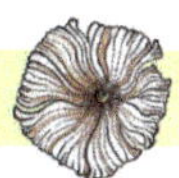

Notes & Ideas

Notes & Ideas

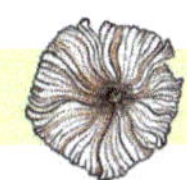

Notes & Ideas

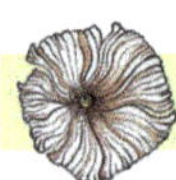

Notes & Ideas

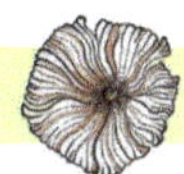

Notes & Ideas

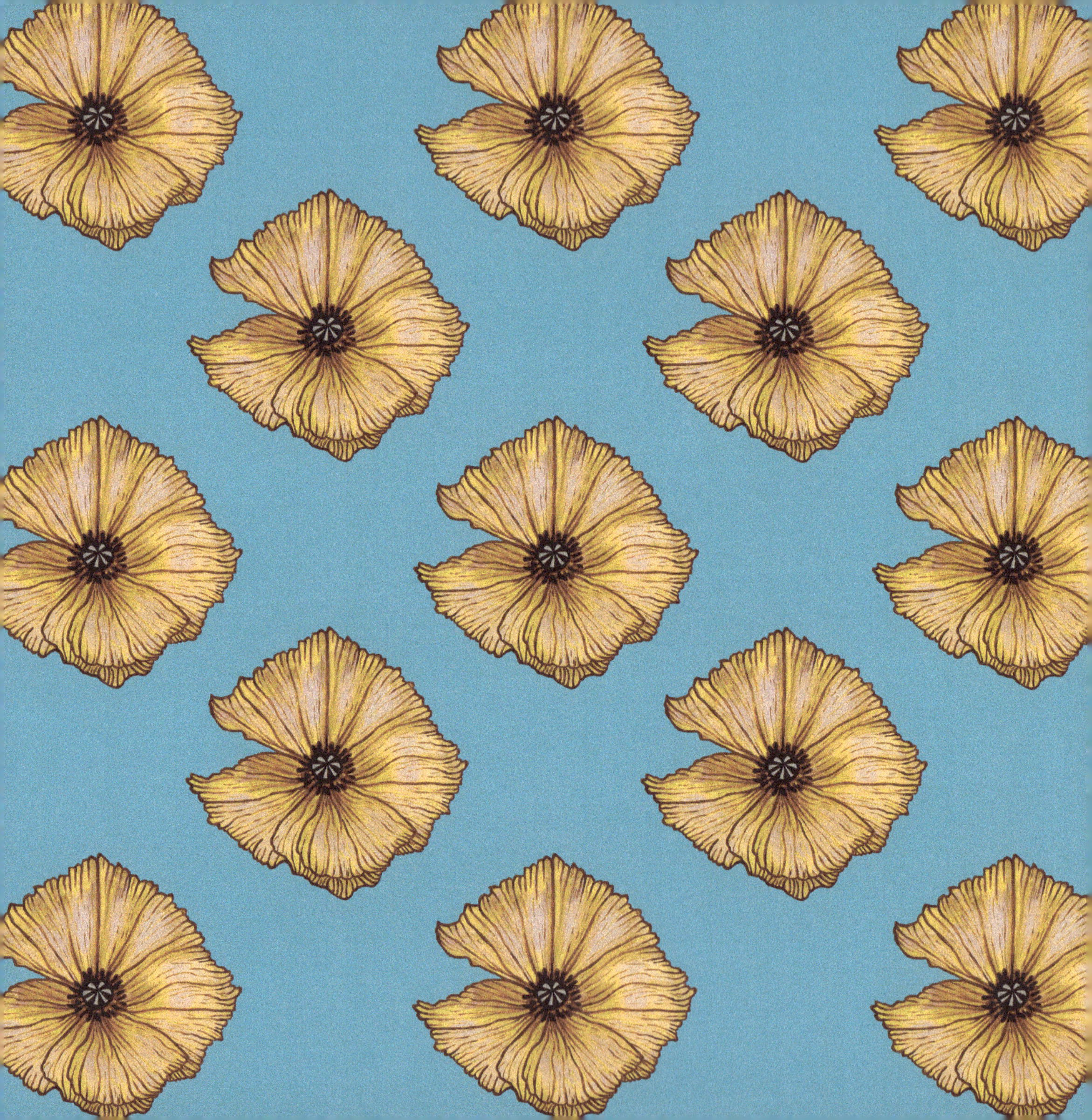

How to See Like an Artist!

PHOTO CREDITS

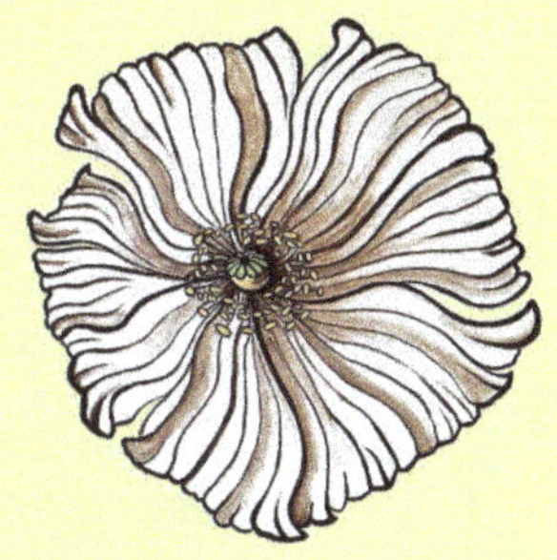

Photo Credits

All photos used in this book were taken by Ariane Trifunovic Montemuro except for the ones that are listed below. Those come from a variety of resources including but not limited to public domain, Creative Commons, stock photography, and others.

Page 4
Green background
Elysium, Decorative Panel, 1906, Léon Bakst
Wikimedia Commons
Public Domain

Page 5
Anna Pavlova
Public Domain

Page 7
Poppy Drawing
www.unsplash.com
Florence Skyline
www.istock.com
Face Illustration
www.istock.com
Pencils
www.unsplash.com

Page 17-18
Poppies
Hailey and Victoria Hodge
www.vinoevinci.com

Page 21
Colored Box Perspective
www.unsplash.com
Woman Tinted Illustration
www.istock.com

Page 42-44
Green Leaves
Salix Babylonica
Pierre Joseph Redouté
Wikimedia Commons
Public Domain
Poppy
Papaver bracteatum
John Lindley
Collectanea botanica
Wikimedia Commons
Public Domain

Page 47
Egyptian Hieroglyphics
Amador Loureiro
www.unsplash.com

Page 63
Flowering Garden
www.pxhere.com

Page 65
David Sculpture
www.unsplash.com
Church Dome
www.flickr.com
Woman's Back Silhouette
www.unsplash.com

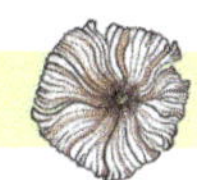

Page 67
Michelangelo's David
Wikimedia Commons
Creative Commons Attribution-Share Alike 4.0
Standing Woman
Wikimedia Commons
Creative Commons by 2.0 Deed (2.0 Generic)

Page 82
Le Pont L'Europe
Gustave Callebotte
Public Domain
Adapted

Page 99
Filippo Bruinelleschi
Public Domain

Page 101
Color Wheel
www.istock.com
Colored Wall with Decorative Iron Gate
www.unsplash.com

Page 122
The Great Wave off Kanagawa
Katsushika Hokusai
Wikimedia Commons
Creative Commons CCO 1.0 Universal Public
Domain Dedication

Page 127
Sunflowers
www.pxhere.com

Page 134
Georgia O'Keeffe
Alfred Stieglitz
Wikimedia Commons
Creative Commons CCO 1.0 Universal Public
Domain Dedication

Page 135
The Grand Canyon
Arthur Wesley Dow
The Seattle Art Museum
Public Domain

Page 140-141
The Waterseller of Seville
Diego Velázquez
Public Domain

Page 143
Trompe L'Oeil Pear Still Life
www.1stdibs.com

Page 144
The Starry Night
Vincent van Gogh
Public Domain

Page 145
Still Life
Pieter Claesz
Public Domain

Page 149
Gathering Women
Stepan Kolesnikoff
Public Domain

Page 157
Self-Portrait as an Artist
Vincent van Gogh
Wikiart
Public Domain

Page 159
The Red Vineyard at Arles
Vincent van Gogh
Wikimedia Commons
Public Domain

Page 166
Guitar on a table
Juan Gris
Google Art Project
Wikimedia Commons
Public Domain

Page 167
Abstraction
Juan Gris
Google Art Project
Wikimedia Commons
Public Domain

Page 168
Black Guitar (still life)
Juan Gris
www.arthive.com
Public Domain

Page 169
La table du musicien (The Musician's Table)
Juan Gris
Google Art Project
Wikimedia Commons
Public Domain

Page 170
Le Pain
Wikimedia Commons
Public Domain

Page 172
The Bordeaux Bottle
Juan Gris
WikiArt
Public Domain

Page 174
La guitare aux incrustations
Juan Gris
Google Art Project
Wikimedia Commons
Public Domain

Page 175
Juan Gris
Public Domain

Page 176
Portrait of Pablo Picasso
Juan Gris
Google Art Project
Wikimedia Commons
Public Domain

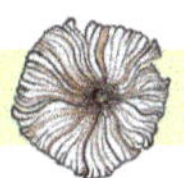

Page 177
Portrait of Juan Gris
Amedeo Mondigliani
Wikimedia Commons
Public Domain

Page 185
Michelangelo
Poeta DPLA
Public Domain

Page 187
Porphyrios Kaysokalivitis
Saint Porphyrios of Kafsokalyvia
Wikimedia Commons
Creative Commons Attribution-Share Alike 4.0

Page 189
Poppies, Isles of Shoals, 1891
Childe Hassam
National Gallery of Art
Public Domain

Page 192
Santa Cruz Cueva Manos
Wikimedia Commons
Public Domain

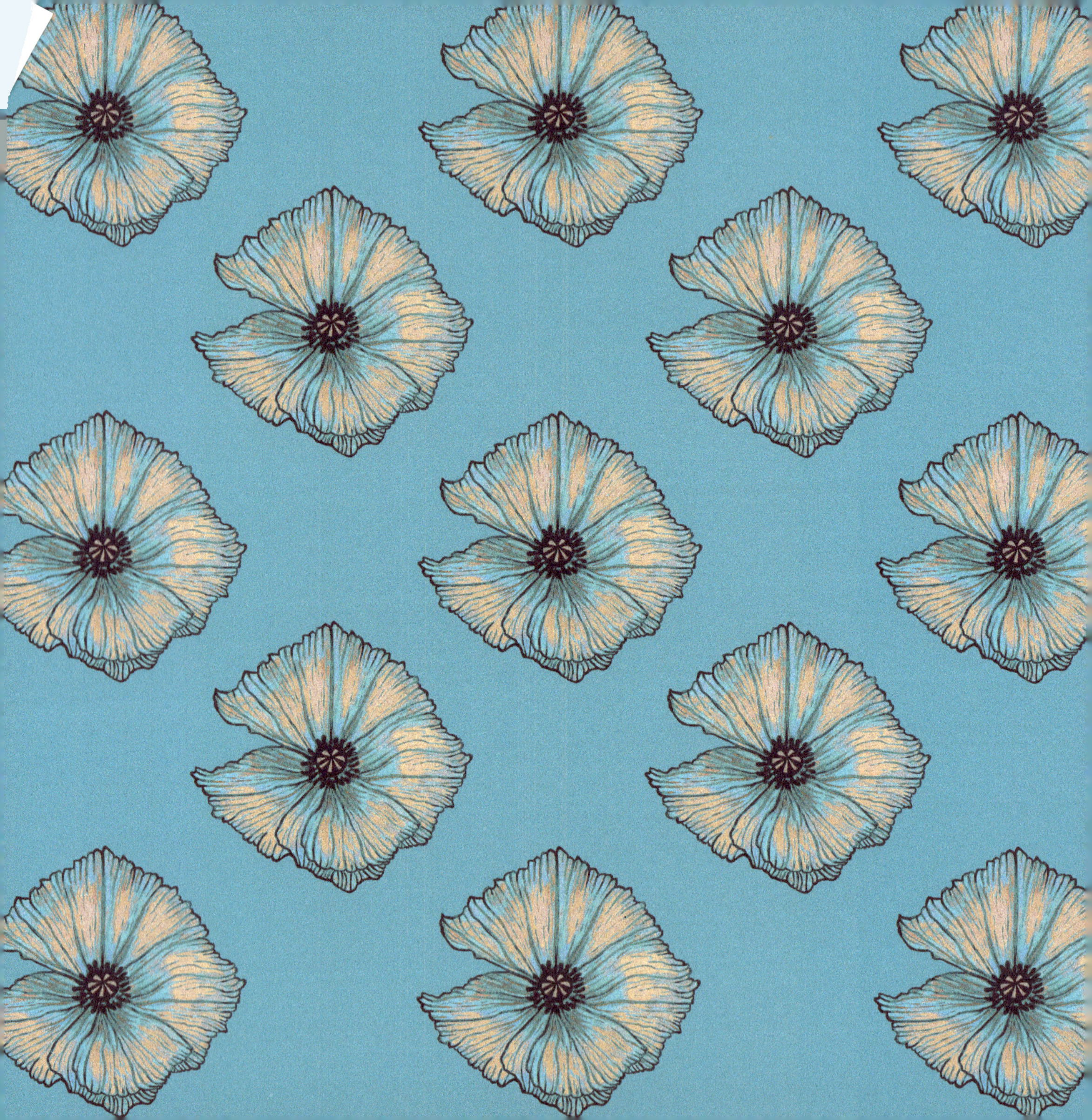